Psychology

in

Progress

General editor: Peter Herriot

Issues in

Person

Perception

Psychology in Progress

Already available

Philosophical Problems in Psychology
edited by Neil Bolton

The Pathology and Psychology of Cognition
edited by Andrew Burton

Thinking in Perspective
Critical essays in the study of thought processes
edited by Andrew Burton and John Radford

The School Years
Current issues in the socialization of young people
edited by John C. Coleman

Applications of Conditioning Theory
edited by Graham Davey

Personality
Theory, measurement and research
edited by Fay Fransella

Aspects of Memory
edited by Michael M. Gruneberg and Peter Morris

Issues in Childhood Social Development
edited by Harry McGurk

Developing Thinking
Approaches to children's cognitive development
edited by Sara Meadows

Brain, Behaviour and Evolution
edited by David A. Oakley and H. C. Plotkin

Small Groups and Personal Change
edited by Peter B. Smith

Issues in
Person
Perception

edited by
MARK COOK

METHUEN

LONDON AND NEW YORK

First published in 1984 by
Methuen & Co. Ltd
11 New Fetter Lane, London EC4P 4EE

Published in the USA by
Methuen & Co.
in association with Methuen, Inc.
733 Third Avenue, New York, NY 10017

This collection © 1984 Methuen & Co. Ltd
Individual chapters © 1984 the respective authors
Printed in Great Britain by
Richard Clay, The Chaucer Press

British Library Cataloguing in Publication Data

Issues in person perception
–(Psychology in progress)
1. Social perception
I. Cook, Mark   II. Series
153.7'5   HM132

ISBN 0-416-32450-9
ISBN 0-416-32460-6 Pbk

Library of Congress Cataloging in Publication Data

Main entry under title:
Issues in person perception.
(Psychology in progress)
Includes bibliographies and indexes.
1. Social perception – Addresses, essays,
lectures.
2. Personality – Addresses, essays, lectures.
3. Employment interviewing – Psychological
aspects – Addresses, essays, lectures.
I. Cook, Mark. II. Series.
HM132.I87   1984   302'.12   83-25097

ISBN 0-416-32450-9
ISBN 0-416-32460-6 (pbk.)

Contents

vi   Contents

Notes on the contributors

Robin M. Akert is Assistant Professor of Psychology at Wellesley College, Mass.

Dane Archer is a Professor at Stevenson College, University of California, Santa Cruz.

Richard D. Arvey is Professor of Industrial Relations at the University of Minnesota.

James E. Campion is Associate Professor of Psychology at the University of Houston.

Mark Cook is Lecturer in Psychology at University College Swansea.

Rob Farr is Professor of Social Psychology at the London School of Economics.

Sarah E. Hampson is Lecturer in Psychology at Birkbeck College, University of London.

Douglas N. Jackson is Senior Professor of Psychology at the University of Western Ontario.

Alexander Lovie is Lecturer in Psychology at the University of Liverpool.

Serge Moscovici is Professor at the Ecole des Hautes Etudes en Sciences Sociales, Paris.

Geraldine F. Nagy is a co-worker with James Shanteau in the Department of Psychology, Kansas State University.

Mitchell Rothstein is a consultant in the Human Resource Planning Department, Ontario Hydro, Toronto.

James Shanteau is in the Department of Psychology, Kansas State University.

Editor's introduction

This book is intended to complement my earlier *Perceiving Others* (1979), and specifically to enable the student to study in greater depth some of the issues that *Perceiving Others* hadn't space to describe in full detail.

The four issues selected for analysis in greater depth are: inference from multiple cues; methodology of measuring accuracy of perception; selection for employment; and the relationship between person perception and personality. These are not, of course, the only four important issues in the area; two were selected because they are currently at the forefront of attention (multiple cues, and person perception and personality), one because it is of enduring practical importance (selection for employment), and one because it has been neglected of late, unreasonably so in the opinion of myself and another contributor (accuracy). Among the issues that might have been included, but weren't, are stereotypes, psychiatric diagnosis (and other forms of applied person perception besides employment selection), and various issues derived loosely – isn't everything? – from attribution theory. I had originally intended to include a critique of attribution theory – by myself – but found little to add to what I had already said in Chapter 5 of *Perceiving Others*, so I chose instead a more constructive chapter outlining another solution to the accuracy problem. Moscovici and Farr's chapter describes the origin and philosophical standing of attribution theory.

Chapters 3 (Shanteau and Nagy) and 4 (Lovie) provide complementary discussions of how people draw inferences from more than one piece of information, and discuss particularly how people resolve discrepancies in the information available. It is very easy for people to draw an inference from a single piece of information – attractive people are nice, people who wear glasses are intelligent – as numerous unimaginative contributors to social psychology journals continue to demonstrate annually. It is reasonably easy to draw an inference when provided with several pieces of information all pointing the same way – although too much information tends to confuse both lay and expert judges of others. Life gets difficult for the judge when he is given six or more facts about someone which all point in different directions, or when, as often happens in personnel selection, they don't point very clearly in any direction at all.

Chapters 5 (Archer and Akert) and 6 (Cook) both consider research on the accuracy of people's judgement of each other. This is a somewhat unfashionable issue, and the inclusion of two chapters on it represents an effort on my part to re-awaken interest in it. It has become unfashionable partly because apparently simple techniques prove to be methodologically complex, but also because talking of 'accuracy' of perception implies a reality to be perceived, and the current resurgence of phenomenological approaches to social psychology tends to deny any such reality. Archer and Akert and I consider emotional states, interpersonal relationships and personality traits to be sufficiently real to be distinguishable from people's perceptions of them, and also that the accuracy of such perceptions is a real and important issue. Both chapters emphasize methodological aspects, giving a review of past research and its failings, before outlining a method that avoids these difficulties. Archer and Akert concentrate on the accuracy of inference of moods, emotions and relationships from expressive behaviour, and discuss the problem of constructing a criterion – what is to count as the real answer. My chapter considers the problems of studying accuracy of perceiving personality traits.

Chapters 7 (Rothstein and Jackson) and 8 (Arvey and Campion) both concern selection for employment – an issue that follows on logically from the two preceding chapters on accuracy. The aim of employment selection is to choose the right man for the job, an aim which obviously supposes there are real and perceivable differences between candidates. Arvey and Campion's chapter gives an up-to-date review of research on the employment interview, to complement the earlier reviews of Wright (1969) and Ulrich and Trumbo (1965). Rothstein and Jackson provide an analysis of implicit personality theories used by personnel selectors to complement their previous research on implicit personality theories in psychiatric diagnosis, as well as a challenging discussion of whether personality judgements are made, or made accurately, in the employment interview.

The fourth issue, discussed in the first two chapters, is the place of person perception in psychology, and its links with Gestalt psychology and the study of personality. In Chapter 1, Moscovici and Farr trace the development of attribution theory from Gestalt psychology, bringing in the important work of Mead, Ichheiser and Goffman. In Chapter 2, Hampson discusses the relations between person perception and personality, starting from the fundamental ambiguity of certain types of research. Are ratings by one person, of another person's personality, a measure of the true personality of the perceived? Or are they a measure of the way the rater sees other people? Hampson concludes that such ratings serve both functions.

I would like to thank my contributors for writing such useful contributions so promptly, and Methuen for giving me the chance to publish them in their Psychology in Progress series.

MARK COOK

1 On the nature and role of representations in self's understanding of others and of self

Rob Farr *and*
Serge Moscovici

The historical background

Since the mid-1960s, the study of person perception in particular, and of social psychology in general, has come to be increasingly dominated by attribution theory. The aim of this contribution is to place attribution theory in its historical context, to illustrate how it developed from other schools of psychology, and how it relates to them, and tentatively to suggest that some of its ideas are not all that new.

The impetus for the study of how it is that we perceive others is to be found in the work of Gestalt social psychologists such as Asch (1946), Heider (1944, 1946, 1958) and From (1971, but Danish original in the early 1950s). It will be helpful to look briefly at the historical antecedents of those Gestalt social psychologists. They are 'social' psychologists precisely because they recognize the distinction between the perceiver (P) and the 'other' (O) whom P perceives. Whilst the flowering of social psychology, as Allport (1954) noted some time ago, is a peculiarly American phenomenon, its historical roots are to be found in European movements of thought in philosophy and the social sciences. The pioneers of Gestalt psychology, in its classic phase, were more directly concerned with the perception of objects and events in the physical environment than they were with the perception of such social stimuli as other persons.

The Gestalt psychologists, in the days when the movement centred primarily on Berlin, comprised a distinct 'school' of psychology. Within the newly developing science of psychology they adopted a uniquely phenomenological perspective. Phenomenology, as a more general movement within philosophy, was broadly concerned with the description of the world as it 'appears' to P (i.e. the perceiver). Gestalt psychologists, however, differed from pure phenomenologists when they went on to claim that man's experience of the world is isomorphic with certain neural events in the cortex of the brain.

Gestalt psychologists, as a school, were opposed to the Leipzig tradition of experimental psychology which Wundt had inaugurated in 1879 and which was concerned with the analysis of the contents of consciousness by means of introspection. Gestalt psychologists believed that man experienced the world as an organized and meaningful whole. If this experience is broken down into the basic 'elements' of sensation which underlie it, then organization and meaning are lost or destroyed as qualities of immediate experience. It was a clarion call of the Gestalt movement that 'the whole may be different from its parts studied in isolation.' This slogan epitomized their opposition to the analytic introspectionism of the Leipzig laboratory.

In those days, when it was accurate to describe psychology as the science of mental life, Gestalt psychologists were opposed to an exclusive reliance upon introspection as the most suitable technique for exploring mental phenomena. Thus it was that they were opposed to the use of introspection long before they emigrated to America where they encountered, on their arrival, a well-established, but different form of opposition to Wundtian introspectionism – namely American behaviourism. We propose shortly to argue that, in the history of American psychology, Gestalt psychology has always provided a viable 'alternative' to the dominant tradition of behaviourism. It is, thus, important, at this particular juncture, to appreciate the nature of the relationships between the psychologies of Wundt and the Gestaltists and the relationship of both to American behaviourism.

It is not always appreciated, especially in the official North American histories of psychology as an experimental science, that

Wundt himself had been clearly aware of the limitations of the new experimental science which he had helped to create. He believed, for example, that it was not possible to study man's higher cognitive processes within the confines of the laboratory by means of introspection. (For a fuller exposition of this point see Farr, 1978b, 1980a, b, 1981.) The Gestaltists, like Wundt, were also interested in the study of man's higher cognitive processes, for example Köhler's classic study of the mentality of apes (1925) and Wertheimer's study of productive thinking (1945, 1959). Also, like Wundt, they appreciated that these studies could not be carried out by means of introspection. Köhler chose to observe a colony of nine chimpanzees at the Anthropoid Station in Tenerife between 1913 and 1917. Thus observation, even of the higher primates, could shed some interesting light on thought processes in man. Wertheimer was more interested in studying the thought processes of such highly creative persons as distinguished scientists, for example Galileo and Einstein.

Wundt, however, preferred to explore the close relationship between language and thought. This was an important theme in the ten volumes of his *Völkerpsychologie* which appeared between 1900 and 1920. He was even prepared to speculate on how, in man's remote past, language may have evolved from human gestures (Farr, 1980a). He derived his conception of the human gesture from Darwin. G. H. Mead took Wundt's conception of the human gesture as the starting point for the development of his social psychology (Mead, 1934). Thus Wundt and Köhler were more directly influenced by Darwin than was either J. B. Watson or B. F. Skinner, the founders of American behaviourism. Wundt, and the Gestalt psychologists generally, were not averse to psychology being considered as the science of mental life. This was a conception of psychology to which the behaviourists were adamantly opposed.

Those whom Wundt influenced, especially the pioneers of experimental psychology in America, were not prepared to accept that the 'new experimental psychology' had its limitations. For them Wundt was a pioneer in that he had demonstrated the feasibility of establishing psychology as an independent, experimental, laboratory science. They easily ridded themselves of the limitations which Wundt saw in his new laboratory science by abandoning introspection as a methodology. Watson strove to make psychology a branch of natural science by declaring it to be the science, not of experience, nor of mind, but of behaviour. This was part of what Danziger (1979) referred to as the positivist repudiation of Wundt.

When the major Gestalt theorists (e.g. Wertheimer, Koffka, Köhler and Lewin) migrated from Berlin to America they no longer formed a clearly identifiable and coherent school of psychology. This was in part because they migrated at different times and went to separate institutions. Some held appointments at élite East Coast colleges which were distinguished for the quality of their under-graduate teaching but which lacked large graduate research pro-grammes (Ash, 1980). Lewin did much to stimulate the development, in America, of an experimental social psychology. Heider, as we shall see, also made significant contributions to the development of social psychology in America. The dominant form of psychology which the Gestaltists found firmly established when they arrived in America was, as noted above, behaviourism. The 'new experimental psy-chology' which Titchener and others had brought with them from Leipzig had scarcely survived the transatlantic crossing. The func-tionalism of William James (defined as such in contrast to the struc-turalism of Titchener who was the representative, in America, of the Wundtian orthodoxy) was a peculiarly American flowering. The psychology of William James was still rooted very much in man's *experience* of the world. James was interested in exploring the nature of man's consciousness and his experience of selfhood. He conceived of human consciousness in a more dynamic and fluid manner than did Wundt. Wundt's conception of consciousness owed more to Descartes than it did to Darwin. James's conception of it, however, owed more to Darwin than to Descartes. For James psychology was still very much the 'science of mental life' (indeed, this was the opening sentence of his famous *Principles of Psychology* (James, 1890)). Func-tionalism, however, was but a half-way house on the road to the full-blown behaviourism which was to become the dominant force in American psychology for most of the present century. When the Gestalt psychologists came to settle in America and re-oriented themselves with respect to their new environment they found them-selves united in their opposition to behaviourism (Ash, 1980). This was how Gestalt psychology came to be an alternative tradition to behaviourism in the history of American psychology. It was due to the influence of Gestalt psychologists that social psychology in America became a cognitive science even in the heyday of behaviourism.

From the science of mind to the science of behaviour

When psychology first began as an experimental science it did so within the framework of philosophy. The early pioneers began to use the experimental methods of the physiologists in order to tackle the problems which psychology inherited from philosophy (for a fuller exposition of this, see the chapter on Wundt in Miller, 1966). Psychology was born as an experimental science out of the liaison between German sensory physiology and the long tradition in philosophy of the British Associationists. 'The Germans knew how the receptors worked; the British knew why they were important. Given the positivistic spirit of the times it was inevitable that the two lines of thought should converge. When this happened, psychology became an experimental science' (Miller, 1966, p. 29). The ghost of Descartes haunted the birth of psychology as an experimental discipline. His dualism of mind and body is evident in the science of the early German psychological laboratories. The science of 'psycho-physics' was concerned with relating mental events (the 'psychics') to physical events (the physical nature of the stimuli impinging upon the sense organs). The characteristics of the physical stimuli were precisely known; what remained to be determined were the mental events. The 'contents' of consciousness were explored by means of introspection. This was the analytic introspectionism of the laboratory which Wundt established at Leipzig in 1879.

Psychology at this time was really the science of experience from the standpoint of the observer. Here, however, observer and observed were one and the same person. This is a distinctive feature of introspection as a method of research. Philosophers knew very well that one cannot 'observe' or study, in any reliable or valid sense, what is going on in other peoples' minds. One can only report on those things of which one is aware – what is going on in one's own mind. Philosophers had been using introspection for centuries, but usually only from the depths of their own armchairs. Their introspections were casual and occasional, rather than rigorous and systematic. Wundt's new laboratory science was both highly controlled and strictly circumscribed, and was therefore quite unlike earlier forms of introspection. Not everyone could introspect reliably – a rigorous training was often called for. Only certain people could provide data which were sufficiently reliable to be usable for scientific purposes. The untrained layman, for example, might refer his mental experience to the object which occasioned it. For example, he might 'refer' the colour and fragrance to the rose rather than reporting them as basic sensory experiences. Titchener called this interpretation the 'stimulus error'.

> A coin, for example, cannot be described as a 'shilling'. The introspective observer must strip off meanings and values. Although those are indeed present in the experience, they are not elements, they are elusive compounds which must be analysed if possible. One who reports objects inferred from elements commits the stimulus error. (Woodworth, 1965, p. 28)

Today, following Heider and others, we would classify this as an attributional error. It is an 'error', however, only with respect to the canons of acceptability for introspective reports in the Leipzig and Cornell laboratories of yesteryear. In everyday life this is a natural phenomenon with a high degree of functional utility in terms of its evolutionary significance. The man in the street could not survive if he attended only to raw sensory data. Apprentice experimenters in the Leipzig and Cornell laboratories had to shed the habits of a lifetime in order to make such valid introspective reports.

It is important for the theme of this chapter to appreciate the nature of the distinction between 'self' and 'other' with respect to mental events. There was one thing which Descartes in the course of his *Meditations* could not doubt and that was that he did doubt – hence his famous 'cogito ergo sum' statement. His one certainty related to his own mental experience. If one adopts his method of radical doubt, however, it makes one's belief in the existence of minds other than one's own problematic. This form of doubt was not conducive to the development of a serious social psychology. Friedman (1967) expressed it this way: 'Philosophical concentration on the problem of the relation of the mind to the body reduced the study of society to the problem of whether other minds existed' (p. 163).

From serious doubt, on the part of *self*, that *others* have minds which are amenable to investigation it is but a short step to the development of doubt, on the part of those others, that self has valid experiences on which he can reliably report. Evidence of 'reliability' is usually social in form, i.e. several observers agree on what it is that they observe. Self-reports, therefore, are suspect because they cannot be checked independently. The making of observations without reference to the consciousness of the other first occurred in the study of infants and animals. Watson made a significant contribution to the study of animals by dispensing with the mandatory reference to the consciousness of the animal which was required after one had carefully described its actual behaviour. Such reference could only be by way of analogy to what occurred in the mind of the observer of the animal. The dangers of anthropomorphism are obvious. By dispensing with such references to consciousness, Watson was able to improve the quality of scientific observation in the study of animal and child behaviour. The absence of speech in other species and in the human infant made such methods of observation inevitable. With their perfection, behaviourism became established as a dominant force in psychology. Success in the study of the behaviour of animals and of young children led to an extrapolation of the same methods of investigation to the study of the human adult.

Watson sought to make psychology a branch of natural science by declaring it to be the science of behaviour. Behaviourism was a systematic programme for ridding psychology of mentalistic concepts. It is a measure of its success as a programme that, for most of this century, it would have been plainly inappropriate to refer to psychology as being the science of mental life. With behaviourism there came into psychology the concept of the 'empty organism' and the 'black box'. Speculation as to what might be going on 'inside' the organism or the black box was ruled out in the interests of methodological rigour. This was part of the programmatic attempt to eliminate from psychology all reference to consciousness or mind. An early behaviourist text, in which Meyer (1921) adopted a consistent methodological stance, was interestingly entitled *The Psychology of the Other One*. Meyer set out, in his writing, to provide Robinson Crusoe on his desert island with the one book in psychology which would enable him to figure out what sort of man Man Friday was, and what he was, and was not, capable of doing. The advice to the methodological purist is to approach the other (whether machine, plant, animal or human) as though 'it' were a total stranger. This was the thoroughly objective stance that it was necessary to adopt if psychology was to become a branch of natural science. Meyer believed that in the past we had a psychology of self – this was part of the inheritance from philosophy. Now, he felt, it was time to develop the psychology of the 'Other-One' (i.e. what we now recognize as behaviourism). 'There is a special fact which has greatly retarded the advancement of the psychology of the Other-One – the fact that the psychology of the Self appears so much easier, so much more promising' (p. 4).

It was necessary in psychology, from the standpoint of behaviourism, not only to avoid all reference to the minds of others but also to keep a tight rein on the development of theoretical ideas in the mind of the observer. In the radical behaviourism of B. F. Skinner one is admonished *not to go beyond the evidence* available to the senses. Skinner criticized Pavlov for speculating about the neural states of excitation and inhibition in the cortex of the brain on the basis of purely behavioural evidence, namely the sequencing of stimuli and responses. These cortical states were not directly visible and hence were conceptual rather than factual. Yet Pavlov had originally provided Watson with the model of what a purely objective psychology might be like. Skinner also criticized Hull, a neo-behaviourist, for inventing such theoretical notions as 'drive', 'habit', etc. Skinner believed such notions to be unnecessary in accounting for the facts of learning. Tolman (1935) had put forward the idea of 'intervening variables' which, whilst they were not directly visible, nevertheless could be defined in terms of variables which were observable – for example, whilst hunger or thirst as drive states are not directly observable they can be operationally defined in terms of the number of hours since the organism had last had either food or drink. Hull had made extensive use of intervening variables in the development of his highly systematic theory of learning. These intervening variables were quite closely related, either to stimulus events or to response events which were directly observable. Whilst the constraints of defining variables operationally kept a tight rein on speculation, such practices were not approved of by radical behaviourists. There is thus in behaviourism a certain theoretical impoverishment. This stems from a deliberate decision to avoid all reference either to the minds of others or to events (such as inferences) going on in the minds of the observers of those others.

From the perception of objects and events to the perception of persons

Early research in Gestalt psychology was concerned with the perception of such dramatic events as movement and such basic distinctions in our perception of the world as that between figure and ground. Persons stand out as figures against the background of the physical environment and also as important sources of movement or action. Behaviour (whether of man or animals) is a highly salient aspect of man's experience of the world around him. The major Gestalt theorists were aware of the dramatic implications for psychology of taking behaviour as the subject matter of their discipline. Koffka has this to say: 'if we start with behaviour it is easier to find a place for consciousness and mind than it is to find a place for behaviour if we start with mind or consciousness' (Koffka, 1936, p. 25). This could well have been a suitable epitaph for the life and work of the American philosopher, George Herbert Mead.

Early in his *Principles of Gestalt Psychology* Koffka recounts the following German legend:

> On a winter evening amidst a driving snowstorm a man on horseback arrived at an inn, happy to have reached a shelter after hours of riding over the wind-swept plain on which the blanket of snow had covered all paths and landmarks. The landlord who came to the door viewed the stranger with surprise and asked him whence he came. The man pointed in the direction straight away from the inn, whereupon the landlord, in a tone of awe and wonder, said: 'Do you know that you have ridden across the Lake of Constance?' At which the rider dropped stone dead at his feet. (Koffka, 1936, pp. 27, 28)

Koffka then goes on to ask the following interesting question: 'In what environment, then, did the behaviour of the stranger take place?' His answer is important for anyone who considers psychology to be a branch of natural science:

> The Lake of Constance. Certainly, because it is a true proposition that he rode across it. And yet, this is not the whole truth, for the fact that there was a frozen lake and not ordinary solid ground did not affect his behaviour in the slightest. It is interesting for the geographer that this behaviour took place in this particular locality, but not for the psychologist as the student of behaviour; because the behaviour would have been just the same had the man ridden across a barren plain. But the psychologist knows something more: since the man died from sheer fright after having learned what he had 'really' done, the psychologist must conclude that had the stranger known before, his riding behaviour would have been very different from what it actually was. Therefore the psychologist will have to say: There is a second sense to the word environment according to which our horseman did not ride across the lake at all,

but across an ordinary snow-swept plain. His behaviour was
a riding-over-a-plain, but not a riding-over-a-lake. (Koffka,
1936, p. 28)

There is clearly a divergence in perspective here as between the
observer and the rider. This is comparable to that divergence in perspective which exists between an experimenter and those who participate in his research as subjects. This brings us straight into the
heartland of that area of research which the contemporary reader will
immediately recognize as the social psychology of the experiment.
Indeed, it was part of Koffka's original intent to raise just such an
issue: 'Does the rat run in the maze *the experimenter* has set up?'
(Koffka, 1936, p. 28, italics in the original). It is sufficient that Koffka
suggested that the perspective of the experimenter or observer might
be *different* from that of his research subject or the observed. I am
seeking here to make *explicit* the social psychology which is *implicit* in
Koffka's original distinction between the geographical and the behavioural environments. The social psychology is quite explicit, however,
in Heider's *Psychology of Interpersonal Relations* (1958); it is also quite
explicit in Ichheiser's 'Misunderstandings in Human Relations'
(1949).

With behaviourism there came into psychology a different version
of the stimulus error from the one which Titchener had originally
identified. The error is the tendency on the part of the observer to
believe that he has correctly identified which aspects of the environment 'cause' the behaviour he observes. As observer and observed
are here two different persons or organisms this inevitably involves
more than one perspective. In order to explain the behaviour of other
it may be necessary for self to understand the environment as other
believes it to be rather than as self knows it to be. This essentially
Gestalt perspective is enshrined in the social science literature in what
has come to be known as Thomas's theorem: 'if men define situations
as real, they are real in their consequences' (Thomas and Thomas,
1928, p. 567).

When behaviourism became the dominant force in American psychology, experimentalists directly related observable stimuli to
observable behaviour, thus neglecting, as an area of serious scientific
study, the *meaning* of those stimuli for the organism whose behaviour
they were observing. This question of meaning, however, was central
to the interests of the Gestalt theorists. The Gestalt theorists strongly

influenced the development of social psychology in America – especially Lewin, Heider and Asch. They laid the foundations of an experimental social psychology and established such fields of empirical inquiry as person perception, consistency models of attitude change, attribution theory and the dynamics of small groups. Thus the influence of Gestalt psychology on the development of social psychology in America is pervasive. Campbell (1963), in his classic article on 'Social attitudes and other acquired behavioural dispositions', noted how the 'view of the world' approach to the study of attitudes came to prevail over the 'consistency of response' approach. This represented, in an area of study of major significance for social psychologists, a victory for Gestalt theory over behaviour theory. It also represents a victory for those methodologists who prefer to elicit accounts from actors rather than stick strictly to what observers can record.

Elsewhere, one of us has tried to show how the theory to which an experimenter subscribes influences his actual experimental practice (Farr, 1976, 1978a). The main contrast in the history of experimental social psychology is between those who were influenced by Gestalt theory (e.g. Lewin, Asch, Festinger, etc.) and those who were influenced by behaviour theory (e.g. Allport, Dashiell, Dollard and Miller, Hovland, etc.).

> Allport adopted the perspective of the experimenter and saw himself as operating within a natural science tradition of experimentation. Minimising the interactional aspects of the basic experimenter–subject dyad, he faithfully recorded the behaviour of his experimental subjects and inferred this to be a function of physically identifiable aspects of the subject's environment. Asch on the other hand, adopted the perspective of a subject in one of his own experiments and attempted to aim at an understanding of the meaning for the subject of the experimental situation. (Farr, 1976, p. 229)

This approach to the social psychology of the experiment is thought to have arisen only in recent years with the work of Martin Orne (1962). As an alternative perspective to the dominant behavioural one it is, at least, as old as Gestalt theory. Looking back on his seminal paper, and speculating on why it turned out to be so significant, Orne had this to say: 'It seemed naive to assume that human subjects respond only to those aspects of the experiment that we define as stimuli' (1979).

It appears to me that the difficulties with psychological experiments can best be conceptualised by assuming that in all studies there are two experiments: the one which the investigator intends and the one which the subject perceives. The ecological validity of the inferences drawn from any given experiment will largely depend upon how closely the experiment the subject perceives approximates the one the experimenter intends. We cannot assume the nature of the relationship, and our methodology must concern itself with assessing it empirically. (Orne, 1979, p. 26)

Here we are back again with the innkeeper and the rider on horseback.

Once *self* (i.e. P) acknowledges that the perspective of *other* (i.e. O) may differ from his own perspective one of several things may follow:

(a) With a sympathetic leap of the imagination self may try to put himself in the place of other and attempt to see the world as other sees it. This is what Lewin tried to do in his concept of the psychological life-space of the individual. In so doing he failed to retain his own separate perspective as an observer of that other.

(b) P may retain his perspective on O whilst appreciating that the perspective of O will differ from his own. This is Heider's model which he adopts as a basis for his psychology of interpersonal relations. It is a much more inherently social model than the one developed by his good friend and fellow Gestaltist, Lewin. 'It is difficult or impossible to describe in topological terms how one person's life-space is represented in another person's life-space – how, for instance, the sentiment of A can be a goal for B, or how A reacts to what B does to him'. (Heider, 1958, p. 14)

(c) P can bring out the divergence in perspective between himself and O by inviting O to tell him about the world as he sees it. P can question O about his actions. O need not remain silent in the presence of P. They can converse. This is a useful introduction to what, elsewhere, one of us has described as 'the social psychology of the inter-view' (Farr, 1982). The interview is a useful research strategy for establishing that there are perspectives on events other (i.e. O) than that of the person (P) initiating the inquiry. Harré and Secord (1972) argue that a new methodology is called for in the social sciences. They accept Strawson's characterization of a person as someone who can monitor his own behaviour and give an account of it. They therefore suggest that the most appropriate methodology for the social sciences is the elicitation, collection and analysis of 'accounts'. Their quite ready acceptance that 'accounts' might need to be negotiated suggests that they retain a quite healthy belief in the existence of perspectives other than those of the narrator.

Whilst the approach in this chapter is an explicitly social one it is phenomenological in orientation, without being hostile to purely behavioural approaches. Meyer, in his *The Psychology of the Other-One*, says:

> If we call psychology a Natural Science, it is the study merely of the nature of 'the Other-One *in relation to us*'. And if we call psychology a Social Science, it is the fundamental social science. The social sciences in the common use of this term must then be regarded more properly as the 'special' or 'applied' social sciences. (Meyer, 1921, italics added)

The forms of behaviourism which have been of significance in the history of psychology have focused on the individual organism. They have therefore been non-social in their conceptions of man. This, however, need not have been the case. We have just noted how Meyer could conceive of psychology as being *either* a natural science *or* a social science. Watson could only consider it as being a branch of natural science. In Meyer's view *if* psychology were a natural science *then* it was the study of the behaviour of the Other-One *in his relation to us*; that is to say, his conception of behaviourism was a social one. In an interesting sense Heider's perspective, whilst being a Gestalt one, is quite close to this. He is concerned with the study of O (the 'Other-One', in Meyer's terminology) *from the perspective of P*. He is interested in the *representations* which P has of O which enable him to anticipate the other's actions and which serve as a guide to P in his interactions with O. When P stands for psychologist *these representations correspond to psychological theories*. We have already noted above how behaviourists in psychology traditionally have played down the role of theory in their particular brand of psychological science. The representations to which we have referred are social in two senses: (i) in terms of their on-going dynamics they refer to the representations which P has of O, that is, they relate to at least two different persons; and (ii) they are social *in origin* and arise out of P's personal and social experience within a particular culture at a particular point in time in the history of that culture. We use the term 'representation' here in Durkheim's original sense of 'collective' representation, that is, by way of contrast to the 'individual' representations which operate at a purely psychological level. Later in this chapter we shall see how contemporary work in the area of attribution theory derives from, and constitutes part of, the study of social representations.

This approach to the study of the representations which P forms of O is highly compatible with new developments in the general area of cognitive science, for example the work of Sanford and Garrod (1981) on understanding written text. Sanford and Garrod are interested in the representation of the reader in the mind of the writer in so far as this enters into and affects the process of writing. In the study of dialogue they are similarly interested in the representation of the listener in the mind of the speaker in so far as this enters into and affects the development of discourse. This is a far more inherently social approach than is traditional in the field of psycholinguistics.

In concluding this section we wish to make reference to one other version of behaviourism (apart from that of Meyer) which is inherently social in form – the social behaviourism of Mead (1934). One of us has written extensively elsewhere on the contemporary significance of Mead's work (Farr, 1980a, c, 1981). The relevance of Mead in the present context is that he developed a form of behaviourism which was explicitly opposed to that of Watson who had been a junior colleague of his at Chicago. Unlike Watson he singled out for explanation those very characteristics which set man apart from other species – language, thinking, self-awareness and mind. He found, in Darwin's *The Expression of the Emotions in Man and Animals* (1872), the key to understanding the social nature of mind in man. Mead (1934) further developed Wundt's concept of the human gesture which the latter, in turn, had developed on the basis of some of Darwin's observations. Both Mead and Wundt were concerned with speculating on how, in man's remote past, language may have evolved from gesturing. Mead, in particular, was interested in the 'conversation of gestures' which occurs when one animal orients itself with respect to another.

For Mead, 'self' emerges out of social interaction. An individual is an object in the social world of other people and as a result of interacting with them he becomes an object to himself – he becomes a 'person'. Man, uniquely as a species, can act towards himself as an object. Man is thus a 'minded organism'. For Mead the *meaning* of an action was to be found in the response which it elicited from others. This was the sense in which it was accurate to describe Mead as a *social behaviourist*. The significance, for man, of language resides in its power to evoke in the speaker a response analogous to that which it evokes in a listener from the same culture. As man can normally hear himself talk he is more self-reflexive in the auditory, than he is in the visual, modality. This asymmetry between the two modalities springs from the simple biological fact that man's eyes are at the front of his head and so he is only rarely an object in his own visual field. This asymmetry between the two modalities is important for the theme of the next section of this chapter. There is a divergence in perspective between 'actors' and 'observers' (Jones and Nisbett, 1971) if one considers the visual domain. There is not, however, the same divergence in perspective between speakers and listeners in the oral/aural domain.

Attribution theory and social representations

The study of attribution processes is very much a vogue topic of research in experimental social psychology. Heider (1958) in his highly seminal volume, *The Psychology of Interpersonal Relations*, identified the nature of some of the basic attributional processes. The study of attributions thus initially arose in psychology out of adopting a phenomenal perspective. It is, historically speaking, firmly rooted in Gestalt psychology.

Heider was concerned with taking stock of the rules of inference whereby the layman *goes beyond* the purely behavioural evidence available to him (as an *observer* of the actions of (O)ther and their consequences) when he infers the opinions, attitudes, motives, goals, intentions, traits, abilities, etc. of that particular O which would account for those actions. These are all 'constructs' in the mind of P which enable him to predict and anticipate the actions of O. The notion of mind is crucial for identifying the precise location of these constructs. Since psychology ceased to be the science of mind there has been much confusion in these matters. When P is a psychologist it is necessary to enquire about the ontological status of those mental constructs. For Freud the concepts of ego, id and super-ego were clearly constructs *in his own mind* which enabled him to interpret the psychological phenomena which he observed in his consulting room.

16   Issues in person perception

Observation, for Freud, always took precedence over theory. This was what made him the distinguished scientist he was. However, many of the pioneers of the mental test movement, as well as certain personality theorists, believed that the abilities and traits for which they devised tests were characteristics inherent in the Os who performed on those tests. These pioneers were dazzled perhaps by the magic of measurement. When they first began to conceive of themselves as scientists engaged in the serious business of measurement, rather than as practitioners wrestling with the practical problems of appraisal, they committed, we submit, an attributional error.

In the heyday of behaviourism theorists were always careful to distinguish between intervening variables, a notion first introduced by Tolman (1935), and hypothetical constructs (see MacCorquodale and Meehl, 1948). Both of these were constructs in the mind of P, the observer (for an illuminating contemporary discussion of this issue, see Hyland, 1981). The critical difference between the two was that hypothetical constructs carried 'surplus meaning', i.e. they were thought to refer to entities which were independent of the thinker; for example, genes and atoms were hypothetical constructs long before the entities in the real world to which they correspond had been identified and isolated. The pioneers of the mental test movement believed intelligence to be a hypothetical construct in this sense. They might have been wiser to have stuck to the type of operational definition advocated by the physicist Bridgman (1927): 'intelligence is what intelligence tests measure.' This is often thought, wrongly, to be a simple device for opting out of the problems involved in defining theoretical concepts. It is, instead, a suitably cautious approach when the theorist is unsure whether or not the entity to which he refers exists independently of his notion of it. Even when the theorist *does* believe that his key idea corresponds to something 'out there', his use of the adjective hypothetical to qualify construct reminds him of the *provisional* nature of his theoretical construct as he does not *yet* have 'evidence' of its independent existence. In their eagerness to achieve scientific respectability some of the early pioneers in psychology may well have thrown caution to the wind.

This is all the more surprising in view of a highly sophisticated early warning about the unconscious nature of attributional errors in research. We refer here to the pioneering experimental studies of Stumpf and Pfungst into the non-verbal system of signals which passed between questioner and horse in the famous case of Clever

Hans. Hans's reputed powers of mathematical calculation were of considerable interest, at the turn of the century, to psychologist and biologist alike. That was an era in which there was considerable interest in the nature of animal intelligence. Hans, on being presented with various mathematical problems, tapped out the answers with his hoof. In 1904 some thirteen professionals, including a professor of psychology, a physiologist, a vet, a director of the Berlin Zoo and a circus manager, certified that, in their opinion, Hans was receiving no intentional cues from his owner (Mr von Osten) or any other questioner: 'This is a case which appears in principle to differ from any hitherto discovered.' Pfungst first established that Hans was, in fact, clever and that his cleverness did not depend on the presence of his master: Almost any questioner could elicit accurate answers. Pfungst then introduced into his experimental procedures various control conditions, such as putting Hans in blinkers so that he could not see the questioner. This reduced Hans's cleverness. Other conditions also reduced his accuracy; for example, if the questioner did not know the answer to the question neither did the horse. Hans's accuracy also diminished as the physical distance between him and his questioners increased. Hence, Pfungst concluded, Hans was clever only when he had visual access to a source of the correct answer. It was likely therefore, that visual cues were involved (though no specific ones had been discovered).

Pfungst then carried out further experimental investigations to identify precisely the system of cues. A slight forward inclination of the questioner's head, to see the horse's hoof more clearly, was the signal to begin tapping. This did not need to be accompanied by a question. For a large answer questioners inclined their heads further forward and this controlled the rate of tapping; Hans tapped faster because it appeared that he 'knew' a longer answer was called for. A critical factor was the questioner's expectancy of obtaining a correct answer. The questioner tended to straighten up when the correct number of taps was reached. The horse was highly sensitive to tiny upward motions of the questioner's head – even the raising of an eyebrow or the dilation of the nostrils. Anyone could start, or stop, Hans tapping by using these cues.

After their careful experimental investigations, Stumpf and Pfungst were able to identify precisely the nature of the error to which they, in company with many others, had been subject. 'We were looking, in the horse, for what should have been sought in the man.' It was a striking instance of what, today, we would classify as an attributional error. Clearly the stimulus to which the horse was responding was the behaviour of the questioner rather than the mathematical problem written on the board. This is an interesting example of the type of stimulus error identified above. It is also an instance of an early failure to appreciate fully the situation to which the animal was responding (i.e. the *social* nature of that situation) and of the 'bias' on the part of spectators for making dispositional attributions (Ichheiser, 1943, 1949; Jones and Nisbett, 1971). (A bias because they ascribed 'powers' of mathematical computation to the horse.) Pfungst's classic study has now been re-issued, with an interesting introduction by Rosenthal, whose own experimental studies of the social psychology of the experiment are perhaps better known to the contemporary reader (Pfungst, 1965).

In their eagerness to improve on the layman's understanding of his fellow man, psychologists have sought, in matters of research method, to be purists. It is all too easy however for them to forget the perspective from which they themselves view events. We refer here to what Allport (1940) and Ichheiser (1943) called 'the psychologist's frame of reference'. This is the perspective of P in the social psychology envisaged by Heider (1954). There are two broadly contrasting strategies of research which have been important in the history of psychology. There are the two traditions of scientific psychology which Cronbach (1957) first identified in his presidential address to the American Psychological Association – 'correlational' and 'experimental' psychology. A good example of the former type of psychology is the psychometric tradition to which Cronbach himself has contributed in such a distinguished manner. It is not generally appreciated, however, that there are certain assumptions of an attributional nature built into these various methods of research. The bias in the psychometric approach lies in the decision to standardize the conditions of observation or testing and then to *attribute* all of the variance in what one observes to individual differences. The psychologist, in his professional role, is here making *dispositional attributions* in the manner identified by Ichheiser (1943) and by Jones and Nisbett (1971). The striving after increased precision in measurement led to the development of this particular bias. A useful antidote to this particular bias is the adoption of a Bayesian perspective (see, for example, Cronbach and Gleser, 1957). Here the emphasis is on the use of psychometric data to reduce uncertainty in the mind of the decision-maker (the educator) or the personnel selector. This switch in the focus of attention from the person being tested to the person doing the testing is almost as dramatic as Pfungst's decision to concentrate his investigations on the questioner rather than on the horse. The psychology of the Other-One has a nasty habit of reflexively turning one's attention back on the psychology of self. It is important to be clear in one's own mind as to whose mind one is talking about – that of other or that of self. This is where the special expertise of the social psychologist is needed, even in such an apparently non-social field as classical psychometrics.

Cronbach (1957) drew a sharp distinction, in the history of psychology, between the psychometric tradition and the tradition of experimental research. He saw both as being equally venerable, albeit separate and even opposed, traditions. The methodologies associated with the two traditions were often antithetical to each other both in pure and applied research. A large 'within group' variance, due to too wide a range of individual differences, reduces the significance of the 'between group' variance which the experimenter creates when he manipulates the independent variable. The greater prestige has tended to attach to the use of experimental methods. Built into the use of experimental methods are certain assumptions of an attributional nature. In an internally valid experiment (Campbell, 1957) the experimenter can, with confidence, uniquely attribute the difference he obtains on his dependent variable to his manipulation of the independent variable. By the skilful use of control groups he can neatly anticipate any rival explanations that others might wish to make of his results. A well-designed experiment is thus a highly persuasive communication. Not only is the experimenter (or self) justified in the conclusions he draws, but he controls the attributions that any other can make on the basis of his results. All explanations which rival the experimenter's (that X has caused the difference on his dependent variable) have been anticipated and the appropriate controls included in the design (Campbell, 1957). In this lies the secret of the experiment's persuasive impact – at least in the scientific community of other experimenters.

In deciding to tackle a problem experimentally, the psychologist has selected a methodology in which there is a built-in bias favouring the making of a *situational attribution*; the experimenter creates a difference between two situations (his experimental and his control groups) and ascribes the difference he obtains on his dependent variable to the difference between the two situations which he devised. This

situational ascription thus runs counter to the normal bias charac-
terizing the perspective of the observer, overestimating the importance
of traits and dispositions and seriously underestimating the effect of the
situation (Ichheiser, 1943, 1949; Jones and Nisbett, 1971). When the
same social issue is tackled using both scientific traditions outlined by
Cronbach, the contrasting conclusions arrived at can best be explained
in terms of the differing attributional assumptions of the two traditions.
Let us take as an example the issue of Fascism in Nazi Germany. The
pioneering work in this field was Adorno *et al.*'s (1950) study of *The
Authoritarian Personality*. The methodology here was correlational or
psychometric – the use of projective tests, clinical interviews, attitude
and opinion scales, etc. The underlying theory was the psychoanalytic
one of personality development. The burden of the explanation for
what happened in Germany was being carried by postulating a certain
personality type – the Fascist or proto-Fascist – which in turn was
related in a fairly systematic manner to certain styles of child rearing.
When Milgram (1974), much later in the day, came to tackle some of the
same issues, he used experimental methods. It is hardly surprising that
he should end up by stressing situational, rather than dispositional,
determinants of behaviour. He demonstrated how the majority of persons in his experiment continued to obey instructions coming from a
legitimate source of authority even though these involved inflicting
what they believed to be pain on a reluctant fellow subject. The whole
point of Milgram's experimental studies is that he highlights the very
powerful, though invisible, social forces which constrain behaviour. In
an appendix to his research monograph he notes: 'For the social psychology of this century reveals a major lesson: often, it is not so much the
kind of person a man is as the kind of situation in which he finds himself
that determines how he will act' (Milgram, 1974, p. 205). Here is the
antidote to the bias of the observer – and the evidence for it is experimental. Milgram's studies provide convincing evidence of the truth of
Ichheiser's observation:

> Thus, the persisting pattern which permeates everyday life of inter-
> preting individual behaviour in the light of personal factors [traits]
> rather than in the light of situational factors must be considered one
> of the fundamental sources of misunderstanding personality in our
> time. It is both the cause and the symptom of the crisis of our society.
> (Ichheiser, 1943, p. 152)

We have referred several times to Ichheiser's work. He is, for us, a key figure in developing the theme of this chapter. His approach to understanding interpersonal relations is firmly rooted in the Durkheimian study of collective representations. One of us, some time ago, suggested that the term 'representation' could usefully replace 'opinion' in social psychology (Moscovici, 1963). At the time this suggestion was not taken up and developed. Ichheiser identifies what he called the 'mote-beam mechanism'. It 'consists in perceiving certain characteristics in others which we do not perceive in ourselves and thus perceiving those characteristics as if they were peculiar traits of the others' (Ichheiser, 1949, p. 51). Ichheiser chose prejudice as a particularly telling example of how this mechanism operates. 'The concept of prejudice tends rather to camouflage than to illuminate the essential factors in inter-group tensions' (p. 42). This is because prejudice is seen to be a characteristic of individuals, and the observer (who, for Ichheiser, could have been either the social scientist or another layman) fails to 'see' that he himself is also prejudiced. It is this 'failure of insight' which is at the root of much misunderstanding in human relations in everyday life.

Until the recent work of the Bristol school (Turner and Giles, 1981; Tajfel, 1981), the study of prejudice and the study of inter-group relations were two separate and unrelated areas of study within social psychology. This illustrates the force of Ichheiser's original observations that social scientists are not themselves exempt from the operation of the mote-beam mechanism. Ichheiser arrives at the very Socratic conclusion that 'if people who do not understand each other at least understand that they do not understand each other, then they understand each other better than when, not understanding each other, they do not even understand that they do not understand each other' (Ichheiser, 1949, p. 37). The mote-beam mechanism, as identified by Ichheiser is a failure of insight. He distinguishes it quite clearly from the psychoanalytic defence mechanism of projection which 'consists in attributing to other people certain characteristics which we do, but they actually do not, possess' (p. 51). He believed that these two rather different mechanisms were often, in practice, confused.

Ichheiser stressed the importance of attitudes *and images* as basic elements in human relations. The 'images' to which he referred are social representations in the Durkheimian sense.

To define the attitudes which two individuals (or two groups) take with regard to each other is meaningless if we do not define simultaneously the images which they have in their minds about each other. . . . The interpersonal significance of an attitude always depends on the content of the image about the other person to which it refers. (Ichheiser, 1949, p. 58)

One of us has been arguing for some time that the study of social representations could be of central significance to the whole of social psychology (Moscovici, 1961/72): 'the concept of social representation could usefully replace those of opinion or image, which are relatively static and descriptive' (Moscovici, 1963, p. 252). Ichheiser did have a proper appreciation of the role of social representations in the dynamics of interpersonal relations:

Certainly, very often distorted images and misinterpretations are the consequences of conscious and unconscious hostilities. But also the opposite is often true: many hostilities are not the cause but the consequence of distorted images and misinterpretations . . . very frequently, if not always, people who are persecuting others are not aware that they are persecuting, for, in the light of the images which they have in their minds, it looks to them that they are 'fighting for a worthy cause' or are 'liberating the world from an evil thing'. (Ichheiser, 1949, p. 59)

Ichheiser drew an important distinction between 'expression' and 'impression'. 'Impressions' form in the minds of others who witness or observe that expressive behaviour. Ichheiser argued that it was important to study the impressions that people form of the personality of others. Impressions, of course, may or may not be accurate. A recognition of this distinction provides plenty of scope for understanding why there is so frequently a mismatch between the two. Ichheiser's monograph, after all, was 'a study in false social perception'. He was concerned with identifying the analogues, in the field of social perception, to the visual illusions which can occur in our perception of the physical world. He did this from the perspective of a sociology of knowledge. His work provided the basis, which they readily acknowledge, for the distinction mady by Jones and Nisbett (1971) concerning the divergent perspectives of 'actors' and 'observers'.

The mismatch between expression and impression is of crucial significance. They relate to *two* different persons or organisms. Hence we are dealing with a *social process* even in the study of animals lower than man in the evolutionary hierarchy. Ichheiser points out, in a succinct footnote, 'This fundamental discrepancy between expression and impression incidentally explains why physiognomics was never able to achieve the status of a science. Physiognomics could be legitimate only if expressive and impressive values would coincide. But this is not the case' (p. 9). Mead believed that the single most important textbook in psychology in his day was Darwin's *The Expression of the Emotions in Man and Animals*, which for him, contained the clue to understanding the nature of language in man (see Farr, 1980a). For Mead the *meaning* of an expressive act was the *response* it elicited in observing others. Thus he was interested in the 'conversation of gestures' *between* organisms as they co-oriented to each other. The hiss of the snake evoked attack by the dog. The attack was the *meaning* of the hiss; it was not, however, an *intentional* meaning. Language is a peculiar form of gesturing in man which enables him to evoke in others meanings which he 'intends'. Intentionality is much more a characteristic of the behaviour of humans than it is of the behaviour of other species. It has emerged in the course of human evolution and there is nothing 'mysterious' about it. Mead, Wundt and Darwin were interested in the study of expressive behaviour. Ichheiser is more directly concerned with impression. At the end of the day the two need to be interrelated and that was something of which Ichheiser was clearly aware. The most useful starting-point, according to him, is to assume that they are different.

Impressions are important because they are of direct consequence to the actor of whom they are impressions. The impressions that others form of self are of importance to self in his relation to those others. They are autonomous 'social facts' (in the Durkheimian sense) of which self needs to take cognizance. This is the counterpart of 'the behavioural environment' (or Lewin's 'psychological life-space') which Gestalt theorists first identified and which we discussed fairly fully earlier in this chapter, namely, the observer of others needs to take account of how those others (as 'actors') define the situation. Here actors need to take account of the impressions that others (as observers) form of them on the basis of their actions. The influence of Ichheiser on Goffman is clear and explicitly acknowledged. Goffman (1956) in his *The Presentation of Self in Everyday Life*, has brilliantly portrayed how self as actor endeavours to control the impressions that others form of him. He distinguishes between impressions which are 'given off' (and over which self has little or no control) and others which are 'managed'. Those which are given off correspond quite closely to Ichheiser's expression.

Ichheiser also influenced Heider, and Heider is the source of modern research on attribution theory. Whilst Ichheiser was more directly concerned with the sociology of interpersonal relations Heider was more narrowly concerned with their psychology. In moving from socio-logy to psychology there is inevitably some loss in the richness of the social context. Almost a decade ago, one of us could ask in a rhetorical manner: 'What is social about social psychology?' and expect the reply 'Not very much' (Moscovici, 1972). Much of the research in experi-mental social psychology on 'impression formation', 'person percep-tion' and 'attribution theory' is devoid of social significance. Yet it was the *social significance* of impressions which originally led Ichheiser to devote a whole monograph to an explication of them. The impressions which subjects in psychology laboratories form of others, and the attri-butions which they make concerning the 'causes' of their behaviour, are usually trivial in a social sense. This is because the others whom they perceive or of whom they form impressions *do not exist as real people*. To study the mechanisms of attribution in isolation from the social contexts in which they normally operate is a serious impoverishment of the subject-matter of social psychology. Kelley's recent work on *Personal Relationships* (1979) is exempt from this criticism.

The antidote to the social impoverishment of much contemporary work in attribution theory is to reinstate Ichheiser and to study *social representations* as they operate in the social world outside of the labora-tory. Heider was much influenced by Ichheiser's original discussion of success and failure:

> The misinterpretations which consist in underestimating the impor-tance of situational and in overestimating the importance of personal factors, do not arise by chance. *These misinterpretations are not personal errors committed by ignorant individuals.* They are, rather, *a consistent and inevitable consequence of the social system and of the ideology of the nineteenth century,* which led us to believe that our fate in social space depended exclusively, or at least predominantly, on our individual qualities – that we, as individuals, and not the prevailing social conditions, shape our lives. (Ichheiser, 1943, p. 152, italics in original)

This social representation of 'persons' as being responsible for their outcomes is taken over by Heider but in a somewhat diluted form. We would wish to stress the more explicit recognition in the work of Ichheiser of this as being a social representation in the Durkheimian sense of the term. Ichheiser's observations in America in the aftermath of the Depression have an uncannily modern ring about them:

With millions of people suffering the shocks of continued unemployment, with business failures one after the other, banks closing, etc., it was vividly revealed to the man in the street that he was not, as he had been led to believe, the master of his fate, because clearly his fate depended upon forces over which he had no control. (Ichheiser, 1949, p. 62)

References

Adorno, T., Frenkel-Brunswik, E., Levinson, D. J. and Sanford, R. N. (1950) *The Authoritarian Personality*. New York: Harper & Row.

Allport, G. W. (1940) The psychologist's frame of reference. *Psychological Bulletin 37*: 1–28.

Allport, G. W. (1954) The historical background of modern social psychology. In G. Lindzey (ed.) *Handbook of Social Psychology*, vol. 1. Cambridge, Mass.: Addison-Wesley.

Asch, S. (1946) Forming impressions of personality. *Journal of Abnormal and Social Psychology 41*: 258–90.

Ash, M. G. (1980) Gestalt psychology as a case study in the social history of science. Paper presented to the XXIInd International Congress of Psychology, Leipzig, GDR, July.

Bridgman, P. W. (1927) *Logic of Modern Physics*. New York.

Campbell, D. T. (1957) Factors relevant to the validity of experiments in social settings. *Psychological Bulletin 54*: 297–312.

Campbell, D. T. (1963) Social attitudes and other acquired behavioural dispositions. In S. Koch (ed.) *Psychology: A Study of a Science*, vol. 6. New York: McGraw-Hill.

Cronbach, L. J. (1957) The two disciplines of scientific psychology. *American Psychologist 12*: 671–84.

Cronbach, L. J. and Gleser, G. C. (1957) *Psychological Tests and Personnel Decisions*. Urbana: University of Illinois Press.

Danziger, K. (1979) The positivist repudiation of Wundt. *Journal of the History of the Behavioural Sciences 15*: 205–30.

Darwin, C. (1872) *The Expression of the Emotions in Man and Animals*. London: Appleton.

Farr, R. M. (1976) Experimentation: a social psychological perspective. *British Journal of Social and Clinical Psychology 15*: 225–38.

Farr, R. M. (1978a) On the social significance of artifacts in experimenting. *British Journal of Social and Clinical Psychology 17*: 299–306.

Farr, R. M. (1978b) On the varieties of social psychology: an essay on the relationships between psychology and other social sciences. *Social Science Information 17* (4/5): 503–25.

Farr, R. M. (1980a) On reading Darwin and discovering social psychology. In

R. Gilmour and S. Duck (eds) *The Development of Social Psychology*. London: Academic Press.

Farr, R. M. (1980b) *Homo loquens* in social psychological perspective. In H. Giles, W. P. Robinson and P. M. Smith (eds) *Language: Social Psychological Perspectives*. Oxford: Pergamon Press.

Farr, R. M. (1980c) Homo socio-psychologicus. In A. J. Chapman and D. M. Jones (eds) *Models of Man*. Leicester: British Psychological Society.

Farr, R. M. (1981) The social origins of the human mind: a historical note. In J. P. Forgas (ed.) *Social Cognition: Perspectives on Everyday Understanding*. London: Academic Press.

Farr, R. M. (1982) Interviewing: the social psychology of the inter-view. In A. Chapman and A. Gale (eds) *Psychology and People: A Tutorial Text*. London: Macmillan and The British Psychological Society.

Friedman, N. (1967) *The Social Nature of Psychological Research: The Psychological Experiment as a Social Interaction*. New York: Basic Books.

From, F. (1971) *Perception of Other People*. Translated by Brendan Maher and Erik Kvan. New York: Columbia University Press.

Goffman, E. (1956) *The Presentation of Self in Everyday Life*. Edinburgh: University of Edinburgh Social Sciences Research Centre.

Harré, R. and Secord, P. H. (1972) *The Explanation of Social Behaviour*. Oxford: Blackwell.

Heider, F. (1944) Social perception and phenomenal causality. *Psychological Review 51*: 358–74.

Heider, F. (1946) Attitudes and cognitive organisation. *Journal of Psychology 21*: 107–12.

Heider, F. (1958) *The Psychology of Interpersonal Relations*. New York: Wiley.

Hyland, M. (1981) *Introduction to Theoretical Psychology*. London: Macmillan.

Ichheiser, G. (1943) Misinterpretations of personality in everyday life and the psychologist's frame of reference. *Character and Personality 12*: 145–60.

Ichheiser, G. (1949) Misunderstandings in human relations: a study in false social perception. Supplement to the September issue of the *American Journal of Sociology*. Chicago: University of Chicago Press.

James, W. (1890) *Principles of Psychology*, 2 vols. New York: Holt, Rinehart & Winston.

Jones, E. E. and Nisbett, R. E. (1971) The actor and the observer: divergent perceptions of the causes of behaviour. In E. E. Jones, D. E. Kanouse, H. H. Kelley, R. E. Nisbett, S. Valins and B. Weiner (eds) *Attribution: Perceiving the Causes of Behaviour*. Morristown, N. J.: General Learning Press.

Kelley, H. H. (1979) *Personal Relationships: Their Structures and Processes*. Hillsdale, N. J.: Laurence Erlbaum Associates.

Koffka, K. (1936) *Principles of Gestalt Psychology*. London: Routledge & Kegan Paul.

Köhler, W. (1925) *The Mentality of Apes*. Harmondsworth, Middlesex: Penguin Books, 1957 edition. Translated by Ella Winter from the second revised

German edition. First published in Germany, 1925.

MacCorquodale, K. and Meehl, P. E. (1948) On a distinction between hypothetical constructs and intervening variables. *Psychological Review 55*: 95–107.

Mead, G. H. (1934) *Mind, Self and Society: From the Standpoint of a Social Behaviourist.* Edited, with an introduction, by C. W. Morris. Chicago: University of Chicago Press.

Meyer, M. F. (1921) *The Psychology of the Other-One: An Introductory Textbook.* Columbia, Missouri: The Missouri Book Co.

Milgram, S. (1974) *Obedience to Authority: An Experimental View.* London: Tavistock.

Miller, G. A. (1966) *Psychology: The Science of Mental Life.* Harmondsworth, Middlesex: Penguin Books.

Moscovici, S. (1961) *La Psychanalyse: Son image et son public.* Paris: Presses Universitaires de France (2nd edn, 1976).

Moscovici, S. (1963) Attitudes and opinions. *Annual Review of Psychology 14*: 231-60.

Moscovici, S. (1972) Society and theory in social psychology. In J. Israel and H. Tajfel (eds) *The Context of Social Psychology: A Critical Assessment.* London: Academic Press.

Orne, M. T. (1962) On the social psychology of the psychological experiment: with particular reference to demand characteristics and their implications. *American Psychologist 17*: 776-83.

Orne, M. T. (1979) This week's citation classic. *Current Contents 11*(13): 26.

Pfungst, O. (1965) *Clever Hans: The Horse of Mr. von Osten.* Edited by Robert Rosenthal. New York: Holt, Rinehart & Winston.

Sanford, A. J. and Garrod, S. C. (1981) *Understanding Written Language: Explorations of Comprehension Beyond the Sentence.* Chichester: Wiley.

Tajfel, H. (1981) *Human Groups and Social Categories.* Cambridge: Cambridge University Press.

Thomas, W. I. and Thomas D. S. (1928) *The Child in America.* New York: Knopf.

Tolman, E. C. (1935) Psychology versus immediate experience. *Philosophy of Science 2*: 356-80.

Turner, J. C. and Giles, H. (eds) (1981) *Intergroup Behaviour.* Oxford: Blackwell.

Wertheimer, M. (ed.) (1945) *Productive Thinking.* Enlarged edition, 1959. New York: Harper & Brothers.

Woodworth, R. S. (1965) *Contemporary Schools of Psychology.* London: Methuen.

2 Personality traits: in the eye of the beholder or the personality of the perceived?

Sarah E. Hampson

Consider the following situation. A group of students who live on the same floor of a student residence, and hence know each other fairly well, have taken part in a psychological study. It involved each student rating every other on a series of personality scales, such as good-natured versus irritable, and talkative versus silent. The average of all the ratings for each person in the group on each scale was calculated. It was then possible to determine the pattern of relations between the personality scales by intercorrelating them, and to discover the smaller number of underlying dimensions by factor analysing these intercorrelations.

The question is, do these results tell us about the personality characteristics of the students as *ratees*, or do they tell us about the way the students as *raters* perceive the personality of the ratees? In other words, would such a study be an investigation into personality or a study of person perception? This is the central question to be explored in this chapter.

The answer to be offered is that such a study is an investigation into both personality *and* person perception, since personality traits are as much a social construction of the perceiver (rater) as characteristics of the perceived (ratee). By arriving at a new conceptualization of what personality traits actually are, the traditional boundary between personality and person perception disappears.

Hitherto, personality has generally been regarded by personality theorists as a set of characteristics which may be said to exist within the individual causing her or him to behave in certain ways. Personality researchers such as Cattell (Cattell and Kline, 1977) and Eysenck (1953) define these internal characteristics as personality traits; traits are used for describing individual differences, explaining past and present behaviour, and predicting future behaviour. In this discussion, the personality traits believed by personality theorists to be located within the individual and investigated by trait theorists will be referred to collectively as 'actual personality'.

The personality traits that observers believe to be present in the targets of their observations and which are the focus of person perception studies will be referred to as 'perceived personality'. Perceived personality traits are also used for descriptive, explanatory or predictive purposes.

It has been assumed that while personality theorists are attempting to come to grips, albeit indirectly, with 'real' personality, person perception is only concerned with people's beliefs about 'real' personality and that to study these beliefs will not contribute to an understanding of actual personality. It is this traditional assumption which constitutes the boundary between the fields of personality and person perception, and it is this boundary which is being questioned here.

What do personality ratings measure?

Since both perceived and actual personality traits are regarded as internal factors, they can never be studied directly but only inferred from observations of overt behaviour. For this reason, personality researchers have to rely upon measures of their subjects' behaviour such as observers' ratings, subjects' responses on self-report questionnaires or subjects' performance scores on tasks assumed to have relevance to personality (Cattell, 1965; Block, 1977). It is with the first two measures that we are concerned here. The term 'personality rating' will be used to cover both observers' ratings and self-reports. The rating scales used by observers and items found in self-report questionnaires vary considerably in terms of how far they refer to specific behaviours versus abstract personality attributes. For example, a rating scale may require the observer to assess how much time the subject 'spends playing football' or how 'active' the subject is. A questionnaire item might ask the respondent if she 'talks to strangers' or is 'outgoing'. Thus some personality ratings require reference to particular behaviours while others demand an inference based on a more general impression. Do these ratings measure actual personality, perceived personality or something else?

Personality ratings and actual personality

The hypothetical study described at the beginning of the chapter was not merely a flight of imagination. Studies designed more or less along these lines have been carried out independently by researchers claiming to be investigating actual personality (e.g. Cattell, 1946; Norman, 1963), as well as by researchers who believed they were studying the perception of personality (e.g. Wishner, 1960; Dornbusch et al., 1965). It is important to remember that both the major trait theorists arrived at their initial theories of the structure of actual personality by analysing rating data (Eysenck, 1944; Cattell, 1947). While they went on to seek additional support for their theories using self-report questionnaires and objective tests, nevertheless the first findings, which shaped the course of subsequent investigations, were derived from observers' ratings. Thus there is a contradiction here. The same measures (ratings) have been used to investigate perceived and actual personality despite the fact that the two have been regarded as different entities. The contradictory ends to which ratings have been put is highlighted in an investigation by Passini and Norman (1966).

They followed the same design as Norman (1963), by having the members of small groups assign one another to either pole of a series of bipolar personality scales. They succeeded in replicating Norman's results by obtaining the same factor structure with each of the five factors characterized by the same high-loading scales. The one difference in Passini and Norman's study was the fact that the subjects were all complete strangers to one another, whereas in Norman's studies the subjects all knew each other reasonably well. Passini and Norman had shown, therefore, that the pattern of personality characteristics regarded as going together is the same regardless of how well raters know the ratees.

This surprising result was used to good effect by Mischel (1968) as part of his multipronged attack on the personality trait. He used it to strike at the heart of the validity of personality ratings as indices of actual personality. He argued (Mischel, 1968, p. 44) that if the same pattern of ratings is obtained, regardless of whether raters have any information on which to base their judgements, then raters cannot be relied upon as veridical sources of actual personality data. He concluded that personality ratings tell us far more about the pre-existing beliefs of the raters than they do about the nature of the actual personality of the ratees.

Personality ratings and perceived personality

If personality ratings tell us more about the beliefs raters hold about the pattern of relations between personality scales than the pattern of relations actually exhibited by the subjects of their observations, then the accuracy of these beliefs is inevitably suspect. The implication is that person perception is not a process of discerning the actual personalities of the people around us, but instead involves our projection of perceived personalities on to them. The question then becomes one of determining whether the projection of perceived personality overlaps with actual personality, or whether perceived personality is a gross distortion of actual personality. Is it the case that personality ratings measure a set of beliefs which constitute perceived personality, and that perceived personality is really nothing more than a figment of the imagination having no relation to actual personality? This point was taken up in a series of studies by D'Andrade (1965, 1974) and Shweder (1975, 1977).

These studies attempted to distinguish between three possible interpretations of what personality ratings are measuring. First, as personality research assumes, they could be measuring actual personality. Second, as person perception assumed, they could be measuring perceived personality, which may or may not correspond to actual personality. Finally, they could be measuring neither of these things, but instead be an index of the semantic or conceptual similarity between the personality terms used as the labels for the rating scales.

The semantic similarity interpretation suggests that traits overlapping in meaning, such as talkative and friendly, are attributed to the same individual purely because of the semantic similarity between the terms, without any consideration of whether the individual is actually a friendly and talkative person: 'items alike in concept are judged to be characteristic of the same person even when the conceptual relationships among the items do not correspond to the relationships among items in actual behaviour' (Shweder, 1975, p. 476). Shweder and D'Andrade (1979) specified that this 'systematic distortion' is particularly likely to occur under difficult memory conditions, such as those encountered by raters making their judgements days or weeks after exposure to the behaviours concerned.

To distinguish operationally between these three interpretations of personality traits, a reliable measure of actual personality was needed against which personality ratings and the conceptual similarity ratings could be compared. The measure selected by D'Andrade (1974) and Shweder (1975) was the immediate, on-the-spot behaviour rating of subjects. These ratings were then compared with ratings of the same subjects on the same scales made after a delay of a few weeks. They were also compared with conceptual similarity ratings of the scales obtained from an independent group of raters who were instructed to rate all possible combinations of scale-pairs for similarity in meaning. In both studies, the pattern of ratings found under immediate, on-the-spot conditions was only weakly related to the pattern of ratings obtained under delayed conditions and the pattern obtained from the conceptual similarity ratings. In contrast, the delayed ratings and the conceptual similarity ratings were very closely related. Both Shweder and D'Andrade concluded that ratings from memory are liable to distortion arising from the semantic overlap between rating scales. They argued that people cannot be relied upon to make accurate ratings of actual personality, when there is a delay between exposure to the ratees and the rating exercise. In addition they claimed that a reasonable inference to make from these findings is that peoples' beliefs about personality, or their 'implicit personality theories' (see Chapter 7), are merely the product of the overlap in meaning between trait terms and not accurate reflections of reality.

Shweder (1977) suggested that the systematic distortions found in personality ratings made from memory are further examples of a cognitive-processing limitation of the human mind. Difficulty with correlational reasoning has been observed in a variety of contexts (Chapman and Chapman, 1967, 1969; Tversky and Kahneman, 1973, 1974); Shweder argued that personality raters' failure to appreciate that two items may be similar in meaning, without necessarily being found to co-occur in the same individual, is an extension of this difficulty into social information processing.

The Shweder–D'Andrade critique of personality ratings amounts to as powerful an attack on perceived personality as Mischel's critique of actual personality. Taken together, the two critiques imply that the 'personality' purported to have been discovered by personality researchers, and the 'personality' that we attribute to one another via the processes of person perception, are to be dismissed as figments of the imagination. The combination of these arguments leads to the conclusion that personality ratings measure nothing more than people's beliefs about the conceptual similarity or semantic overlap between the rating scales. However, this conclusion has not gone unchallenged.

Personality ratings and constructed personality

Not surprisingly, the Shweder–D'Andrade critique of personality ratings has itself been the subject of both methodological and conceptual criticisms (Block *et al.*, 1979; Lamiell, 1980; Lamiell *et al.*, 1980).

Both Shweder and D'Andrade attempted to obtain an objective measure of actual personality by using immediate, on-the-spot behaviour ratings but, as Block, Weiss and Thorne (1979) stressed, such ratings do not constitute a truly objective criterion. Rating scales vary in the degree to which they refer to specific behavioural acts or require inference from a general impression. Some of the rating scales used in this research were highly inferential: for example, category 6 'Shows antagonism, deflates others' status' (D'Andrade, 1974). Even where relatively specific behaviours are implied by the wording of the item, such as 'Was he fond of swimming?' (Shweder, 1975), there is still scope for distortion by the human observer. 'Behavior in the raw has an infinite variety of facets and pattern possibilities and therefore can only be studied by selection. The act of selection, however done, represents a constructive and theoretical assertion about the world' (Block *et al.*, 1979, p. 1062).

Shweder and D'Andrade's critique collapses because of their failure to locate a truly objective criterion against which to assess perceived personality or beliefs about semantic similarity. They failed because they based their arguments on rating data, but personality ratings, even when made under optimal on-the-spot conditions involving specific concrete behaviours, are inevitably a representation of reality that has been filtered through the human information processing system. As such, the ratings will always be contaminated by characteristics of that system. There can never be truly objective personality ratings because ratings are more than just frequency counts of actual behaviours. If that is all they were, they would not be *personality* ratings. A personality rating, even when it directs the rater's attention to a specific behaviour such as 'Does he like football', involves the rater in distinguishing certain events in the behaviour stream and drawing inferences from these events to a more abstract concept. Perceived personality is bound to involve a 'theoretical and constructive assertion about the world'.

In acknowledging this, we do not have to conclude that perceived personality is merely the projection of beliefs about semantic similarity. Indeed the results obtained both by Shweder and by D'Andrade can be used to support the argument that perceived personality is distinct from semantic similarity. If perceived personality is merely a reflection of semantic similarity, then raters should be insensitive to characteristics of ratees that contradict the semantic similarity between ratings scales. For example, since talkative and friendly are semantically similar a ratee rated as highly talkative should, according to the semantic similarity hypothesis, be rated as highly friendly too, regardless of whether the ratee actually is friendly or not. Alternatively, if perceived personality is more than just the projection of semantic similarity beliefs, then raters should be able to perceive discrepancies such as a talkative ratee who is not friendly. Since immediate, on-the-spot behaviour ratings cannot be truly objective personality measures, they can therefore be measures of perceived personality. In both Shweder's and D'Andrade's studies, these immediate ratings did not bear such close resemblance to semantic similarity ratings as did the delayed ratings. This finding therefore supports the argument that raters are capable of making observations that contradict their pre-existing beliefs about semantic similarity. The fact that these discrepant observations tend to be forgotten after a delay, resulting in the correspondence between delayed ratings and semantic similarity ratings, is in accord with what we know about human memory and its tendency to organize material in a consistent and coherent way at the expense of discrepant information.

The ability of the rater to make observations that contradict semantic similarity was demonstrated more directly in the work of Lamiell and his colleagues. Lamiell took a closer look at the assertions made concerning the similarity between memory-based personality ratings and conceptual similarity ratings of the rating scales themselves. Note that Lamiell's criticisms are not concerned with ratings as measures of actual personality, but with the comparison between ratings as measures of perceived personality and as measures of semantic similarity.

Lamiell drew attention to the fact that Shweder's assertion states that, at the level of *individual ratees*, the rater's beliefs about conceptual similarity between items will be reflected in his or her ratings: 'items alike in concept are inferred to be behaviourally characteristic *of the same person*' (Shweder, 1975, p. 482, emphasis added), yet his evidence is derived from studies where results are pooled across individual ratees. Lamiell argued that the critical test of Shweder's claim is achieved by looking for correspondence between conceptual similarity and perceived personality ratings at the level of individual ratees.

Lamiell, Foss and Cavenee (1980) compared teachers' conceptual similarity ratings of adolescents' activities with their ratings of a group of adolescents on the same activities. In a Shweder-type analysis, the pattern of ratings for the ratees as a group was compared with the conceptual similarity ratings, and the two patterns were found to be highly similar. However, when the pattern of conceptual similarity was compared with each teacher's ratings of each adolescent on a ratee-by-ratee basis, the relationship was much weaker. So raters are capable of noting discrepancies between their beliefs about which rating scales are related, and their perceptions of particular instances of these relations as exhibited by individual ratees. From this study it may be concluded that personality ratings can measure perceived personality.

In attempting to establish what personality ratings measure, the shallowness of the distinction between actual and perceived personality becomes apparent. A personality rating is the product of a constructive process in which the rater observes the ratee through a cognitive filter which imposes structure on what is seen. Personality traits are therefore neither in the eye of the beholder nor in the personality of the perceived. Rather, they are constructed out of the behaviour of the perceived and the mind of the beholder in a mutually dependent process. Personality traits are social constructions and, as such, may be metaphorically located not *within* individuals but *between* them.

The social construction of personality

The attempt to resolve the contradiction over what personality ratings actually measure has led to an alternative conceptualization of the nature of personality in which the perception of personality plays an important part. Doing away with the boundary between actual and perceived personality has highlighted the significance of the perceiver. We have seen that a person's behaviour may be observed by someone else who then makes a personality inference, but a person may also be a self-observer and hence the role of the self-perceiver must also be accommodated in this new conceptualization of personality. The constructivist view of personality regards personality as involving three components: the perceived, the perceiver and the self-perceiver (Hampson, 1982).

The components of constructed personality

In stressing the socially constructed aspect of personality, the component that the person, as a biologically distinct organism, brings to the social arena should not be underestimated. It is the individual who provides the raw material (behaviour) from which personality is constructed. In part this behaviour is the product of the person's biological endowment. We know rather little about the way inherited characteristics actually result in individual differences in behaviour (Wells, 1980), although some personality researchers (e.g. Eysenck, 1967) have speculated about the possible biological bases of specific personality traits. The constructivist view is aimed at redressing the balance in personality research, which has emphasized internal factors at the expense of social and cultural factors. Hence the characteristics of the person that are of a non-social nature will not concern us further here.

Of more direct concern is the component provided by the perceiver in personality construction. The perceiver component refers to the beliefs people hold about personality or their 'implicit personality theories'. Behaviours performed in a social context are imbued with social meaning by those observing them. They are used as the basis for making personality inferences which assist in understanding and predicting behaviour.

In the same way that we can observe other people's behaviour and make personality inferences about them, we can also observe ourselves and hold beliefs about our own personalities. Indeed, we can go further and decide what sort of person we would like to appear to be, and attempt to create particular personality impressions by behaving in particular ways (Goffman, 1959). Thus the third component of constructed personality is the contribution from the self-perceiver.

In arriving at a conceptualization of personality in which the traditional distinction between actual and perceived personality has been removed, it is necessary to show how socially constructed personality can fulfil the functions of its predecessors. The chief distinction between the trait theorists' approach to actual personality, and the traditional views on perceived personality, is that trait theorists regard personality as a motivating force that causes behaviour, whereas perceived personality serves descriptive, explanatory and descriptive functions for the perceiver. While it is clear how the constructivist view incorporates the functions of perceived personality, it is less apparent how it can take over the motivating functions of actual personality. However, each of the three components of the constructivist view of personality contributes towards the understanding of the causes of behaviour. First the perceived component, the person as a biologically distinct organism, allows for the role of biological factors in causing behaviour. But personality is not just a set of motivating forces locked up inside the individual, causing her or him to behave in ways perhaps beyond the individual's control or understanding. Social behaviour is used by the self and others to make inferences about the person performing the behaviour. Thus social behaviour is open to social control. We are often aware of the fact that our social behaviour is being used by others as the basis of personality inferences, and this awareness exerts a control over our behaviour. It causes us to choose between different courses of action on the principle of maximizing the likelihood of achieving the sort of appearance to which we are currently aspiring. This point is central to Harré's (1979) concept of the 'expressive order'. Harré argues that much of human activity revolves around the pursuit of reputation: 'the formation of an impression of ourself in the eyes of others' (Harré, 1979, p. 19). In addition, we are concerned with forming an impression in our own eyes that is compatible with our self-image, and therefore the self-perceiver component also plays a causative role.

In arguing that personality is a social construction, the language of personality description becomes the main focus of study. Trait words form a substantial chunk of the English language amounting to around 18,000 words in all (Allport and Odbert, 1936), and the constructivist view demands a reappraisal of the concept of the personality trait.

Trait as cognitive categories

Let us consider exactly what traits refer to. They do not refer directly to observable phenomena: there is no such 'thing' as friendliness or dependability in existence in the real world. However, there are all sorts of behaviours which people would agree constitute instances of friendliness and dependability. Traits are categories for social behaviour, and these categories only have meaning in so far as they have generally recognized social significance. We, as social actors and observers, share a common set of understandings about the meaning of social behaviour; personality traits are used as a way of summarizing and communicating this meaning.

The view of traits as cognitive categories is an extension of the concept of semantic categories, found in cognitive psychology. The work of Eleanor Rosch and her colleagues is of particular relevance here (Rosch *et al.*, 1976). They investigated concrete object categories, such as 'furniture', 'clothing' and 'birds', and the relation between the words used to describe these objects and actual instances of these objects in the real world. The real-world manifestations of these categories are clusters of co-occurring attributes, such as feathers, beak and wings, in the case of 'bird'. Such a model lends itself readily to an extension into the social domain, with traits being regarded as semantic categories referring to clusters of co-occurring behavioural and situational attributes (Hampson, in press).

The constructivist view of personality, and the associated cognitive view of traits as categories, thus reconceptualizes personality traits. Nevertheless it does not turn them into abstractions with no bearing on reality. The constructivist view asserts that traits are built out of the raw material of actual behaviour which is perceived by observers and categorized in trait terms. The constructivist view repudiates Shweder's and D'Andrade's claims that beliefs about traits are erroneous and that they result in systematic distortion of the real world. The controversy over what personality ratings measure resulted in doubt being cast, both on the validity of actual personality and perceived personality. The constructivist view adopts a different position on this issue: the distinction between perceived and actual personality is collapsed, since socially constructed personality is seen as the substitution of perceived real-world behaviour by cognitive trait categories. Personality traits, redefined as part of a socially constructed reality, are nevertheless still open to investigation by personality researchers and investigators of person perception, although a rather different approach is called for.

Socially-constructed personality traits are assumed to be anchored in the real world, in the sense that they are used as categories to apply to perceived behaviour. Of course, observations of behaviour are never truly objective, but are *perceptions* and therefore open to the influence of the perceiver's information processing system. This point, while damaging to the traditional view where a distinction between actual and perceived personality is made, is entirely compatible with the constructivist view. For the constructivist view, evidence is required that observers are capable of perceiving patterns of behaviour on which to base the personality construction process. These patterns must 'exist' in so far as the trait labels applied to them are useful for communicative and predictive purposes. Thus the constructivist view is supported by evidence of behavioural consistency derived from observations of behaviour. Lamiell's work described above suggests that people are capable of perceiving others' distinctive patterns of behaviour; in the next section further evidence will be presented to support the view that patterns of consistent behaviour do occur, and are perceived as such.

From our growing understanding of the workings of human cognition we know that information processing is open to error and bias, and there is no reason to suppose that the processing of personality information should be immune from these problems. Therefore, it is to be expected that socially-constructed personality will at times be over-applied or unjustifiably inferred. Recent research into social cognition, also to be described in the next section, is beginning to elucidate the conditions under which such misconstructions will occur.

Behaviour consistency and personality misconstruction

Most people are consistent much of the time

Mischel (1968) coined the derisory term 'personality coefficient' for the correlation of between 0.2 and 0.3 typically found when a measure of a personality trait was correlated with a behaviour. He concluded from this that people are far less consistent and hence less predictable than we like to suppose. However this conclusion is looking distinctly implausible in the light of more recent research which has succeeded in boosting the coefficient, under certain conditions, to between 0.8 and 0.9.

Two modifications to the research on behavioural consistency have resulted in this dramatic improvement in the personality coefficient. First, the research by Epstein (1979) has demonstrated that one-off samples of behaviour are unreliable measures to correlate with personality scale scores, and that the more appropriate measure to use is an average of a number of behaviour samples. A similar line of reasoning underlies Buss and Craik's (1980) finding that questionnaire measures of dominance predicted multiple acts more accurately than single acts, replicating Jaccard's (1974) earlier study. The scale measures were also better predictors of more prototypical dominant acts than less prototypical acts. These studies indicate that only a slight modification to the conventional procedures for locating behavioural consistency can result in strong evidence for consistency.

The second modification is somewhat more elaborate, because it depends on the idea that consistency is the product of interactions as opposed to main effects. Bem and Allen first advanced the view that it is possible to predict 'some of the people some of the time' (Bem and Allen, 1974, p. 517). The critical moderator in the search for consistency turned out to be people's self-perceptions. When Bem and Allen divided their subjects into those who regarded themselves as highly variable in their expression of the personality traits 'friendly' and 'conscientious' and those who did not regard themselves as variable on these traits, they found that there was far more consistency between different measures of these traits for the low than the high variability subjects. The importance of self-perceived consistency for determining which personality traits are likely to be useful for predicting behaviour for which subjects has been confirmed in a number of subsequent studies (Turner, 1978; Vestewig, 1978; Turner and Gilliland, 1979; Kenrick and Stringfield, 1980; Tunnell, 1980). In addition to demonstrating that behavioural consistency can be found, these studies also support the constructivist view of personality by showing how including the self-perceiver leads to a more complete account of personality.

Cognitive studies of person perception and misperception

The constructivist view of personality traits as cognitive categories suggests that one future direction for personality research will be to focus on the way information about behavioural consistency is encoded, stored and retrieved. There is already a substantial amount of research on social cognition in which models and techniques from cognitive psychology are being applied to the understanding of social information processing (Hastie *et al.*, 1980; Higgins *et al.*, 1981). Much of this research has been concerned with the processing of personality-related information.

The essential features of a model of person cognition have been specified by Hastie and Carlston (1980). The model requires three stages for the acquisition, retention and retrieval of information. At acquisition the stream of behaviour has to be segmented in some fashion to form units of raw perceptual information which can then be transformed into mental representations for retention. These representations are then retrieved for social judgement purposes. The work on person cognition can be organized in terms of the stage of the model to which it applies.

The acquisition stage is of particular importance in the understanding of personality construction, since it is the interface between the perceiver and the real world. It is at this stage that behavioural consistency has to be perceived and encoded. Funder (1980) pointed out that the perceiver may be sensitive to *patterns of consistent* behaviours, rather than to *specific* behaviours, in accord with the approach to behaviour consistency advocated for personality researchers by Epstein (1979). This view is not supported in a series of studies by Newtson and his colleagues which suggest that behaviour is perceived as discreet action units with the break points between the completion of one action and the commencement of the next carrying the most information (Newtson, 1973; Newtson and Engquist, 1976; Newtson *et al.*, 1977; Newtson *et al.*, 1978). In contrast, Ebbesen's investigations, using Newtson's techniques, have led him to develop an alternative model more in line with Funder's proposal. Ebbesen argued that behaviour is simultaneously encoded in two forms: an abstract, global code and a more concrete and detailed code (Ebbesen, 1980, 1981). A problem with choosing between models of the acquisition stage is that subjects may be able to process the incoming behavioural information in a variety of ways depending on the task set by the experimenter.

The stages of retention and retrieval have received more attention from investigators into social cognition. Research has been addressed to the nature of the mental representation of the perceptual information and to an account of the processes involved in retrieval of these representations for judgement purposes. A range of solutions to the problem of mental representation has been offered. For example, traits have been represented as nodes in a mental network (Harris and Hampson, 1980), and as lists of features (Ebbesen and Allen, 1979). At the more global level, individuals may be represented in terms of their correspondence to particular prototypes of person categories (Cantor and Mischel, 1979), or to particular themes or schemata such as occupations (Ostrom *et al.*, 1980; Taylor and Crocker, 1981).

An account of the way these representations change over time, are used in social judgement, and are influential in subsequent information processing, is necessary for the understanding of personality construction. For it is in the operation of these processes that the basis for misconstruction of personality may be discerned. One reliable finding is the strong effect on recall and recognition of the way material is organized in memory. Once incoming information has been organized around a particular trait, theme or schema, then information consistent with that organizational focus tends to be better recalled than inconsistent information (Cantor and Mischel, 1979; Lingle *et al.*, 1979). There is also a tendency to recognize or recall consistent but non-presented information (Cantor and Mischel, 1977; Snyder and Uranowitz, 1978). A related finding is the demonstration of illusory correlation effects in the social domain: subjects tend to ignore the actual patterns of correlations between traits present in the stimulus material, and perceive illusory correlations corresponding to their pre-existing beliefs (Berman and Kenny, 1976; Hamilton and Rose, 1980). Together, these studies are beginning to sketch out the mechanisms by which observers may tend to perceive more consistency than is warranted, and ignore information contrary to an initial impression or pre-existing beliefs.

Conclusions

In this chapter a new conceptualization of personality traits has been offered in response to evidence from studies of both personality and person perception, drawing attention to the weaknesses of the traditional definition. Within the framework of a socially constructed personality, personality traits take on the form of categories applied to patterns of behaviour with agreed social significance. Traits therefore do not reside exclusively in the eye of the beholder nor in the personality of the perceived, since traits are constructed by the beholder in the process of observing the perceived.

What are the implications of the new conceptualization for future research in personality and person perception? Since Mischel's initial critique of the trait concept and his subsequent reflections on personality (Mischel, 1968, 1973, 1977, 1979), personality researchers have been reconsidering their subject matter. Some (e.g. Eysenck and Eysenck, 1980), after due consideration of the criticisms, have not believed it necessary to come up with any fundamental change in their approach. However, this is not true of them all.

One trend that is now emerging, which has its roots in the pre-trait theory era of personality, may be termed the biographical approach (De Waele and Harré, 1979; Block, 1981; Lamiell, 1981; Levinson, 1981). Here, investigators concentrate more on individuals than groups, and study the consistencies and inconsistencies in personality over a person's life-span. It is less of an individual difference approach, in the sense of finding ways of ordering people with respect to one another along the same dimension, and more of an individualistic approach, in so far as the aim is to arrive at a description and understanding of particular persons. There is less stress on quantitative data collection, and more value is placed on qualitative information, including the individual's own perceptions of her- or himself, and other people's perceptions of that individual. The biographical approach therefore takes all three components of socially-constructed personality into account: the perceived, the perceiver and the self-perceiver.

References

Allport, G. W. and Odbert, H. S. (1936) Trait names: a psycholexical study. *Psychological Monographs 47*: Whole No. 171.

Bem, D. J. and Allen, A. (1974) On predicting some of the people some of the time: the search for cross-situational consistencies in behaviour. *Psychological Review 81*: 506–20.

Berman, J. S. and Kenny, D. A. (1976) Correlational bias in observer ratings. *Journal of Personality and Social Psychology 34*: 263–73.

Block, J. (1977) Advancing the psychology of personality: paradigmatic shift or improving the quality of research? In D. Magnusson and N. S. Endler (eds) *Personality at the Crossroads: Current Issues in Interactional Psychology*. Hillsdale, N. J.: Lawrence Erlbaum Associates.

Block, J. (1981) Some enduring and consequential structures of personality. In A. I. Rabin, J. Aronoff, A. M. Barclay and R. A. Zucker (eds) *Further Explorations in Personality*. New York: Wiley.

Block, J., Weiss, D. S. and Thorne, A. (1979) How relevant is a semantic similarity interpretation of personality ratings? *Journal of Personality and Social Psychology 37*: 1055–74.

Buss, D. M. and Craik, K. H. (1980) The frequency concept of disposition: dominance and prototypically dominant acts. *Journal of Personality 48*: 379–92.

Cantor, N. and Mischel, W. (1977) Traits as prototypes: effects on recognition memory. *Journal of Personality and Social Psychology 35*: 38–48.

44   Issues in person perception

Cantor, N. and Mischel, W. (1979) Prototypes in person perception. In L. Berkowitz (ed.) *Advances in Experimental Social Psychology*, vol. 12. New York: Academic Press.

Cattell, R. B. (1946) *Description and Measurement of Personality*. London: Harrap.

Cattell, R. B. (1947) Confirmation and clarification of primary personality factors. *Psychometrika 12*: 197–220.

Cattell, R. B. (1965) *The Scientific Analysis of Personality*. Harmondsworth, Middlesex: Penguin Books.

Cattell, R. B. and Kline, P. (1977) *The Scientific Analysis of Personality and Motivation*. New York: Academic Press.

Chapman, L. J. and Chapman, J. P. (1967) Genesis of popular but erroneous psychodiagnostic observations. *Journal of Abnormal Psychology 72*: 193–204.

Chapman, L. J. and Chapman, J. P. (1969) Illusory correlation as an obstacle to the use of valid psychodiagnostic signs. *Journal of Abnormal Psychology 74*: 271–80.

D'Andrade, R. G. (1965) Trait psychology and componential analysis. *American Anthropologist 67*: 215–28.

D'Andrade, R. G. (1974) Meaning and the assessment of behaviour. In H. M. Blalock Jr (ed.) *Measurement in the Social Sciences*. Chicago: Aldine-Atherton.

De Waele, J.-P. and Harré, R. (1979) Autobiography as a psychological method. In G. P. Ginsberg (ed.) *Emerging Strategies in Social Psychological Research*. Chichester: Wiley.

Dornbusch, S. M., Hastorf, A. H., Richardson, S. A., Muzzy, R. E. and Vreeland, R. S. (1965) The perceiver and the perceived: their relative influence on the categories of interpersonal cognition. *Journal of Personality and Social Psychology 1*: 434–40.

Ebbesen, E. B. (1980) Cognitive processes in understanding ongoing behaviour. In R. Hastie, T. M. Ostrom, E. B. Ebbesen, R. S. Wyer, D. L. Hamilton and D. E. Carlston (eds) *Person Memory: The Cognitive Basis of Social Perception*. Hillsdale, N. J.: Lawrence Erlbaum Associates.

Ebbesen, E. B. (1981) Cognitive processes in inferences about a person's personality. In E. T. Higgins, C. P. Herman and M. P. Zanna (eds) *Social Cognition: The Ontario Symposium*. Hillsdale, N. J.: Lawrence Erlbaum Associates.

Ebbesen, E. B. and Allen, R. B. (1979) Cognitive processes in implicit personality trait inferences. *Journal of Personality and Social Psychology 37*: 369–486.

Epstein, S. (1979) The stability of behaviour: I. on predicting most of the people much of the time. *Journal of Personality and Social Psychology 37*: 1109–26.

Eysenck, H. J. (1944) Types of Personality – a factorial study of 700 neurotic soldiers. *Journal of Mental Science 90*: 851–961.

Eysenck, H. J. (1953) *The Structure of Personality*. London: Methuen.

Eysenck, H. J. (1967) *The Biological Basis of Personality*. Springfield, Ill.: C. C. Thomas.

Eysenck, M. W. and Eysenck, H. J. (1980) Mischel and the concept of personality. *British Journal of Psychology 71*: 191–204.

Funder, D. C. (1980) On seeing ourselves as others see us: self–other agreement and discrepancy in personality ratings. *Journal of Personality 48*: 473–93.

Goffman, E. (1959) *The Presentation of Self in Everyday Life*. New York: Doubleday.

Hamilton, D. L. and Rose, T. L. (1980) Illusory correlation and the maintenance of stereotypic beliefs. *Journal of Personality and Social Psychology 139*: 832–45.

Hampson, S. E. (1982) *The Construction of Personality: An Introduction to Experimental Personality Research*. London: Routledge & Kegan Paul.

Hampson, S. E. (in press) Person memory: a semantic category model of personality traits. *British Journal of Psychology*.

Harré, R. (1979) *Social Being*. Oxford: Blackwell.

Harris, P. L. and Hampson, S. E. (1980) Processing information within implicit personality theory. *British Journal of Social and Clinical Psychology 19*: 235–42.

Hastie, R. and Carlston, D. E. (1980) Theoretical issues in person memory. In R. Hastie, T. M. Ostrom, E. B. Ebbesen, R. S. Wyer, D. L. Hamilton and D. E. Carlston (eds) *Person Memory: The Cognitive Basis of Social Perception*. Hillsdale, N. J.: Lawrence Erlbaum Associates.

Hastie, R., Ostrom, T. M., Ebbesen, E. B., Wyer, R. S., Hamilton, D. L. and Carlston, D. E. (eds) (1980) *Person Memory: The Cognitive Basis of Social Perception*. Hillsdale, N. J.: Lawrence Erlbaum Associates.

Higgins, E. T., Herman, C. P. and Zanna, M. P. (eds) (1981) *Social Cognition: The Ontario Symposium*. Hillsdale, N. J.: Lawrence Erlbaum Associates.

Jaccard, J. J. (1974) Predicting social behaviour from personality traits. *Journal of Research in Personality 7*: 358–67.

Kenrick, D. T. and Stringfield, D. O. (1980) Personality traits and the eye of the beholder: crossing some traditional philosophical boundaries in the search for consistency in all of the people. *Psychological Review 87*: 88–104.

Lamiell, J. T. (1980) On the utility of looking in the 'wrong' direction. *Journal of Personality 48*: 83–8.

Lamiell, J. T. (1981) Toward an idiothetic psychology of personality. *American Psychologist* in press.

Lamiell, J. T., Foss, M. A. and Cavenee, P. (1980) On the relationship between conceptual schemes and behaviour reports: a closer look. *Journal of Personality 48*: 54–73.

Levinson, D. J. (1981) Explorations in biography: evolution of the individual life structure in adulthood. In A. I. Rabin, J. Aronoff, A. M. Barclay and R. A. Zucker (eds) *Further Explorations in Personality*. New York: Wiley.

Lingle, J. S., Geva, N., Ostrom, T. M., Leippe, M. R. and Baumgardener, M. H. (1979) Thematic effects of person judgments on impression organization. *Journal of Personality and Social Psychology 37*: 674–87.

Mischel, W. (1968) *Personality and Assessment*. New York: Wiley.

Mischel, W. (1973) Toward a cognitive social learning reconceptualisation of personality. *Psychological Review 80*: 252–83.

Mischel, W. (1977) On the future of personality measurement. *American Psychologist 32*: 246–54.

Mischel, W. (1979) On the interface of cognition and personality: beyond the person–situation debate. *American Psychologist 34*: 740–54.

Newtson, D. A. (1973) Attribution and the unit of perception of ongoing behaviour. *Journal of Personality and Social Psychology 28*: 28–38.

Newtson, D. A. and Engquist, G. (1976) The perceptual organization of ongoing behaviour. *Journal of Experimental Social Psychology 12*: 436–50.

Newtson, D. A., Engquist, G. and Bois, J. (1977) The objective basis of behaviour units. *Journal of Personality and Social Psychology 35*: 847–62.

Newtson, D. A., Rindner, R. Miller, R. and Lacross, K. (1978) Effects of availability of features changes on behaviour segmentation. *Journal of Experimental Social Psychology 14*: 379–88.

Norman, W. T. (1963) Toward an adequate taxonomy of personality attributes: replicated factor structure in peer nomination personality ratings. *Journal of Abnormal Social Psychology 66*: 574–83.

Ostrom, T. M., Lingle, J. S., Pryor, J. B. and Geva, N. (1980) Cognitive organization in person impressions. In R. Hastie, T. M. Ostrom, E. B. Ebbesen, R. S. Wyer, D. L. Hamilton and D. E. Carlston (eds) *Person Memory: The Cognitive Basis of Social Perception*. Hillsdale, N. J.: Lawrence Erlbaum Associates.

Passini, F. T. and Norman, W. T. (1966) A universal conception of personality structure? *Journal of Personality and Social Psychology 4*: 44–9.

Rosch, E. M., Mervis, C. B., Gray, W. D., Johnson, D. and Boyes-Braem, P. (1976) Basic objects in natural categories. *Cognitive Psychology 8*: 382–439.

Shweder, R. A. (1975) How relevant is an individual difference theory of personality ratings? *Journal of Personality 43*: 455–85.

Shweder, R. A. (1977) Likeness and likelihood in everyday thought: magical thinking in judgments about personality. *Current Anthropology 18*: 637–58.

Shweder, R. A. and D'Andrade, R. G. (1979) Accurate reflections or systematic distortion? A reply to Block, Weiss and Thorne. *Journal of Personality and Social Psychology 37*: 1075–84.

Snyder, M. and Uranowitz, S. W. (1978) Reconstructing the past: some cognitive consequences of person perception. *Journal of Personality and Social Psychology 36*: 941–50.

Taylor, S. E. and Crocker, J. (1981) Schematic bases of social information processing. In E. T. Higgins, C. P. Herman and M. P. Zanna (eds) *Social Cognition: The Ontario Symposium*. Hillsdale, N. J.: Lawrence Erlbaum Associates.

Tunnell, G. (1980) Intra-individual consistency in personality assessment: the effect of self-monitoring. *Journal of Personality 48*: 220–32.

Turner, R. G. (1978) Consistency, self-consciousness, and the predictive validity of typical and maximal personality measures. *Journal of Research in Personality 12*: 117–32.

Turner, R. G. and Gilliland, L. (1979) The comparative relevance and predictive validity of subject generated trait descriptions. *Journal of Personality 47*: 230–44.

Tversky, A. and Kahneman, D. (1973) Availability: a heuristic for judging frequency and probability. *Cognitive Psychology 5*: 207–32.

Tversky, A. and Kahneman, D. (1974) Judgment under uncertainty: heuristics and biases. *Science 184*: 1124–31.

Vestewig, R. (1978) Cross-response mode consistency in risk-taking as a function of self-reported strategy and self-perceived consistency. *Journal of Research in Personality 12*: 152–63.

Wells, B. W. P. (1980) *Personality and Heredity: An Introduction to Psychogenetics*. Harlow: Longman.

Wishner, J. (1960) Reanalysis of 'impressions of personality'. *Psychological Review 67*: 96–112.

3 Information integration in person perception: theory and application

James Shanteau *and* Geraldine F. Nagy

Introduction

Many decisions of important consequence involve forming impressions about other people. Decisions of guilt or innocence by jurors about defendants in courts of law, judgments of the desirability of prospective dating partners, and judgments about the ability and qualifications of job applicants all involve processing information about people. In short, forming some kind of an overall 'picture' of what other people are like is basic to a great many decisions.

Traditionally, the study of impression formation has been associated with the person perception task. In this task, individuals are presented with personality trait information about another person and then asked to describe their impression of the stimulus person. One purpose of this chapter is to present some of the key findings from research conducted within the basic person perception paradigm. An even more important purpose, however, is to show how the basic paradigm has been extended recently to study a variety of important interpersonal decisions. These decisions, such as those listed initially, are of considerable societal relevance. But in order to place this more current emphasis in perspective, it is first necessary to review the earlier person perception research. Thus, the chapter will provide an overview of both traditional and current approaches to impression formation.

This overview will be placed within the framework of *Information Integration Theory* (Anderson, 1974, 1981). The Information Integration (IIT) approach has been central in person perception research for nearly twenty years. Moreover, it has been adapted to a number of applied social judgment situations (e.g. Kaplan and Kemmerick, 1974; Shanteau and Nagy, 1976, 1979; Nagy, 1981). Additionally, IIT has been used to study a variety of psychological judgments outside of social perceptions. Some examples include gambling and risky decision-making (Shanteau, 1974; Lopes, 1976; Anderson and Shanteau, 1970), psychophysical judgments (Anderson, 1974a), judgments by children (Butzin and Anderson, 1973) and decisions made by expert livestock judges (Phelps and Shanteau, 1978). Although there are other approaches to person perception, we chose to discuss the one with which we are most familiar. For presentation of an alternative view, see chapter 4 in this book.

Information integration theory

Before turning to the main body of the chapter, it is first necessary to provide a brief overview of some of the major principles and procedures within IIT. The basic premise underlying IIT is that human judgments (including judgments that are made about other people) are the outcome of evaluating and combining information about the judged objects (persons). The major goal of IIT is to derive a quantitative description of the way that information is processed to arrive at a final judgment. In effect, this quantitative description is a representation of the subjects' 'judgmental strategy'.

The basic elements of the IIT approach are illustrated in Figure 3.1 (adapted from Shanteau and Nagy, 1976). The explicit stimuli (which can be pieces of information about another person such as personality traits) are denoted by S_1, S_2, and S_3. These explicit stimuli are formed into a judgment via two processes. The first is *stimulus evaluation*. This process involves transforming the external stimulus into subjective values which reflect the assessment of the meaning and relevance of each item of information for the task at hand.

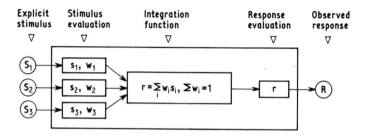

Fig. 3.1 Diagram of Information Integration Theory showing three processes of stimulus evaluation, integration function and response evaluation. Diagram adapted from Shanteau and Nagy (1976).

Specifically, each item of information can be summarized by two subjective parameters. One is the subjective stimulus *scale value* (s) which refers to the location of the stimulus along the particular dimension of judgment, e.g. likeableness of another person. The fact that the scale value depends on the dimension of judgment is worth emphasizing. For instance, the description 'very humorous' may be perceived as highly favorable when the dimension of judgment is the dateability of a person of the opposite sex. But the scale value may be unfavorable when the dimension of judgment is the effectiveness of a plumber (Anderson and Lopes, 1974).

The second descriptive parameter within IIT is the *weight* (w) of the particular stimulus or item of information. This weight value can generally be thought of as the importance or relevance of that item. Again, the weight value depends on the dimension of judgment. For instance, scholastic standing may carry a much greater weight when evaluating the abilities of a prospective employee than when judging the guilt of a defendant in court.

Once the stimuli have been evaluated, the weights and scale values are integrated or combined into an overall response (r). The combination rules, formally called integration functions, can be generally described using various arithmetic or algebraic operations. A number of different combination rules have been explored within IIT. This discussion will, however, focus on *adding* and *averaging*; both are members of the larger class of linear models which have played a central role within the area of impression formation. Additionally, the *differential-weighted averaging* and *multiplying* rules will be presented since they have been used increasingly in more recent interpersonal judgment studies. Each of these rules will now be discussed in turn.

Adding and averaging

Adding and averaging rules both imply that when information is combined the effect of one piece of information is independent of any others. Despite a surface similarity between the two rules, they imply quite divergent psychological processes. Adding, in simple terms, states that the component information about a stimulus person is summed to form a final judgment. One consequence of this rule in impression formation is that the more information of like value that one receives about another person, the more extreme or polarized one's judgment should become (i.e. 'the more the better').

In contrast to adding, averaging states that the overall judgment is the mean of the individual components of information. Furthermore, averaging implies that when one already has highly favorable information about another person, the availability of moderately favorable information will decrease the polarity of the final impression. In effect, averaging can be likened to a 'center of gravity' notion.

Despite these differences, the initial test for adding and averaging is identical. Both adding and averaging imply that information should combine non-interactively. Given that stimulus combinations have been constructed from factorial (fully crossed) designs, this means that subjects' evaluations should plot as parallel lines (see Figure 3.2 for an example). Statistically, both models require that interactions in an

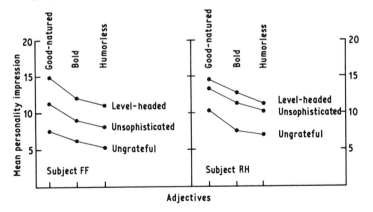

Fig. 3.2 Plot of two-factor design for two subjects from Anderson (1962). Subjects judged likeableness of hypothetical persons described by adjectives indicated from row and column factors. Results reveal parallelism expected by additivity prediction of constant-weight averaging model.

analysis of variance be non-significant. This test simply determines whether any observed deviations from parallelism are due to other than chance factors.

Once the above tests of fit have been met, further tests can be performed to differentiate between adding and averaging. Efforts to test between these two models, in fact, dominated much of the early impression formation research. These tests will, therefore, be discussed further when the historical roots of the IIT approach are presented in the next section.

Differential-weighted averaging

Differential-weighted averaging refers to the case in which information is averaged, but, unlike the simple averaging rule described above, the weights given to the pieces of information change. When this occurs, the averaging model becomes more complex, and deviations from strict parallelism will be found (see Figure 3.3 for an example). Statistically, there will be significant interactions in an analysis of variance.

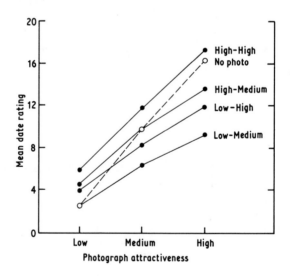

Fig. 3.3 Plot of mean attractiveness of dates described by adjectives and/or photographs. Solid lines show diverging pattern expected from differential-weighted averaging model. Dotted line reveals cross-over test in support of averaging over adding. Results taken from Lampel and Anderson (1968).

Multiplying

The multiplying rule has been explored most extensively in areas of risky judgment and gambling (Shanteau, 1974), but has also been studied within the area of social judgment. Briefly, multiplying applies when one piece of information modifies or modulates another. If multiplying holds, the data should plot as a fan of diverging straight lines (see Figure 3.6 for an example). Statistically, a significant interaction should be obtained in an analysis of variance with the interaction concentrated in its bilinear component (see Anderson and Shanteau, 1970 for further details on this bilinear analysis).

Functional measurement

The key to the IIT approach is the ability to describe the subject's judgment strategy (i) by testing the fit of alternative rules for the integration function, and (ii) by deriving quantitative estimates of the weights and scale values. These two steps are accomplished by a set of procedures called *Functional Measurement* (FM). The details of these procedures, which vary depending on which rule is being applied, have been described elsewhere (e.g. Anderson, 1974, 1981) and will not be repeated here.

Nevertheless, the logic behind FM deserves emphasis. According to FM, measurement is dependent on having an adequate understanding of the subject's integration function. At the same time, knowledge of the function provides a frame for estimating weights and scale values. In effect, the integration rule and the estimation of values are mutually dependent on each other. This differs from other approaches to social judgment in that the integration rules are not assumed *a priori*, but rather are derived from the pattern of responses.

Although most research using FM has focused on the integration function, there has been an increasing concern recently with estimation of weights and scale values. In part, this shift in emphasis has reflected the trend towards research of more applied interest. As will be argued below, the subjective values used by subjects can be quite informative when the judgment task is of more substantive interest.

While there are other approaches to measurement and model testing (e.g. Fishbein and Ajzen, 1975), the use of the FM approach has several advantages. First, FM has incorporated well-developed statistical analyses for testing between alternative algebraic rules. These techniques are usually based on factorial designs and ANOVA techniques (see Anderson, 1974 and 1981, for a detailed explanation of FM methodology and statistical analyses). Second, parallel to these statistical analyses are graphical analyses which allow direct visual inspection of the fit of alternative rules. These graphical analyses will, in fact, form the basis of most of the results presented in this chapter. A final advantage is that these statistical and graphical analyses have been developed to deal with individual subject data. This is important because group analyses can conceal real individual differences that are often important in applied settings. Within this chapter, efforts will be made to present some individual data; when group data are presented, they will reflect individual results.

Organization

The remainder of this chapter will be organized into three parts. In the first part, five selected studies will be presented which illustrate the early development and the basic principles of Information Integration Theory. In the second, five studies which demonstrate the expansion of the IIT approach into other areas of social judgment will be reviewed. Finally, the third section will explore some trends for future research on impression formation; also, within this section, we shall attempt to synthesize some of the findings presented here with findings in other areas of human judgment.

Historical roots

In this and the next section, we shall review various empirical studies. These studies are either central to, or representative of, various important research trends. Rather than extensively discussing each study, we begin by presenting those aspects of each study which we feel are most relevant. We then comment on each study and point out how it influenced subsequent research. Interested readers are, of course, encouraged to read the original papers for further details concerning methodology, analytic procedures, and so on.

Initial research

Asch (1946) Any historical discussion of personality impression research must begin with Asch's classic paper (1946). This paper was largely responsible for the initial interest in impression formation and for the personality trait task which has dominated much of the impression formation research. Asch (1946) presents a series of ten experiments in which subjects were presented with personality trait adjectives and then asked for their impression of the person described. Subjects indicated their impressions by writing a short paragraph describing the stimulus person and by selecting from among pairs of opposing adjectives those traits they felt would best describe the person.

Asch's contention was that the subject's final impression of the stimulus person reflected a dynamic process in which the separate traits would interact to form a unitary impression. Various results obtained within the ten studies supported this contention. For example, in one of the major studies, Asch found that changes in certain key traits ('warm' versus 'cold') produced widespread changes in the final impression. These results were interpreted as supporting the existence of 'central' traits which are not simply incorporated into the impression, but actually change the meaning or interpretation of other available traits.

Another example is a 'primacy effect' which was observed. Asch found that when sequences of the same adjectives were read in opposing order, the adjectives which were read first were most predictive of the final impression. This primacy effect was interpreted as being supportive of Asch's proposed interactive theory. Specifically, Asch suggested that a primacy effect occurs because the initial traits in a stimulus sequence set the direction for the interpretation of later ones. In other words, the adjectives did not operate independently of one another; rather, each new adjective was interpreted in the light of ones that had already been received.

Comment   Asch's proposal that impression formation is an interactive process sparked a considerable amount of subsequent work on impression formation. The primacy effect, in particular, was central to much of this early work. Many of the studies dealing with the primacy effect were concerned with exploring alternatives to Asch's interactive or change-of-meaning hypothesis. Among other hypotheses, two in particular were explored extensively: (i) discounting, and (ii) attention decrement. Under the discounting hypothesis, later adjectives are seen not as changing meaning but as being given less weight owing to their inconsistency with earlier traits. Attention decrement, on the other hand, refers to the possibility that later adjectives have less effect because the subject's attention wanes as more adjectives in a sequence are read.

Stewart (1965)   While numerous studies have explored the primacy effect, the study by Stewart (1965) deserves special attention. Stewart was one of the first to propose that primacy did not reflect a change in the meaning of later adjectives, but instead only reflected a change in their importance (referred to as *weight* in later research). Specifically, Stewart (1965) advocated the attention decrement hypothesis and set up a unique experiment to test its viability. He reasoned that if attention decrement is responsible for the primacy effect, then manipulating the experimental task so that subjects are forced to attend to later adjectives should diminish the effect. In contrast, a change-of-meaning hypothesis would predict no difference or an even more pronounced primacy effect under these circumstances.

Stewart (1965) tested the attention decrement hypothesis by asking subjects to rate the *likeableness* of stimulus persons described by a sequence of personality trait adjectives. Subjects were split into two groups. In the first group, the entire stimulus sequence was read prior to the subjects' making their likeableness ratings (end responding). In the second group, however, subjects responded after each adjective in the stimulus sequence was read (continuous responding).

Consistent with previous results, Stewart found a primacy effect when subjects responded only at the end of the stimulus sequence. However, for the continuous responding group this effect was reversed; adjectives presented later in the sequence actually had a greater effect for these subjects, namely, a recency effect. Since continuous responding forced the subjects to attend to later adjectives, Stewart interpreted these results in support of the attention decrement hypothesis.

Comment   Numerous studies since Stewart (1965) have attempted to clarify the primacy effect. Several studies have shown that a primacy effect can be reversed to recency using a variety of attentional manipulations (e.g. Hendrick and Constantini, 1970). Such reversals have been found using both sequential presentation (Briscoe, Woodyard, and Shaw, 1967; Tesser, 1968) and simultaneous presentation (Kaplan, 1971b).

The importance of Stewart (1965) and the other papers cited above is that they emphasize the role of the weighting process in impression formation. This, in effect, set the stage for further study and clarification of the role of weights in the judgment process.

In addition, Stewart's study may be seen as exemplifying various changes made in the basic Asch paradigm. Although Stewart borrowed heavily from Asch by using adjective trait sets to explore impression formation, he incorporated a great deal more stimulus control. Also, the use of likeableness ratings provided a form of responding which was easier to analyze. Both stimulus control and likeableness ratings would become major characteristics of the IIT approach to impression formation.

Combination rules

In addition to the primacy effect, early research was directed towards understanding *how* individual items of information were combined to form a final impression. Consistent with the idea that impression formation was a dynamic process, Asch believed that the final impression could not be accounted for by some simple (i.e. linear) combination of component parts. This proposal initiated numerous studies which attempted to explore the applicability of linear combination rules in impression formation.

Anderson (1962) Anderson's 1962 study was a significant development in the area of impression formation because it introduced procedures which allowed a direct test of a linear combination rule. In this study, subjects rated the likeableness of twenty-seven hypothetical persons, each described by three adjectives; the twenty-seven stimuli were constructed by combining adjectives in a 3^3 factorial design.

It was within this study that Anderson introduced the use of ANOVA as the basis of testing linear integration rules. Anderson reasoned that if subjects combined the personality traits via a dynamic interactive process, then significant interactions in an ANOVA would be observed. Furthermore, the interaction should be visualized by deviations from parallelism when the data were plotted. On the other hand, support for a linear rule would involve non-significant interactions and produce parallelism in plots.

Results of Anderson's (1962) study are graphically presented in Figure 3.2. Each of the panels within this figure represents a 3 × 3, row × column design. The adjectives are listed next to the rows and columns of the factional plots, with representative results shown for two subjects. As can be seen, the lines are close to parallel which is consistent with a linear processing rule. This was supported by statistical analyses which revealed non-significant interaction terms at both the group and individual subject levels. Numerous subsequent experiments (see Anderson, 1974, for a review) have replicated these results.

Comment   While the Anderson (1962) study supported the notion that personality trait information about others is combined according to some linear process, it did not discriminate between two alternative rules, adding and averaging, which both can lead to linearity. Although an averaging interpretation of the above data has been favored by Anderson and his colleagues, the adding rule is not without its supporters (Triandis and Fishbein, 1963). In response to these opposing views, much of the later impression-formation research, particularly within IIT, focused on testing between these two rules.

Anderson (1965)   A major development in the testing of combination rules came in a study conducted by Anderson in 1965. In this study, Anderson proposed a *qualitative* test between adding and averaging rules. Specifically, subjects evaluated the likeableness of persons described by sets of either two or four adjective traits which varied in polarity. Two different types of sets were used in which stimulus persons were described by (i) two highly favorable adjectives – HH, (ii) two highly favorable and two mildly favorable adjectives – HHM + M + , (iii) two very unfavorable adjectives – LL, and (iv) two very unfavorable and two mildly unfavorable adjectives – LLM – M + .

Anderson reasoned that if an adding rule described the integration of information in the impression-formation task, then providing the subject with additional information of like polarity should cause the final impression to become more polarized. For example, combining mildly favorable (M + M +) with highly favorable information (HH) would simply increase the favorability of the overall impression (HHM + M + > HH). Similar predictions would apply to negative trait sets (LLM – M – < LL).

While adding implies more polarized impressions, averaging makes the opposite prediction. Specifically, if traits are averaged, the subject's response should be higher for persons described only by two highly favorable adjectives than for persons described by two highly and two mildly favorable ones (e.g. HH > HHM + M +). This occurs because the presence of the mildly valued traits decreases the average value of the stimulus information. A similar prediction can be made for unfavorable trait sets (LLM – M – > LL).

Within the Anderson (1965) study, the two critical comparisons described above supported averaging. As predicted, HHM + M + yielded a less favorable response than HH. Similarly, for negative information LLM – M – yielded a less unfavorable response than LL. This result has been obtained repeatedly in subsequent studies (Hendrick, 1968; Leon *et al.*, 1973).

Comment The qualitative test developed by Anderson (1965) has several advantages over other model testing techniques. For one thing, the critical test described above predicts differences in the direction of the final response and, therefore, does not depend on the linearity of the response scale. Additionally, the test not only supports averaging but also eliminates a whole class of models which are based on the general adding formulation. Finally, by emphasizing differences in the direction of the final response, this critical test underlines the psychological differences between the two rules.

Lampel and Anderson (1968) The Anderson 1962 and 1965 studies essentially set the stage for the use of IIT procedures in the study of social judgment. Later studies attempted to extend the generalizability of the averaging rule.

One of the earliest studies to go beyond the simple personality trait task was reported by Lampel and Anderson in 1968. These investigators had female college students evaluate the dateability of males described by either a photograph and two personality trait adjectives, or a photograph presented alone. The purpose of this study was to explore how subjects integrated heterogeneous information, in this case verbal and visual.

The results of the Lampel and Anderson (1968) study are graphically displayed in Figure 3.3. This figure plots the mean dateableness ratings for each of the photograph and personality trait adjective combinations. The photographs are spaced along the horizontal from low to high attractiveness. The adjective trait pairs are listed vertically next to their respective curves, where H, M and L correspond to adjectives of High, Medium and Low value, respectively. The curve denoted by 'NONE' represents the subjects' mean response to the photographs when presented alone.

Several aspects of Figure 3.3 are of importance. First, consider the 'NONE' curve. As can be seen, this curve crosses over the remaining ones. This cross-over eliminates a simple adding rule for the combination of the photograph and adjectives information. Clearly, if the HM adjectives add to the unattractive (low) photograph, they cannot simultaneously subtract from the attractive (high) photograph as this cross-over would imply. While adding cannot handle such data, averaging does predict these results.

The graphical tests of averaging presented above is based on similar logic to the qualitative test introduced in Anderson's (1965) article. However, the Lampel and Anderson test is a superior one. While the Anderson (1965) test requires separate verification that mildly positive information is indeed positive and that mildly negative information is indeed negative, the Lampel and Anderson test requires only that the added information be near neutral value. Also, the procedure used by Lampel and Anderson is based on a *quantitative* test as opposed to the qualitative test used in Anderson (1965).

In addition to providing an improved test of averaging versus adding, the Lampel and Anderson study provides a clear example of a more complex form of averaging, namely differential-weighted averaging. As noted previously, the linear (parallel) form of averaging is based on the assumption that the levels within stimulus factors have the same weight. However if the weight varies across the different levels, then the results will no longer be linear, but will be non-parallel. Specifically, a model in which the weight on one factor (e.g. the adjectives) depends on the level of the other factor (e.g. the photographs) will produce interactive, divergent results. This is a differential-weighted averaging rule.

Such a pattern of divergence can be seen in the solid lines in Figure 3.3, that is, the curves diverge towards the right. This can be explained by differential-weighted averaging in that less importance is attached to personality adjectives when the photograph is unattractive. For more attractive photographs, greater weight is given to the personality traits. Technically, since averaging requires that the weights sum to 1, the relative importance of the personality traits is less in the context of the unattractive than in the context of the attractive photographs.

Comment   Similar examples of differential weighting have been obtained in many other settings. Differential-weighting appears to be most likely to occur when judgments other than likeableness are required (Nagy, 1981). Additionally, there is increasing evidence that differential-weighting applies when extremely negative stimuli are involved (Leon, *et al.*, 1973).

The significance of support for the differential-weighted averaging rule is that it gives more flexibility to the averaging rule in that it allows certain deviations from parallelism to be accounted for in terms of the weight parameter. Additionally, support for differential weighting is an important development because it exemplifies the psychological importance of weights within the judgment process.

Another important contribution of the Lampel and Anderson paper is that it was one of the first applications of IIT to judgments of personal relevance to the subjects. Thus, by providing photographic information the realism of the impression formation task was greatly increased.

Conclusions

The studies discussed thus far not only provided convincing evidence that averaging describes the integration of information in impression formation, but were critical steps in the theoretical and methodological development of IIT. These and supporting studies, in effect, provided the initial impetus for the IIT approach. Many of the methods and theories which would later be applied to a variety of social judgments were developed in this early research.

We will now turn towards some of these more recent applications. Although the areas discussed in the following section differ from the traditional concept of 'impression formation', they share the property of being based on judgments about other people. The assumption is that these judgments involve a common process and, therefore, are an extension of basic impression formation work.

Applications

Through selected examples, this section will show how IIT can be extended to the analysis of interpersonal decisions of social relevance. Specifically, we will review four different areas of applied research involving IIT techniques: jury decisions, dating, choice personnel selection, and consumer judgments. Within each of these areas, one or two major studies will be reviewed. Aside from discussing methods and results in each case, special attention will be paid to the applications and extensions of IIT to this socially relevant research.

Jury decisions

Kaplan and Kemmerick (1975)   Kaplan and Kemmerick's (1975) was one of the first major studies extending the IIT impression formation paradigm to complex social judgments. These authors proposed that jurors' decisions of guilt or innocence could be conceptualized as an information processing task in which information about the defendant is evaluated and integrated. Their overall aim was to describe these processes with the same approach employed to explore the simpler personality impression tasks used in earlier IIT work.

Kaplan and Kemmerick (1975) took this approach in the hope that it would help clarify some issues raised in previous jury judgment studies. They were especially concerned about the role of non-evidential, personality trait information on the jurors' judgments. Although previous studies had provided evidence that non-evidential information influences judicial decisions (e.g. Kalven and Zeisel, 1966), the way this information is combined with evidential information had not been explored. When non-evidential factors such as the defendant's attractiveness (Landy and Aronson, 1969) or attitudinal similarity to jurors (Griffitt and Jackson, 1973; Mitchell and Byrne, 1973) have been studied, the levels of evidential information have not been varied. But without variation, it is not possible to study integration rules. Therefore, a major focus of the Kaplan and Kemmerick (1975) study was on the rules used to integrate evidential and non-evidential information.

Procedurally, Kaplan and Kemmerick had college students evaluate eight defendants in a simulated jury task. The defendants were accused of felony traffic offences and were described by (i) evidential information which accounted for the circumstances of the crime in either a very high or very low incriminating manner, and (ii) non-evidential information in which the defendant's personality was characterized in positive, negative or neutral terms, or not at all. The evidential and non-evidential information was co-varied in a 2 × 4 factorial design. Students rated the guilt of each of the defendants on a twenty-point scale. Additionally, they assessed the punishment of each defendant between 1 (minimum) and 7 (maximum). Finally,

instructions regarding the relevance of non-evidential information
were systematically varied. These instructions either stressed the
personality characterizations as indicators of culpability, questioned
the usefulness of these characterizations, or said nothing either
way.

Several findings of interest were obtained. First of all, subjects
consistently used both the evidential and non-evidential information
when evaluating the defendants. Also, more highly incriminating evidence and negative personality characterizations resulted in higher
responses. This occurred regardless of the instructions about the
relevance of the personality characterizations.

It is noteworthy that a linear rule for the integration of evidential
and non-evidential information was supported. In the left panel of
Figure 3.4, each data point represents the subjects' mean guilt rating
for a defendant; personality characterizations of varied value are on
the horizontal axis with the curves representing high or low incriminating evidence. The right panel shows an analogous plot for subjects'
punishment judgments. In both of these panels the curves are very
near to parallel, as expected from a linear rule. Additionally, this
parallelism was statistically supported by ANOVA analyses: for both
the guilt and punishment ratings, the interaction was non-significant.

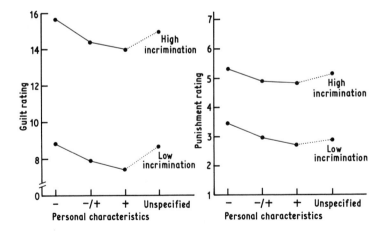

Fig. 3.4 Guilt judgments (left panel) and punishment judgments (right
panel) as a function of degree of incriminating evidence and personality
characteristics of defendant. Parallelism of solid lines supports additivity
prediction of averaging. Data taken from Kaplan and Kemmerick (1974).

On the basis of these findings, Kaplan and Kemmerick concluded that the processes underlying juror judgments could be successfully studied using the IIT approach. They further suggested that one benefit of adopting the IIT framework is that the theory and findings of earlier work on impression formation could provide a basis for studies of juror judgments. Specifically, they proposed that phenomena such as perceiver bias (Kaplan, 1971a), order effects (Anderson, 1971), source credibility (Birnbaum, *et al.*, 1976), amount of information (Anderson, 1967), redundancy (Kaplan, 1972) and consistency of information (Kaplan, 1973) could be of considerable value in the study of juror judgments.

Comment   In addition to exemplifying the extension of IIT to a socially relevant area, the Kaplan and Kemmerick study made some significant contributions towards the understanding of juror judgments. The finding that the defendant's personality characteristics affect jurors' judgments is not surprising (Landy and Aronson, 1969; Mitchell and Byrne, 1973). However, the ineffectiveness of instructions regarding these characterizations has some important implications. Of course, it may be argued that a simulated jury task cannot be directly generalized to actual juror judgments. However, it is important to note that in actual court settings personality information is available in a highly salient form. Such information may have, therefore, an even greater impact than did the simple personality trait adjectives which were used in the study.

Dating

Although Lampel and Anderson (1968) used dating as their research task, their primary interest was not in dating *per se*. In effect, dating was simply the medium for the study of several issues of theoretical interest to IIT. However, two later studies (Nagy, 1976; Shanteau and Nagy, 1979) used the principles of IIT as tools to explore issues of specific interest to dating.

Nagy (1976)   The primary purpose of the Nagy (1976) study was to clarify the role of physical attractiveness in the dating situation. Numerous dating studies had concluded that the dates' physical attractiveness dominated the subjects' decision (Walster, *et al.*, 1966; Huston, 1973). However, these studies had either not provided any additional information about the date, or the additional information had not been systematically manipulated. Additionally, the way information was integrated had not been studied.

Nagy (1976) attempted to clarify these issues by having female college students evaluate the dating desirability of males described by (i) a photograph, and (ii) personal characteristics. For example, subjects rated dates such as:

Joe
Very sexually aggressive

The name referred to a photograph on a nearby display board. These photographs were chosen on the basis of preliminary ratings to cover a broad but representative range of physical attractiveness. The specific characteristics (listed in Figure 3.5) were chosen because preliminary subjects had indicated that these were of particular relevance in the dating situation. The adverb quantifiers were used to manipulate the levels of the characteristics.

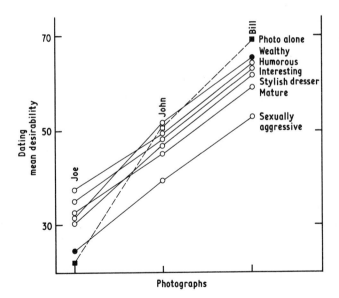

Fig. 3.5 Mean desirability of dates described by photographs and dating characteristics. Solid lines support additivity prediction and dotted line supports cross-over prediction from averaging. Data adapted from Shanteau and Nagy (1976).

In addition to rating the dates as described above, subjects evaluated each of the photographs alone and each of the adverb-modified characteristics alone. These separate ratings allowed a qualitative test of the averaging rule. They were also used as predictors in a regression analysis described below.

As expected, the results showed a significant effect for both the dates' physical attractiveness and personal characteristics. Interestingly, physical attractiveness did not dominate the subjects' judgments. Estimates of the relative impact of physical attractiveness and personal characteristics showed them to be about equal.

Graphical results bearing on the integration of the photographic and personal information are shown in Figure 3.5. Consistent with a linear integration rule, the lines are close to parallel. Furthermore, the dotted line, which reflects the subjects' mean ratings for the photographs when presented alone, crosses over the others as predicted by averaging. The averaging hypothesis was also supported by standard statistical analyses.

Comment   The primary contribution of the Nagy (1976) study was its emphasis on the valuation (e.g. assessment of weights) rather than the integration process. Although the averaging rule was tested, this was done in order to verify the FM procedures used to derive weight estimates. This emphasis on the valuation process contrasts markedly with earlier IIT research which had been concerned almost exclusively with testing integration rules.

Shanteau and Nagy (1979)   As with the Nagy (1976), Shanteau and Nagy (1979) used IIT procedures as a tool to explore some issues of particular interest in the dating area. A recurring question in the literature has been whether individuals consider their chances of being accepted when choosing between alternative dates. That is, do subjects' inferences about their chances of being accepted influence their selection of prospective dates? Initially, investigators felt that subjects would consider their chances for acceptance and, as a consequence, prefer dates of equal attractiveness to themselves (Walster *et al.*, 1966). Although this 'matching hypothesis' seemed reasonable, the results were at best indecisive (Berscheid, *et al.*, 1971; Huston, 1973). Thus, the part that probability of acceptance played in dating choice was not clear.

Shanteau and Nagy (1979) attempted to resolve this ambiguity by using the IIT approach to investigate how (and whether) probability is combined with physical attractiveness. To accomplish this goal, three studies were run. In the first, female college students were asked to make preferential choice between two males described by (i) a photograph, and (ii) a verbal statement giving the probability that the pictured male would accept the subject as a date. For example, the students made preferential choices between alternatives such as:

Fairly likely   Unlikely
Tom   Joe

The names identified photographs of differing attractiveness, and the stimuli were varied in a factorial design.

ANOVA analyses at the individual subject level consistently revealed significant effects for both attractiveness and probability. These results are presented graphically in Figure 3.6. As can be seen, increases in both the attractiveness of the date and the probability of acceptance led to more favorable responses. The graphical results displayed in Figure 3.6 not only show that both physical attractiveness

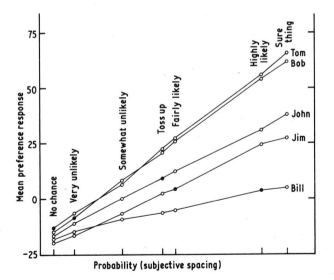

Fig. 3.6 Mean preferential ratings by female subjects for dates described by probability of acceptance and physical attractiveness. Diverging fan of straight lines supports a multiplying model. Data taken from Shanteau and Nagy (1979).

and probability were used, but also reflect on how they were used. Specifically, the divergence of the curves towards the right shows that the date's attractiveness had a greater effect on the subject's judgments as the probability of acceptance increased. This diverging pattern is consistent with a multiplicative rule. Psychologically, this means that probability modified or modulated the effect of physical attractiveness. One outcome of this rule is that a date who is low in either factor, that is, very unattractive or very unlikely to accept the subject as a date, will be seen as undesirable.

An obvious limitation of the first study was that probability of acceptance was explicitly provided to subjects; however, this information is not normally available in most actual dating situations. The second experiment was run to explore the role of probability of acceptance when it was left to the subjects to infer it from the photograph. Procedurally, this involved having the same subjects as in the first experiment make preferential choices between all possible pairs of dates described by photographs alone. At a separate time, subjects rated the physical attractiveness of each of the seven photographs and also estimated the probability that they (the subject) would be accepted by the pictured dates.

The purpose of the second experiment was to determine whether subjects would made inferences about probability and, if so, to determine how these probability inferences were used in conjunction with physical attractiveness to arrive at a decision. Results for three representative subjects are presented in Figure 3.7. The spacing along the horizontal axis reflects the rated attractiveness of the photographs. The probability estimates are indicated by asterisks. The filled circles give the relative preference values for each date compared to all others.

The left and center panels (S 1 and S 5) present results similar to those obtained for the majority of subjects. As can be seen, the probability values do differ for dates of varied attractiveness. Furthermore, the similarity of the probability and preference curves, particularly for the upper levels of attractiveness, is striking. This suggests that probability inferences are made, and that they are reflected in subjects' evaluations of prospective dating partners.

Also, of interest in Figure 3.7 is that these subjects had the greatest preferences for dates of intermediate physical attractiveness. This finding is consistent with the matching hypothesis; as noted before, this hypothesis predicts that subjects will prefer moderately rather

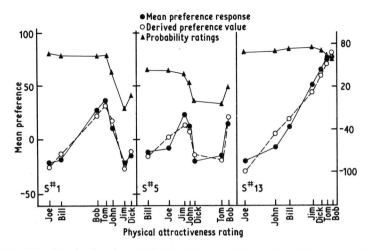

Fig. 3.7 Results for three individual female subjects from Shanteau and Nagy (1976). Solid points represent mean preference ratings for dates described by photographs only. Rated attractiveness of dates shown by spacing along horizontal, and rated probability shown by asterisked points at top. Dotted line gives predicted values derived from a multiple regression analysis based on multiplication of probability and attractiveness ratings. Left and center panels are representative of most subjects who had peak preference for dates of intermediate attractiveness. Right panel is representative of a few subjects who had peak preference for dates of highest attractiveness.

than highly attractive dates. Of course, some subjects did choose the most attractive dates. This approach is exemplified by S 13 in the right panel of Figure 3.7. Also of interest is that this subject rated all of dates as highly likely to accept.

In addition to the above graphical analyses, statistical analyses were performed. Specifically, regression procedures were used to determine how subjects combined probability with attractiveness of the date. The basic approach involved using probability, physical attractiveness and the cross-product of the probability and attractiveness values as predictors in a multiple-regression analysis. The mean preference values (filled circles in Figure 3.7) were used as the criterion. Since probability and physical attractiveness were shown to combine multiplicatively in the preceding experiment, it was expected that the cross-product of these values would account for a significant portion of the variance in the criterion.

As predicted, for most subjects the cross-product term was found to be significant, which supports a multiplying rule. Of special interest was that the cross-product term was found for subjects (e.g. S 1 and S 5 in Figure 3.7) who had shown their highest preferences for dates of intermediate physical attractiveness. Similar results were obtained in a third experiment using subjects who had not been run through Experiment 1 initially.

Comment   The major finding of interest in the Shanteau and Nagy (1979) study was that subjects not only used probability of acceptance when it was provided explicitly, but also when it was left to the subjects to infer it. The ability to deal with probability when it was subjectively inferred represents a major extension of the IIT approach. Prior to this study, only the effect of explicitly provided information had been explored using the IIT approach. Yet in real life, social judgments are not made solely on the basis of explicitly provided information. As has been demonstrated repeatedly by those concerned with implicit personality theory, social judgments often involve a variety of inferences made from other information.

The way these inferences are integrated with other information is an important component of the impression-formation process. Furthermore, such inferences can dramatically effect the final judgment. This later point was nicely demonstrated within the Shanteau and Nagy study by the finding that subjects who made differing probability inferences generally preferred moderately over highly attractive dates. In all, the Shanteau and Nagy study was an important step towards the study of implicit inferences in impression formation (see also Shanteau and Nagy, 1976).

Another contribution of the Shanteau and Nagy study was the complementary use of ANOVA (in IIT) and regression procedures to study human judgment. Traditionally, these two approaches have been applied separately and have not been employed to mutual advantage. Whereas IIT research has focused on testing integration rules through ANOVA procedures, those using regression procedures have generally been interested in deriving weights for stimulus information (see Slovic and Lichtenstein (1971) for a thorough comparison of these two approaches). Shanteau and Nagy (1979), however, showed that the use of both ANOVA and regression procedures within the same study can be quite beneficial. This strategy, among other things, proved quite useful in exploring alternative combination rules across a variety of situations. In effect, support for multiplying using ANOVA analyses in the first experiment laid the foundation for the exploration of combination rules using regression procedures in the second and third experiments.

Finally, the Shanteau and Nagy study suggests that there may be some continuity in processes between experimentally controlled and more realistic judgment settings. Although simulated judgment tasks have been subject to much criticism (Ebbessen and Konecni, 1975), this study showed that similar processes operated in the controlled setting used in Experiment 1 and the more realistic setting in Experiments 2 and 3.

Personnel selection

Nagy (1981)   Previous research on personnel selection has looked at the effects of a wide variety of applicant characteristics; for instance, the influence of scholastic standing, aptitude test scores, sex, race and physical attractiveness have all been studied (see Schmitt (1976) for a review). In addition, specific variables such as order effects (e.g. Farr, 1973) and negative applicant characteristics (e.g. Bolster and Spring-bett, 1961) have been studied extensively. (See Chapter 8 in this book for a further discusison of some issues related to personnel selection.)

Previous research, however, had not taken advantage of the benefits of a systematic research approach such as that offered by IIT. Nagy (1981) conducted a study of personnel selection which demonstrated how IIT could be profitably employed. Three issues were of major concern in the research. First of all, the effects of legally irrelevant information, such as the applicants' sex, age and physical attractiveness, were of interest. Second, the effectiveness of providing a job description and specific instructions requesting subjects not to use irrelevant information was of concern. Finally, the way that subjects combined information was explored. Since previous studies had suggested that negatively valued information had a greater effect on personnel managers' evaluations than positively valued information, a differential-weighted averaging rule (similar to that obtained by Lampel and Anderson, 1968) was expected.

Three studies were run. In each, subjects evaluated the desirability of various job applicants. In the first study, business students served as subjects. The second study involved having the same students re-evaluate the job applicants with the aid of a job description and specific instructions requesting them not to use irrelevant information. The third experiment involved a replication of Experiment 2 using experienced personnel managers as participants.

In all three experiments, job applicants were described by summary application forms. Each applicant was described by two items of job-relevant information and three items of job-irrelevant information. The job-relevant items consisted of the quality of recommendations by previous employers and the number of years of relevant work experience. The job-irrelevant information was conveyed by photographs which were systematically varied with respect to sex, age and physical attractiveness. In all, there were thirty-two hypothetical applicants who were constructed from a factorial design. The applicants were evaluated for the job of computer programmer analyst.

Results obtained for Experiment 1 showed that business students primarily focused upon the applicant's recommendations and, to a lesser degree, on experience. Nevertheless, significant effects for job-irrelevant items were obtained for many subjects.

An interesting result was obtained involving the subjects' use of experience and recommendations. Representative results are displayed in Figure 3.8. Most of the students showed a pattern similar to that shown for S 8. As can be seen, the curves cross over, which is clearly inconsistent with any linear (i.e. parallel) combination rule. Even those students without a cross-over pattern showed a convergence to the left as is shown for S 13. Nagy (1981) proposed that these patterns in Figure 3.8 are indicative of a differential-weighted averaging rule in which the negatively valued level of experience (1 year) was weighted more heavily than the positively valued level (8 years). This differential-weighting of experience would (consistent with the patterns displayed in Figure 3.8) cause recommendations to have a lesser relative effect in the context of 1 year's experience as opposed to 8 years'.

Similar analyses were performed for Experiment 2 in order to determine the effects of providing a job description and instructions discouraging the use of irrelevant information. Results showed that the effects of irrelevant information were eliminated for nearly all subjects. Also, most subjects revealed a more balanced use of experience and recommendations. Combination rules were, however, unaffected by the job description and instructions.

Analyses for the experienced personnel managers in Experiment 3 revealed several findings of interest. In contrast to students, experienced personnel managers made their judgments exclusively on the

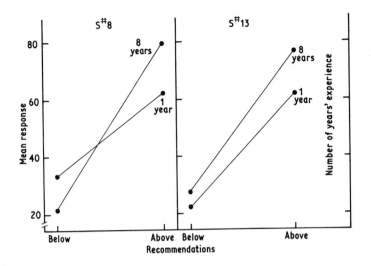

Fig. 3.8 Representative plots of experience X recommendations interactions for two representative business subjects in Nagy (1981). Plotted points
are mean desirability ratings of job applicants. Cross-over interaction in left
panel indicative of differential-weighted averaging. Parallelism in right panel
indicative of constant-weight averaging.

basis of recommendations and experience; none of the personnel
managers showed significant effects for irrelevant items. With regard
to combination rules, the personnel managers showed similar results
to the students in that a differential-weighted averaging rule was supported. However, there were some differences. Unlike the graphical
results obtained for most students, the curves for the personnel
managers did not cross over; instead, they tended to converge towards
the left. Nagy argued that this is probably due to personnel managers
attaching less negative scale values than the students to the below
average recommendation. Theoretically, Nagy argued, if a sufficiently low level of recommendations were added to the design, a
cross-over would occur.

Comment   Overall, the Nagy study revealed several findings of direct
practical importance to the area of personnel selection. Particularly
noteworthy was the evidence for the effectiveness of a job description
in reducing the effects of irrelevant information. Also of practical
interest is that the judgments of experienced personnel managers

differed in significant ways from those of students. This is important in that it implies that students (even those in business) cannot be used as surrogates or replacements for experienced decision-makers (see also Ettenson *et al.*, 1981).

While the basic approach used by Nagy is similar to the one used in other IIT studies of impression formation, there are two differences which deserve comment. First of all, the Nagy study was unique in that it explored social judgments using experts as participants. Second, Nagy specifically studied the effects of an intervention (i.e. providing a job description) on the judgment process. Overall, the significance of these two changes is that the person perception paradigm can be expanded to study and to change the decision processes underlying real decision-makers.

Of course, the Nagy study also has some limitations. In realistic settings, for instance, personnel managers often operate under stress factors (e.g. an excessive number of applicants, time constraints). Thus, their decision processes may differ somewhat from those described by Nagy. This possibility might well be considered in the planning of future research. For example, the effects of job-related stress on experts' decision strategies and their use of irrelevant information could be evaluated. It might also be interesting to compare various techniques, for example, prior training, for coping with job-related stress.

Consumer judgments

Troutman and Shanteau (1976)   Another recent application of IIT has been in the area of consumer decision-making. Although consumer decisions have not traditionally been considered from the perspective of personality impression formation, there have been some interesting trends in this direction. Part of the impetus for this trend has been the increased concern for the evaluation of consumer services (Schneider, 1973). When considering services, the evaluation of other people is often involved.

One of the first studies to recognize the connection between evaluation of consumer services and personality impression formation was conducted by Troutman and Shanteau (1976) on the topic of medical services. As part of a larger project, they asked parents to evaluate medical doctors in pediatrics. Each pediatrician was described by two items of information: (i) a verbal statement describing the doctor's ability to handle children, and (ii) a description of the quality of the staffs' manners. Each of these factors was varied across four levels and combined in a factorial design.

Results from the Troutman and Shanteau study are presented in Figure 3.9. The open data points describe subjects' mean evaluations of pediatricians described by both attributes. As can be seen, these points plot as solid parallel lines, which supports the additivity prediction of both adding and averaging models. To separate the two models, the filled points (connected by a dotted line) were examined. These points, corresponding to the mean evaluation.of pediatricians described only by doctor's ability, are clearly steeper than the solid lines. This graphical test supports an averaging combination rule.

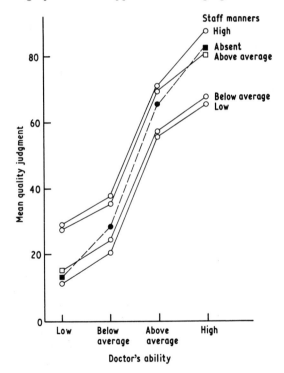

Fig. 3.9 Mean quality judgments of pediatricians described by attributes of staff manners and doctor's ability from Troutman and Shanteau (1976). Parallelism of solid lines supports additivity prediction of constant-weight averaging model. Dotted lines show results when only doctor's ability attribute presented; cross-over supports averaging over adding.

Further support for the averaging hypothesis was obtained by statistical tests performed at both the group and individual subject levels.

Comment   Overall, the Troutman and Shanteau study showed that subjects evaluated pediatricians by averaging attribute information. Specifically, these results show that consumers' evaluations of pediatricians described by both moderately favorable and highly favorable attributes are less positive than their evaluations of doctors described only by highly favorable attributes. From a practical standpoint, this means that the *quality* of information about pediatricians may be more important than the *quantity* of information. In short, averaging implies that 'less may be better'.

While the finding of an averaging combination rule in applied settings is interesting, it is just a beginning. As Troutman and Shanteau point out, the averaging versus adding issue is only the first step in the analysis of consumer strategies in regard to services. While follow-up research has been conducted in the area of medical services (Troutman, 1977; Brien, 1979), there has still been little analysis of other service areas (e.g. repair services, banking services).

Conclusions

As a whole, the studies reviewed in this section provide a demonstration of the flexibility of both IIT and the impression-formation paradigm to deal with issues of practical concern. Indeed, the variety of real-world issues that can be addressed using this approach may be limited only by the imagination of the investigators.

It is also worth emphasizing that there may be considerable benefit in extending basic research approaches into applied settings. On the one hand, demonstrating the generalizability of some basic laboratory findings – averaging, for example˙ – in real-world settings can be of great value. By exploring common issues across a variety of basic and applied settings, it may be possible to provide unification to otherwise disparate areas. On the other hand, some of the methodological and analytic extensions necessitated by the constraints of applied research may prove to be useful in basic research settings. For instance, the techniques developed by Shanteau and Nagy (1979) to study dating have already proved useful in other studies of applied (Shanteau, 1980) and basic issues (Anderson, 1981).

In the next section, some of the other consequences of this trend towards applied research will be discussed. In addition, several of the findings from the studies presented above will be related to trends in the broader domain of human judgment and decision-making. As can be seen, therefore, the research discussed in this section is of importance for a variety of practical and theoretical reasons.

Discussion

In this section, we begin by looking at some of the trends in regard to past and present research. We next try to relate these research trends to some other current approaches to judgment analysis, the study of biases and heuristics, for example. We conclude with a discussion of possible future developments and some final comments on the IIT approach to person perception.

Past and present trends

The preceding sections of this chapter have traced the development and expansion of the Information Integration Theory approach to impression formation. As should be evident from the studies reviewed, the application of IIT has extended far beyond the simple personal perception task originally introduced by Asch. While the focus in the earlier research was to demonstrate support for the IIT approach, the emphasis in more recent studies has been to use IIT to clarify important issues in the content areas themselves. Thus, in each of the applied studies presented, the goal was to study issues of practical or applied interest. In all, the extension of IIT to a variety of areas demonstrates that it can be a valuable tool for studying judgments of social interest.

While the application of IIT to complex social judgments is certainly notable, the contributions of early IIT work should not be overlooked. These initial studies laid the groundwork for later research by contributing to the methodological and conceptual development of IIT. Furthermore, findings obtained in early IIT work on impression formation has been of value in guiding research on applied social judgments. As pointed out by Kaplan and Kemmerick (1974) in their study of juror judgments, basic IIT work provides an extensive background on such phenomena as perceiver bias, other effects, source credibility, information redundancy and stimulus inconsistency. Any and all of these may be of considerable importance in juror judgments. Of course, the same can also be said for judgments in areas such as dating or personnel selection. In our view, investigators concerned with applied social judgment could benefit greatly from careful consideration of the initial personality impression formation research.

Other approaches to judgment

Workers on social judgment would not only benefit from greater concern with early impression formation work but also from more attention to other areas of human judgment. For example, social judgment researchers might profitably draw from research on risky decision-making (Shanteau, 1974, 1975), inferential judgment (Edwards, 1968), and strategies and heuristics (Kahneman and Tversky, 1973). Indeed, a basic premise of IIT researchers has been that many of the same behavioral laws that apply to personality impression formation also apply to other kinds of human judgment. For instance, in addition to the topic areas reviewed here, the IIT approach has revealed consistent patterns of results in areas such as subjective estimates of IQ (Birnbaum and Stegner, 1981), transportation mode choice (Norman and Louviere, 1974; Norman, 1977), marketing judgments (Bettman *et al.*, 1975), job satisfaction (Singh, 1975) and judgments of auditors (Ettenson *et al.*, 1981).

Despite this cross-fertilization within IIT, the majority of research on personal perception has not made connections with other areas of judgment and decision research. The benefits of such connections were illustrated in the Shanteau and Nagy (1979) study of dating judgments. These authors used the findings of risky decision-making studies (i.e. gambling) to arrive at a prediction of how probability and physical attractiveness might operate in the dating context. In fact, the observed results were quite similar to those obtained in studies of gambling. That is, probability operated by modifying or modulating the effect of the date's physical attractiveness; this is similar to the way probability modifies the effect of pay-off value in a variety of gambling situations (Shanteau, 1975). Moreover, many of the analytic techniques used in this research were borrowed from lens model researchers (Hammond *et al.*, 1977) and others involved in multiple-regression research (Slovic and Lichtenstein, 1968, 1971). Thus, as the Shanteau and Nagy study demonstrates, there can be considerable benefit in terms of theory, method and analysis by making use of techniques drawn from other research areas.

Strategies and heuristics   Future investigators of impression formation might look at the research on the use of strategies and heuristics. Tversky and Kahneman (1974) and Slovic (1972) have proposed that within most judgment situations individuals are unable cognitively to handle all the relevant information needed to make perfect decisions. Instead, the individual simplifies the information processing task through the use of various heuristics, or rules-of-thumb.

Several of the heuristics have been studied in various judgment contexts. For example, Kahneman and Tversky (1973; also Tversky and Kahneman, 1973) argued that probability estimates that a certain event will occur will often be based on the number of related instances which can be readily recalled; this heuristic has been called 'availability' (see also Lichtenstein *et al.*, 1978). Other heuristics involve choices among alternatives described by numerous items of information. For example, Slovic and MacPhillamy (1974) showed that when individuals choose among multi-attribute alternatives, they will often focus primarily upon common attributes. In addition, Slovic and Lichtenstein (1968) have shown that the use of heuristics may depend on the response model; for instance, certain information (e.g. payoffs) may be emphasized when it is similar to the final judgment (e.g. estimated value). In all of these cases the use of heuristics may make the individual's judgment more manageable, but may also result in less than optimal decisions (Tversky and Kahneman, 1974).

While numerous heuristics have been explored (e.g. Slovic *et al.*, 1977), they have rarely been studied or even discussed within the personal perception context. However, there is nothing unique about social judgments that would preclude the analysis of heuristics. In fact, within the judgment situations discussed in the previous section, several possibilities for the use of heuristics come to mind. First of all, since Shanteau and Nagy (1979) showed that probability inferences play a major role in dating, it would be worthwhile to determine whether heuristics (such as availability) play a role in making these inferences. Also, in personnel selection and consumer judgment settings, choices among multi-attribute alternatives are involved; it might be interesting to investigate whether heuristics, such as those observed by Slovic and MacPhillamy, are used to ease cognitive strain. Finally, it might be fruitful to explore whether heuristics necessarily lead to biases in impression formation. Hogarth (1981) has argued that heuristics do not always lead to sub-optimal behavior, but may actually be adaptive in some circumstances (for another view of biases and heuristics, see Shanteau, 1978).

Future research directions

The material in the preceding two sections addressed the relationships of social judgment research to early impression-formation work and to work in other areas of judgment and decision-making. In doing so, we have also expressed some general concerns regarding past person perception research. In this final section, we discuss some specific issues which we would like to see explored in future research.

The first issue concerns the need for more penetrating analyses of individual differences. Many of the studies on impression formation have uncovered substantial differences between subjects. With few exceptions, however, the underlying reasons for these differences have not been explored. An example of what might be done appears in Kaplan and Kemmerick (1974). Subjects with high and low predispositions towards innocence or guilt were studied separately and were found to have different strategies of juror judgment; this result has major implications for jury selection. Similar analyses of individual differences in future research may prove to be equally as revealing.

A second change we would like to see is a greater willingness for researchers to intervene and change the subjects' judgment strategies. Up to now, most investigators of impression formation have adopted the 'disinterested observer' approach to research – 'Look, but don't touch' the ongoing processes. However, we believe that researcher intervention can be useful in two ways: (i) it provides a means to understand better the judgment process, and (ii) it provides an opportunity actually to improve the judgment outcome. As an example, Nagy's (1981) study of personnel selection involved an effort to improve the judgments by providing job description and equal-opportunity guidelines. This intervention proved to have a marked impact on the judgment strategies of some subjects. It is worth noting that such interventions have recently become more common in other non-person perception areas of social judgment (e.g. Goodman *et al.*, 1978; Lichtenstein and Fischhoff, 1980; Gaeth and Shanteau, 1981). We believe that person perception researchers would also benefit from a greater willingness to intervene.

A third and final area in which future research would be beneficial is to look beneath descriptions of behavior for deeper levels of understanding. While it is certainly useful to know, for instance, that subjects average personality traits, it would be valuable to know more about why averaging is so pervasive (e.g. see Birnbaum, 1982). Along a similar line, it may also prove useful to inquire further beyond simple measurements into the origins of weights and scale values (Shanteau, 1980). Among other possibilities, such research might enrich our understanding at new levels of the personality impression process.

Final comments on information integration

Because IIT has a somewhat different emphasis from that of traditional approaches, its advantages are often unclear. But, as shown by Shanteau and Nagy's (1979) study of dating, the conceptualization of such judgments as information processing can offer new ways of exploring some longstanding issues. For instance, the matching hypothesis had been studied extensively prior to this study, but evidence either for it or against it was meager. However, Shanteau and Nagy, by focusing on the information processing aspects of dating, provided direct evidence that probability inferences about dates lead some subjects to choose dates of intermediate attractiveness. Thus, a longstanding issue in the dating literature has been, at least in part, clarified by use of the IIT approach.

While there are clearly advantages to IIT, there are also some limitations which deserve discussion. Probably the most frequent source of criticism concerns the relatively rigid and stereotyped manner in which much of the early IIT research was conducted. This led to criticisms that such methodologies were non-representative (Hammond et al., 1975) and would lead to non-generalizable results because of the lack of external validity (Ebbesen and Konecni, 1975). However, as research in the applied section demonstrates, IIT does not rest on any one methodology. Moreover, some basic results, such as averaging, have been found to generalize across a wide variety of content areas and methodologies. Thus, as shown in a number of studies, IIT is far more than a single approach to methodology and analysis.

Another point to bear in mind is that no single study using IIT, or any other approach, is meant to be an end in itself. Rather, as shown by Shanteau and Nagy (1976), research which uses the basic IIT approach initially can be a beginning to a series of studies which move progressively towards greater realism and greater external validity. As such, it will be the cummulative research effort which in the end

82   Issues in person perception

will determine the success or failure of the IIT approach. And, on that score, IIT has led to an impressively large number of studies in a wide variety of content areas; moreover, these studies have repeatedly substantiated the basic premises of information integration theory.

Acknowledgements

The preparation of this chapter was supported in part by U.S. Army Research Institute Contract MDA 903–80–C–0209 to the first author. The unpublished studies described here were supported in part by U.S. Public Health Service Grants from the National Institute of Mental Health (Award MH 26002) and National Institute of Child Health and Human Development (Award HD 11857), and by National Science Foundation Grant (Award BMS-20504).

Correspondence concerning this chapter should be sent to James Shanteau, Department of Psychology, Kansas State University, Manhattan, Kansas 66506, U.S.A. The second author's address is Geraldine Nagy, P.O. Box 591, Bastrop, Texas 78602, U.S.A.

References

Anderson, N. H. (1962) Application of an additive model to impression formation. *Science 138*: 817–18.

Anderson, N. H. (1965) Averaging versus adding as a stimulus-combination rule in impression formation. *Journal of Experimental Psychology 70*: 394–400.

Anderson, N. H. (1967) Averaging model analysis of set size effect in impression formation. *Journal of Experimental Psychology 75*: 158–65.

Anderson, N. H. (1971) Integration theory and attitude change. *Psychological Review 78*: 171–206.

Anderson, N. H. (1974a) Algebraic models in perception. In E. C. Carterette and M. P. Freedman (eds) *Handbook of Perception,* vol. 2. New York: Academic Press.

Anderson, N. H. (1974b) Information integration theory: a brief survey. In D. H. Krantz, R. C. Atkinson, R. D. Luce and P. Suppes (eds) *Contemporary Developments in Mathematical Psychology*, vol. 2. San Francisco, Calif.: W. H. Freeman.

Anderson, N. H. (1981) *Foundations of Information Integration Theory*. New York: Academic Press.

Anderson, N. H. and Lopes, L. L. (1974) The psycholinguistic aspects of person perception. *Memory and Cognition 2*: 67–74.

Anderson, N. H. and Shanteau, J. C. (1970) Information integration in risky decision making. *Journal of Experimental Psychology 84*: 441–51.

Asch, S. E. (1946) Forming impressions of personality. *Journal of Abnormal and Social Psychology 41*: 258–90.

Berscheid, E., Dion, K., Walster, E. and Walster, G. M. (1971) Physical attractiveness and dating choice: a test of the matching hypothesis. *Journal of Experimental Social Psychology 1*: 173–89.

Bettman, J. R., Capon, N. and Lutz, R. J. (1975) Multiattribute measurement models and multiattribute attitude theory: a test of construct validity. *Journal of Consumer Research 1*: 1–15.

Birnbaum, M. H. (1982) Controversies in psychological measurement. In B. Wegener (ed.) *Social Attitudes and Psychophysical Measurement*. Hillsdale, N. J.: Lawrence Erlbaum Associates.

Birnbaum, M. H. and Stegner, S. E. (1981) Measuring the importance of cues in judgment for individuals: subjective theories of IQ as a function of heredity and environment. *Journal of Experimental Social Psychology 17*: 159–82.

Birnbaum, M. H., Wong, R. and Wong, L. (1976) Combining information from sources that vary in credibility. *Memory and Cognition 4*: 330–6.

Bolster, B. I. and Springbett, B. M. (1961) The reactions of interviewers to favorable and unfavorable information. *Journal of Applied Psychology 45*: 97–103.

Brien, M. (1979) Consumer involvement in health care evaluation and decision-making. Unpublished doctoral dissertation, Kansas State University.

Briscoe, M. E., Woodyard, H. D. and Shaw, M. E. (1967) Personality impression change as a function of the favorableness of first impressions. *Journal of Personality 35*: 343–57.

Butzin, C. A. and Anderson, N. H. (1973) Functional measurement of children's judgments. *Child Development 44*: 529–37.

Ebbessen, E. B. and Konecni, V. J. (1975) Decision-making and information integration in the courts: the setting of bail. *Journal of Personality and Social Psychology 32*: 805–21.

Edwards, W. (1968) Conservatism in human information processing. In B. Kleinmuntz (ed.) *Formal Representation of Human Judgment*. New York: Wiley.

Ettenson, R., Krogstad, J. L. and Shanteau, J. (1981) *Materiality judgments: An Analysis of Auditor Expertise*. Technical Report 81-2, Department of Psychology, Kansas State University.

Farr, J. L. (1973) Response requirements and primacy – recency effects in a simulated selection interview. *Journal of Applied Psychology 57*: 228–33.

Fishbein, M. and Ajzen, I. (1975) *Belief, Attitude, Intention and Behavior*. Reading, Mass.: Addison-Wesley.

Gaeth, G. J. and Shanteau, J. (1983) Reducing the influence of irrelevant information on experienced decision makers. *Organizational Behavior and Human Performance*, in press.

84   Issues in person perception

Goodman, B., Fischhoff, B., Lichtenstein, S. and Slovic, P. (1978) *The Training of Decision-makers*. (ARI TR–78–B3) Alexandria, Va.: U.S. Army Research Institute.

Griffitt, W. and Jackson, T. (1973) Simulated jury decisions: influence of jury-defendant attitude similarity–dissimilarity. *Social Behavior and Personality 1*: 1–7.

Hammond, K. R., Rohrbaugh, J., Mumpower, J. and Adelman, L. (1977) Social judgment theory: applications in policy formation. In M. F. Kaplan and S. Schwartz (eds) *Human Judgment and Decision Processes in Applied Settings*. New York: Academic Press.

Hammond, K. R., Stewart, T. R., Brehmer, B. and Steinmann, D. O. (1975) Social judgment theory. In M. F. Kaplan and S. Schwartz (eds) *Human Judgment and Decision Processes*. New York: Academic Press.

Hendrick, C. (1968) Averaging vs. summation in impression formation. *Perceptual and Motor Skills 27*: 1295–302.

Hendrick, C. and Costantini, A. F. (1970) Effects of varying trait inconsistency and response requirements on the primacy effect in impression formation. *Journal of Personality and Social Psychology 15*: 158–64.

Hogarth, R. M. (1981) Beyond discrete biases: functional and dysfunctional aspects of judgmental heuristics. *Psychological Bulletin 90*: 197–217.

Huston, T. L. (1973) Ambiguity of acceptance, social desirability, and dating choice. *Journal of Experimental Social Psychology 9*: 32–42.

Kahneman, D., and Tversky, A. (1973) On the psychology of prediction. *Psychological Review 80*: 237–51.

Kalven, H. Jr and Zeisel, H. (1966) *The American Jury*. Boston: Little, Brown.

Kaplan, M. F. (1971a) Dispositional effects and weight of information in impression formation. *Journal of Personality and Social Psychology 18*: 279–84.

Kaplan, M. F. (1971b) Context effects in impression formation: the weighted average versus the meaning-change formulation. *Journal of Personality and Social Psychology 19*: 92–9.

Kaplan, M. F. (1972) Interpersonal attraction as a function of relatedness of similar and dissimilar attitudes. *Journal of Experimental Research in Personality 6*: 17–21.

Kaplan, M. F. (1973) Stimulus inconsistency and response dispositions in forming judgments of other persons. *Journal of Personality and Social Psychology 25*: 58–64.

Kaplan, M. F. and Kemmerick, G. D. (1974) Juror judgment as information integration: combining evidential and non-evidential information. *Journal of Personality and Social Psychology 30*: 493–9.

Lampel, A. K. and Anderson, N. H. (1968) Combining visual and verbal information in an impression formation task. *Journal of Personality and Social Psychology 9*: 1–6.

Landy, D. and Aronson, E. (1969) The influence of the character of the criminal and his victim on the decisions of simulated jurors. *Journal of Experimental Psychology 5*: 141–52.

Leon, M., Oden, G. C. and Anderson, N. H. (1973) Functional measurement of social values. *Journal of Personality and Social Psychology 27*: 301–10.

Lichtenstein, S. and Fischhoff, B. (1980) Training for calibration. *Organizational Behavior and Human Performance 26*: 149–71.

Lichtenstein, S., Slovic, P., Fischhoff, B., Layman, P. and Combs, B. (1978) Judged frequency of lethal events. *Journal of Experimental Psychology: Human Learning and Memory 4*: 551–78.

Lopes, L. L. (1976) Model-based decision and inference in stud poker. *Journal of Experimental Psychology: General 105*: 217–39.

Mitchell, H. E. and Byrne, D. (1973) The defendant's dilemma: Effects of jurors' attitudes and authoritarianism on judicial decisions. *Journal of Personality and Social Psychology 25*: 123–9.

Nagy, G. (1975) Female dating strategies as a function of physical attractiveness and other social characteristics of males. Unpublished Master's thesis, Kansas State University.

Nagy, G. (1981) How are personnel selections made? An analysis of decision strategies in a simulated personnel selection task. Unpublished doctoral dissertation, Kansas State University.

Norman, K. L. (1977) Attributes in bus transportation: importance depends on trip purpose. *Journal of Applied Psychology 62*: 164–70.

Norman, K. L. and Louviere, J. J. (1974) Integration of attributes in bus transportation. *Journal of Applied Psychology 59*: 753–8.

Phelps, R. H. and Shanteau, J. (1978) Livestock judges: how much information can an expert use? *Organization Behavior and Human Performance 21*: 209–19.

Schmitt, N. (1976) Social and situational determinants of interview decisions: implications for the employment interview. *Personnel Psychology 29*: 79–101.

Schneider, B. (1973) The perception of organizational climate: the customer's view. *Journal of Applied Psychology 57*: 248–56.

Shanteau, J. (1974) Component processes in risky decision-making. *Journal of Experimental Psychology 103*: 680–91.

Shanteau, J. (1975) An information integration analysis of risky decision-making. In M. F. Kaplan and S. Schwartz (eds) *Human Judgment and Decision Processes*. New York: Academic Press.

Shanteau, J. (1978) When does a response error become a judgmental bias? Commentary on 'judged frequency of lethal events'. *Journal of Experimental Psychology: Human Learning and Memory 4*: 579–81.

Shanteau, J. (1980) *The Concept of Weight in Judgment and Decision-making: A Review and some Unifying Proposals*. Technical Report 228, Center for Research on Judgment and Policy, University of Colorado.

Shanteau, J. and Nagy, G. (1976) Decisions made about other people: a human judgment analysis of dating choice. In J. Carroll and J. Payne (eds)

Cognition and Social Judgment. Potomac, Md.: Lawrence Erlbaum Associates.

Shanteau, J. and Nagy, G. F. (1979) Probability of acceptance in dating choice. *Journal of Personality and Social Psychology 37*: 522–33.

Singh, R. (1975) Information integration theory applied to expected job attractiveness and satisfaction. *Journal of Applied Psychology 60*: 621–3.

Slovic, P. (1972) From Shakespeare to Simon: speculations and some evidence about man's ability to process information. *Oregon Research Institute Research Bulletin 12* (2).

Slovic, P., Fischhoff, B. and Lichtenstein, S. (1977) Behavioral decision theory. *Annual Review of Psychology 28*: 1–39.

Slovic, P. and Lichtenstein, S. (1968) The relative importance of probabilities and payoffs in risk taking. *Journal of Experimental Psychology Monographs 78* (3), part 2.

Slovic, P. and Lichtenstein, S. (1971) Comparison of Bayesian and regression approaches to the study of information processing in judgment. *Organizational Behavior and Human Performance 6*: 649–744.

Slovic, P. and MacPhillamy, D. (1974) Dimensional commensurability and cue utilization in comparative judgment. *Organizational Behavior and Human Performance 11*: 172–94.

Stewart, R. H. (1965) Effect of continuous responding on the order effect in personality impression formation. *Journal of Personality and Social Psychology 1*: 161–5.

Tesser, A. (1968) Differential weighting and directed meaning as explanations of primacy in impression formation. *Psychonomic Science 11*: 299–300.

Triandis, H. C., and Fishbein, M. (1963) Cognitive interaction in person perception. *Journal of Abnormal and Social Psychology 67*: 446–53.

Troutman, C. M. (1977) Processes in husband–wife decision-making on health care factors. Unpublished doctoral dissertation, Kansas State University.

Troutman, C. M. and Shanteau, J. (1976) Do consumers evaluate products by adding or averaging attribute information? *Journal of Consumer Research 3*: 101–6.

Tversky, A. and Kahneman, D. (1973) Availability: a heuristic for judging frequency and probability. *Cognitive Psychology 5*: 207–32.

Tversky, A. and Kahneman, D. (1974) Judgment under uncertainty: heuristics and biases. *Science 185*: 1124–31.

Walster, E., Aronson, V., Abrahams, D. and Rottmann, L. (1966) Importance of physical attractiveness in dating behavior. *Journal of Personality and Social Psychology 4*: 508–16.

4 Multiple cue person perception

Alexander Lovie

Shall I compare thee to a summer's day?
Thou art more lovely and more temperate

Shakespeare, Sonnet XVIII

Introduction

How would you feel about someone who was described as 'intelligent, independent and inconsiderate' (Bruner *et al.*, 1958)? If you were told that a gilt (female breeding pig) had few nipples, a heavy bone structure and high muscle trimness, would you judge her to be good or poor breeding stock (Phelps and Shanteau, 1978)? Would you attach much credibility to the estimate of a used car's price provided by an expert mechanic who was also a friend of the seller (Birnbaum and Stegner, 1979)?

These three problems represent only a tiny sample of the multiple cue decisions studied over the last thirty years or so. In addition to the usual trait impression studies, workers in social psychology have also looked at dating behaviour, graduate selection, equity judgments, presumptions of innocence by jurors and the sociability of clinical patients. Although this chapter is concerned primarily with multiple cue work in social perception, it should be realized that many of the ideas and methodologies have been used in areas quite distinct from social psychology. Consequently, certain of the references will not deal *directly* with issues in this area. However, it is impossible to ignore the useful cross-fertilization that has happened between psycho-physics, scaling theory, sequential decision-making for binomial events (usually black and white poker chips), cognitive psychology and person perception. In social psychology the array of concepts and paradigms sampled by this work is extensive, including papers on balance theory, source credibility, set size effects in impression forma-tion and equity theory.

Models of man

There is, however, one unifying thread running through most of the work: that the results can be captured by a limited number of math-ematical models. In other words, most of the recent multiple cue work is self-consciously concerned with the testing of more or less formal models of how information is combined for decision-making purposes (Hoffman, 1960; Goldberg, 1970; Anderson, 1974; Dawes, 1979).

Not surprisingly these fall into the general class of linear models, which includes regression analysis and analysis of variance as special cases. In other words, certain workers have modelled their subjects' responses by means of multiple regression equations where the descriptions (usually traits expressed on a common scale, for example 'honest' and 'confident' rated in terms of their likeability) form the various predictor variables with the subjects' responses (ratings or rankings) forming the criterion variable. Others have described the form and results of such experiments in terms of the familiar linear models of the analysis of variance, where the traits form the factor effects, and the responses act as the dependent variable which the analysis decomposes into these effects. Clearly the latter approach implies some factorial structure to the experiments which employ this form of analysis. For example, in an early paper of Anderson's (see 1974 for a discussion), he employed a simple two-factor design with trait strength for the first word (again on a likeability scale) and trait strength for the second as factors. Further, much of this work has employed some of the most sophisticated experimental designs in psychology because of the problems of obtaining naturally occurring trait combinations and hence of ensuring factor independence or orthogonality (Hoffman, *et al.*, 1968). Non-linear regression models, that is, where the weights or parameters of the predictor variables have been raised to a power, and analysis of variance models which include interaction terms, are sometimes used to model so-called configural or patterned approaches to multiple cue judgments, as will be seen later. Although most workers are content with detecting such patterned responses through the mere presence of non-linear or interaction terms, they do offer possible tests of goodness-of-fit, a feature exploited by few workers with the notable exception of Anderson. Most models, therefore, predict that the responses are linear combinations of these input variables, to put it at its most general.

In addition, a few studies have used Bayesian models to describe the processes of integrating information from a variety of sources but their use has not been as widespread in social perception as in decision-making. Here a series of hypotheses about a person, for example, that they are young or old, are updated as new information (hair colour, say, or walk) comes in, the updating being carried out by Bayes theorem. This changes prior beliefs about the hypotheses into beliefs *a posteriori* in the light of this new information (Lovie and Davies, 1970).

There is an even smaller and somewhat older body of work (not reviewed here) which relies on propositional and logical calculus to model inference in multiple cue perception (see Warr and Knapper (1968) for a review). Strictly speaking, of course, the work on linear models is little more than a probabilistic extension of this logical approach to inference. However, the ability of regression analysis and analysis of variance to cope with response variation makes them of more practical value than a purely logical, deterministic approach.

Before passing to a more detailed coverage of the material it is worth noting that, for the British psychologist at least, it is impossible to ignore the pioneering study of person perception – *Perception of People and Events*, (Warr and Knapper, 1968). Warr and Knapper proposed an information processing/computer analysis of person perception which has continuing interest. Equally important, however, is their emphasis upon the joint contribution of both the stimulus and the perceiver to the perception of people. In addition, their discussion of the problems of measurement on person perception and the influence of individual differences is still worth reading. One could, therefore, view the present chapter as an up-dating of sections of this classic treatment.

Experimental and statistical preliminaries

Stimuli

Most research has used words as stimuli. The classic experiments of Asch (1946), for example, used lists of trait words such as 'warm, intelligent, kind-hearted' to describe a hypothetical person. Other verbal descriptions have included brief phrases or sentences referring to some individual, while yet others have employed personal vignettes as stimuli (see Warr and Knapper, 1968, for a review). Certain of the more applied studies have presented their subjects with psychometric profiles derived, for example, from the MMPI, or hypothetical grade point averages, or SAT (Scholastic Achievement Test) scores. Rarely has the material been in other than verbal form, even in ostensibly realistic or, to use the current jargon, 'ecologically valid' studies. The few exceptions include Lampel and Anderson (1968), Phelps and Shanteau (1978), and Shanteau and Nagy (1979), all of whom used photographs as well as verbal material.

This overwhelming preference for written descriptions does not automatically invalidate the work since, as Warr and Knapper (1968) have argued, trait lists and verbal descriptions are often all the information available in real life, particularly when we have not met the person described. And there are, of course, considerable methodological advantages in using a reasonably controllable set of stimuli.

On the other hand, the few studies which have attempted to cross-validate laboratory findings, for example Phelps and Shanteau (1978), have not shown much generalization from the purely verbal to photographic representations of the items to be judged.

The trait lists have been presented either simultaneously or sequentially, with appropriate changes in some of the models. For example, Anderson (1973a) has suggested that subjects pay less attention to later items when they are sequentially presented, and has allowed for this in his model of information integration.

Responses

Responses have generally been in one of two forms: either ratings on a bewildering array of scales (dichotomous, 6-point, 100-point, etc.), or a mixture of decisions and ratings, again with the same variety of types. There has also been an interest in scaling responses, either to ensure that the scale approximates to a particular scale type (for example, Anderson (1974) argues that his theory of functional measurement yields an interval scale), or to point out the robustness of the analysis in the face of variety of scale type (Dawes, 1979).

Analysis

Finally, analysis of the subjects' responses has depended heavily on the linear model, because it is central to the various conceptual and theoretical positions. For example, Dawes and others are concerned with seeing how good their subjects are when pitted against such a model (so-called 'bootstrapping' studies), while Anderson and his colleagues have been assiduous in seeing how effective certain linear models are as 'models of man'. As mentioned earlier, the linear model has also been used to represent and detect the presence of configural response patterns in subjects' results. Such a Gestalt effect in impression formation was first suggested by Asch (1946), who talked about the centrality of certain traits, for example, warm/cold. For Asch, therefore, changing a 'central' trait in a description resulted in a change in the meaning to the subjects or the other traits in the list. Although the issue of configural versus linear (additive) models has long been debated in the literature, it has yet to be laid to rest (see Birnbaum and Stegner (1979), for a further stir of the pot). Further, I am certain that the continuing argument about the existence of an implicit personality theory will ensure that the search for configural responses continues.

Various approaches

Anderson's integration theory

The single most influential and consistent worker in multiple cue person perception is the American, Norman H. Anderson. Although I shall concentrate on his more recent research, it is worth noting that Anderson has been active in the area for over twenty years: one of his earliest contributions appeared in one of the Yale Studies in Attitude and Communication (Hovland, 1957). Since then he and his students have extended and refined this early model of communication effects into a flexible tool for representing and dissecting a large variety of judgments, including ones like judgments of weight and number which are well outside social psychology. Obviously, each judgment needs a particular version of this basic linear model, but it is possible to detect a prototypical version of the model in many of his papers. This is described next.

Adding or averaging?

Let us say that you have to decide whether you would like someone who was described as 'compassionate and tall'. There are several rather obvious models of how the *separate* likeability ratings for the two adjectives combine to determine the joint attitude. For example, one might predict that the two would summate, or that their ratings might combine as an average of the separate ones. Clearly, for most positively-evaluated trait words, for example 'kind' and 'conscientious', the averaging model for the likeability of these in combination will predict a less extreme score than a summating one. However, more complex trait combinations do not always provide as clear-cut a test between such competing approaches. For example, if one presents subjects with a highly favourable trait and a highly unfavourable one then simple adding and averaging models predict very similar results. Anderson's model has more in common with the averaging representation than the summating one.

Initial bias

Anderson has also included provision for an initial bias in the impression: one might, for example, be predisposed to like people even before meeting them or having them described. Anderson has also allowed for a variety of stimulus context effects through a relative weighting system which modifies the absolute scale values of the stimuli judged in isolation. Given that the weights are usually equal and constrained to sum to unity Anderson's model technically becomes a weighted averaging one.

In a slightly more formal manner, therefore, the response (usually a rating), R, to a collection of N stimuli, S_i, is given as:

$$R = \sum_{i=0}^{N} w_i S_i / \sum_{i=0}^{N} w_i$$

where w_i is the relative (equal) weight. The possibility of a weight coded w_o means that the model can incorporate an initial bias or organismic predisposition. Since the denominator is often arranged so as to sum to 1, the model becomes:

$$R = \sum_{i=0}^{N} w_i S_i$$

a straight averaging process.

Testing the model

The weights – or more precisely the effective stimulus values – are usually estimated from data derived from ANOVA designs (for the technically minded, either a full factorial structure, or a balanced incomplete block, or a fractional factorial with certain unimportant higher order interactions confounded). The estimating equations for the various stimulus values are normally derived from functions of the marginal means of the ratings on the assumption that the averaging model is correct. The use of tractable factorial designs also means that Anderson can use analysis of variance F-tests on interactions to evaluate the averaging model in a very direct way. For example, let us say that we have run a 2-factor experiment, fully crossed, where both factors have two levels, for example, high and low likeability ratings of four adjectives. A trial, therefore, consists of presenting the subject with a pair of adjectives and asking him or her for a likeability rating. If the averaging model is correct, then the rating for the two adjectives together can be predicted from the weighted sum of the two (marginal) adjectives rated separately. The implication here is of zero interaction between the factors and of parallel data lines in the factorial plot. Such statistical and graphical tests are used widely by Anderson and his colleagues as tests for goodness-of-fit for the averaging hypothesis.

Functional measurement

Anderson, through his system of functional measurement (Anderson, 1970, 1971), has claimed that such estimated scale values constitute an interval scale. (Close readers of the non-parametric statistical literature might be surprised to find that Anderson defines an interval scale as one which is monotonic with the appropriate physical scale, although his definition also includes the less controversial points that an interval scale has an arbitrary zero and unit.) One can, therefore, view Anderson's system of functional measurement as a kind of elaborate balancing act where scale type (i.e. interval), substantive concepts (i.e. integration and averaging theory) and analysis (i.e. analysis of variance) simultaneously support and justify each other. In other words, the legitimacy of the use of analysis of variance, with its ability to produce a test of goodness-of-fit through various F-ratios, is dependent upon the response scale being interval scaled (or capable of being monotonically transformed into such). But in turn, whether the scale is interval, or capable of being transformed into such, depends upon the assumption that an averaging model will fit the rating data. Failure of any of the parts could, therefore, bring down the whole edifice, but, because of the interdependency of the structure it would, paradoxically, be difficult to determine which part had failed. No wonder, therefore, that Anderson writes that 'The validity of the functional measurement approach rests on its coherence with an extended network of experimental analysis' (1974, p. 242). Unfortunately, although it is possible within one experiment to provide adequate controls for inferences of some detail, elegance and sophistication, experimenters do not as yet have a theory or methodology for integrating the results of multiple studies whose aims and methods are usually so varied.

However, it is also fair to say that Anderson has been right on more occasions than his critics and that his averaging mechanism has considerable independent support. For example, the important work on subjective categories by Rosch and her co-workers has demonstrated the existence of a prototype category core based on the average of the dimensions defining the category (Mervis and Rosch, 1981).

It is also true to say that the need for linear models to have strong scales of measurement has not appeared so obvious to later workers, and that its support by Anderson is in part a hangover from the great scaling theory debates of the 1950s and early 1960s (see Anderson, 1961). Anderson's main contribution to scaling theory is that he has always been prepared to endorse a particular averaging theory of multiple cue combination, thus cutting the Gordian knot which faces anyone attempting to link theory with scale type via an empirical relational system.

Problems and extensions

Anderson has, therefore, felt it necessary to defend his averaging model from various attacks. One of the earliest argued that a summation model gave a better fit than an averaging one. In the first of two linked papers (1965, 1967) Anderson established that the addition of a less to a more favourable pair of traits produces a less extreme likeability rating than the two favourable traits alone, a result which supports the averaging but not the adding model. The second paper (1967) reformulated the set size effect found in the first study in terms of an extended version of the averaging model. (The set size effect is found in trait studies where the addition of extra homogeneously-rated items produces a more extreme rating response. This poses a problem for a simple averaging model, but not for an addition model, since only the former would predict an unchanging rating.)

Anderson dealt with this problem by invoking the organismic or internal state variable. Specifically he assigned it a weight (w_o) whose value is above zero. Thus if the weights (w_1) and values (s_1) of the stimuli are kept the same, for example, by working only with similarly rated items and constant list lengths, then the original formula can be modified as follows: if there is a list of k items, then R_k, the response rating of these items, can be given as:

$$R_k = \frac{w_o s_o + kw_1 s_1}{w_o + kw_1}$$

which is an increasing function of k, with s_1 as its highest value.

Further, if s_o (the rated value of the internal state) is set at zero by, for example, always starting the subject's rating scale at some neutral value, and if the ends of the response scale are given by the ratings of the highest and lowest valued items on the various lists, then the new averaging equation predicts a constant item weight when the effect of differing list lengths has been allowed for. Anderson published a test of this model in 1967 and found a constant trait weight value, relative to the internal state, for all list lengths.

Anderson and others have also modified the original formula to handle serial or sequential presentation, again by invoking the internal or organismic variable (now reconceptualized as the initial bias variable) and by modifying the equation so that the item weights reflect the serial position of the item in the sequence. Thus a variety of hypothesized primacy and recency effects could be evaluated by the averaging model, and a variety of theories to account for them tested. In general, Anderson has argued against a primacy effect with serial presentation, which has traditionally been thought to support a change-in-meaning hypothesis (Asch, 1946). Instead, he has argued that less attention is paid to later items which is reflected in his model as a decrease in the stimulus weight values with serial position (Anderson, 1973b).

Anderson has also extended the integration model to other central matters in social psychology. For example, in an interesting experimental and theoretical paper with Farkas (Farkas and Anderson, 1979), Anderson has adapted the model to cover equity or reward decisions for one person's effort and performance relative to another's. As with earlier experiments, considerable use is made of analysis of variance and graphical representations to evaluate the model. In particular, the parallelism criterion (i.e. absence of interaction) of earlier tests was used to confirm that reward was a weighted sum of (relative) effort and performance. Further, a test of non-parallelism was employed to evaluate whether the relationship between the persons' performance and effort was ratio. All of these were supported by more detailed analyses of variance and model dissection. Less expected, however, was evidence for a configurational or context determined judgment of reward for certain extreme combinations of effort and performance. Although the paper finishes on a modest note, Anderson and Farkas comment that 'the rule of equity integration may be conducive to a more just society' (p. 894).

Other areas tackled by Anderson are balance theory (Anderson, 1977, 1979; Gollob, 1979). Although it is difficult to summarize so long and complex a paper as his 1977 one on this topic, it is possible to detect a continuing commitment to an averaging model for subject and object adjective relations (e.g. if Joe likes dancing and Jane likes Joe, does Jane like dancing?), to the use of factorial designs and analysis of variance for testing goodness-of-fit for such models, to the value of functional measurement in providing an interval scale for ratings, and to the low value of correlation for model testing.

Students, disciples and converts

Not only has Anderson published many joint papers with his students (see Anderson, 1974, for a representative collection), he has also indirectly inspired other workers. For example, a recent study by Ostrom *et al.* (1978) on jury decisions of guilt or innocence makes explicit use of Anderson's integration theory. Equally interesting is a paper on recall and impression formation by Dreben *et al.* (1979) which describes

Anderson's averaging model as providing 'the most popular and most thorough account for the impression abstraction process in the Asch task' (p. 1759). Further, a recent paper from the committed Bayesian Lee Beach (Beach *et al.*, 1978) concludes that 'opinion revision is not Bayesian' (p. 2), and that a model of the typed favoured by Anderson would account for the discounting effects of a sequence of adjectives of decreasing relevance to the judgment at hand. (See also Beach and Beach, 1978; Ostrom and Davis, 1979, for further applications of functional measurement.)

Of course, Anderson's work is not without its critics (Hodges, 1973; Schönemann *et al.*, 1973; Ostrom, 1977; Gollob, 1979; also the exchange between Anderson and Krantz and Tversky on conjoint and functional measurement in Anderson, 1971) though some of these debates seem either shadow-boxing or exercises in self-propaganda. However, his work shows a singleminded consistency and drive over a twenty-year period that should ensure that this particular show at least will run and run.

Bootstrapping models of man

Early work at Oregon

Anderson's contributions have by and large been to mainstream academic social psychology. His longstanding interest in Asch-type experiments, configurational versus strictly additive theories for such studies, and latterly the topics of balance and equity have also been the concerns of academic workers for at least the last forty years. There is, however, an important group of multiple cue studies which have more applied purposes. And the authors of these studies are less committed than Anderson to a belief in the efficacy of linear models as descriptors of behaviour and judgment. Many of this latter group have been, or are currently, associated with the Oregon Research Institute, whose approach Anderson once described as being 'eclectic' (1974, p. 237). The main figures are Dawes, Hoffman, Goldberg and, to a lesser extent, Slovic and Lichtenstein. A spiritually-linked group, also with applied interests, is centred on the neo-Brunswikian Hammond (Hammond *et al.*, 1975).

For the Oregon group the main early influence was Meehl's '*Clinical versus Statistical Prediction*' (1954) in which Meehl demonstrated the value of a statistical approach, via a linear regression model, over top-of-the-head unaided clinical judgments. The first and, with the benefit of hindsight, most important paper was by Hoffman (1960) on what he termed the paramorphic representation of clinical judgment. What he meant by this was that a linear regression model could capture most aspects of a clinician's judgment at a sufficiently useful level of theoretical and empirical specificity for current scientific purposes; as one substance with an identical chemical, but not molecular, structure to another is said to be a 'paramorph' of that substance. Such a thorough-going instrumentalism is characteristic of most of the other work of the Oregon group, which is not really surprising since such a philosophy also allowed them to use the technology of the linear model for practical purposes.

Hoffman's paper is, however, of considerably more interest than later writers have suggested, since it foreshadows most of the later controversies. For example, Hoffman was careful to point out that the square of the multiple correlation coefficient, R^2, was not a particularly good discriminator between models. He was equally careful to specify the various forms in which configurational effects might reveal themselves in the regression model. The paper also includes four brief case studies on clinical decision-making, including one which showed a limited degree of configurality in the judge's choices. However, as Hoffman pointed out, the R^2 for a linear model for this judge was larger than the configurational one, while both accounted for about 80 per cent of the variance. In other words, the specific form of the model is perhaps less important than its simplicity or its ability to account for a high percentage of the response variance.

The argument as to how best to develop linear models to represent linear and configurational aspects of judgment was continued in Hoffman *et al.* (1968), where an analysis of variance model for a fully crossed factorial design was developed in the practical setting of decisions about gastric ulcer malignancy. Here configurational models were defined in terms of possible interactions between the various symptom signs. (Anderson's 1972 comments on the general problem of detecting configurationality in clinical judgment using analysis of variance is worth reading in conjunction with the Hoffman *et al.* paper, and with the two Goldberg papers cited below.)

Man versus model of man

Paralleling Hoffman's work were two studies by Goldberg (1968,

1970) who, in the first of the two papers, restated the familiar points that inter-clinician reliabilities across a range of tasks were usually low, and that it was possible to operationalize configural effects in terms of interactions in the analysis of variance. In general, Goldberg was unable to find much evidence for configural cue use by clinical judges and concluded that a linear model would account for the overwhelming variance of the clinicians' judgment of MMPI profiles. Goldberg finished this first paper by considering how clinical inference can be improved through extensive feedback. In general, there seemed little improvement over time except for those groups given a simple additive formula made up from five of the MMPI scales for the data *and* the optimum cutting score. All other forms of training, including giving subjects the formula itself but not the cutting score, had much less effect.

In this first paper, Goldberg was careful to point out that his linear models were models of the individual judge and that they were not tested by seeing how well (or badly) the clinician, as modelled by the regression equation, performed in the real world.

In the second paper (1970), however, Goldberg does investigate how well the model actually performs in the real world of MMPI profiles, that is, the clinician is now replaced by a linear model of the clinician, and its performance is assessed. The result, which has been duplicated by many independent researchers, is that the model generally out-performs the clinician even though it is based upon the clinician's own judgments! This somewhat paradoxical finding has been termed 'bootstrapping' by Dawes and others (Dawes, 1971; Hogarth, 1980): replacing man by model of man allows one to raise oneself by one's own bootstraps.

Goldberg's explanation for this is simple: computing a regression equation through least squares minimizes the unreliability of the resulting formula, unlike the performance of the average clinician who, in Goldberg's phrase, 'has his days'. Goldberg is, however, careful to note the specific individuals and groups that the model does (or does not) out-perform. Here the best judge performed almost as well as the best model, while the composite judge out-performed the composite model. However, the typical judge did less well than the typical model. Even more importantly, the simple additive model mentioned earlier (called the actuarial formula by Goldberg; see his 1965 paper for its derivation) out-performed all the other regression models, except a strictly linear one. (Note that Goldberg's regression models for each judge allowed for nonlinear configurational effects: as usual these were small.)

Dawes and bootstrapping

Exploration of bootstrapping has been most vigorously pursued in the last ten years by Dawes (1971, 1976, 1979) and Dawes and Corrigan (1974), graduate selection being the proving ground for such paramorphic representations.

The first paper (1971) is mainly concerned with a practical demonstration of the value of linear regression models in providing composite cutting scores for decisions about graduate entry. The equations performed this task with considerable success, correctly rejecting some 55 per cent of the sample; that is, no student was rejected by the model who was not also rejected by the faculty admissions committee against which the model was validated. In the first paper of the series (but see Dawes, 1964, for some earlier thoughts) Dawes is unable to improve on Goldberg's explanation for bootstrapping, that is, that it worked by minimizing the judges' error variability. However, in a footnote Dawes also suggests that linear models could be useful mimics of many others, providing that the criterion scores for each variable in the models are monotonic, that is, all high and low values of the variables were matched by high and low criterion scores.

The ubiquity and superiority of the linear model is further exploited in Dawes's other three papers which, because of their considerable overlap in material and ideas, will be dealt with together.

Dawes makes an early distinction between 'proper' and 'improper' linear models for judgment. 'Proper' models are those whose weights (usually β- coefficients) have been chosen so as to maximize the relationship between the criterion and the various predictor variables. 'Improper' models are those in which other, usually simpler, rules have been used to generate the weights. Obvious examples are randomly chosen weights and ones which assign equal value to each variable except for sign (so-called unit weighing schemes). Dawes also mentioned that the weights could be chosen by experts.

If bootstrapping appears to lead to paradoxical findings, then replacing people by their improper linear models produced even more counter-intuitive results. For example, improper models with unit weighting schemes out-performed both random and proper linear models. The instrumentalist predilictions of the Oregon group have now taken Dawes from considering the linear model as at least a paramorphic representation of human judges, through questioning its ability to capture the successes of such judges, to considering it purely as an atheoretical tool for dealing with practical situations in as parsimonious way as possible. Clearly, the robustness and flexibility of both proper and improper linear models have reduced their ability to act as models of man. The real question's now are about the relationships between people and this useful technology. This point will be taken up later. As far as Dawes is concerned, the job for people is, first, to select and code the variables for the linear models, that is, to choose the most salient and important variables; and, secondly, to say which of their values have high and low scores on the criterion. (Dawes has repeatedly pointed out that even proper linear models require that the predictor variables be no better than conditionally monotonic in the criterion, for conventional analyses to yield reliable estimates of their coefficients.)

The later papers are concerned with applied examples of bootstrapping. Since Dawes tends to cite repeatedly the same examples, I shall merely list them without more specific references: graduate selection, judgments of marital happiness, choice of handgun ammunition (originally analysed by Hammond and Adelman, see Dawes, 1979), diagnosis from MMPI profiles, and the classic work of Yntema and Torgerson (1961) on the categorization of ellipses. In all cases, linear models, including improper ones, either performed no worse than the subjects in the experiment or out-performed them, at least according to multiple correlational criteria. Dawes does not feel that this is very surprising, particularly as the variability in value of most decision outcomes is usually small enough to allow the judge to arrive at the same decision for quite a wide range of values of the predictor variables (the so-called 'flat maximum problem'). Put more succinctly by Dawes, this latter point amounts to agreeing that 'It is always better to be smarter, more beautiful, closer to age 29, closer to blood pressure 120 over 80, etc.' (1974, p. 105).

Social judgment theory

Although the work of Egon Brunswik has stimulated many multiple cue studies, the general finding of the work (called social judgment theory) is very like that of Dawes in that people's judgments seem to be effectively captured by a regression model (Hammond *et al.*, 1975; Hammond and Wascoe (eds), 1980). Again, like Dawes, the neo-Brunswikians have a liking for instrumentalist philosophies, noting that the large number of competing models for any particular situation has forced them into adopting an applied stance. This implies that the principle guiding choice of model is the model's utility as an aid to better performance rather than how well it provides a fit to the subjects' behaviour or underlying cognitive processes. What is important in their work, however, is the sheer range of applied social settings that they have investigated (see Hammond *et al.*, 1975 for a partial list; and Brehmer, 1976 on interpersonal conflict), their willingness to consider non-linear variants of the basic regression model, and their extensive use of interactive computer graphics as aids to performance. Their work also inspired the development of what is probably the most widely used measure for assessing model fit, that by Tucker (1964), which is based on Brunswik's lens system with its correlational approach to modelling.

Social judgment theory has also emphasized the role of learning in applied social settings and has made important contributions to cognitive approaches to learning, as distinct from the more traditional S – R approach. In essence this has meant that subjects are taught rules and functions, not S – R connections, through complex forms of feedback and feedforward (see Brehmer, 1979 for a recent survey on inference; and Hammond and Summers, 1972 for an earlier theoretical/applied statement on the form that such cognitive learning should take place). Finally, one can view the approach as the extension of multiple cue probability learning into the arena of social judgment. I have not considered this topic in the present chapter since it has not generally concerned itself with social objects. However, its emphasis upon such important matters as cue intercorrelation has made some of its findings of considerable relevance here (see Brehmer, 1979, on multiple cue learning theory; and Einhorn *et al.*, 1979, on cue redundancy and intercorrelation and its effect on iudgment).

Critics of bootstrapping

In general, few people have challenged the existence of bootstrapping, that is, that a linear model (proper or improper) can either equal or out-perform the judge on which it is based. Two such attempts worth mentioning briefly are by Einhorn (1970; see also his 1971) and Libby

(1976a). In the first study, Einhorn attempts to show that non-linear, 'non-compensatory'; 'conjunctive' and 'disjunctive' models can provide a better fit to certain decision-making results than a linear (regression) model, where the results were derived from both experiments and theoretical considerations. What Einhorn means by these various jargon terms is as follows: conjunctive models are those in which a person or object is assessed on a mixture of all their properties. For example, this person is given a job because he is both intelligent and hardworking. By extension, disjunctive models are those in which the choice is made on the basis of either one property (intelligence) or another (perseverence). Such models are said to be non-compensatory, unlike the usual regression ones with their variable coefficients, since it is not possible to include a trade-off measure between the various properties. Since regression models, through their coefficients, can compensate a failing in one variable by increasing the valuation of another, they are said to be compensatory (see also Dawes, 1964, 1971; Hogarth, 1980).

Unfortunately, the conclusions from Einhorn's paper are somewhat unclear, partly because of the very limited amount of experimental work included, partly because the linear model considered was of the proper variety only.

Libby's paper (1976a), the rejoinder to it by Goldberg (1976), and Libby's re-rejoinder (1976b) constitute the more serious of the two attacks on bootstrapping. Briefly, Libby claims that in his particular applied setting (the prediction of business failure by forty-three experienced loan officers), twenty-six of the judges out-performed their optimal models, seven cases equalled them, and ten proved to be less successful. Moreover, unlike Goldberg (1970), both the composite and average judge out-performed their model equivalents. (Note that, because of the nature of the cues, Libby employed a linear discriminant function as the model against which his judges' performance was assessed, not a regression one.) The explanations offered by Libby for these contradictory findings were, first, that the criterion to be predicted was much better defined and more reliably measured than in earlier studies and, second, that his subjects were much more experienced and motivated than those in earlier work. Libby also argued that the skewed distributions over cue weights found in his study were not found in other experiments.

This latter point was taken up by Goldberg (1976), who found that only when the cue distributions were transformed into symmetrical form were the usual bootstrapping effects found. Goldberg, however, employed a regression model instead of the discriminant one used by Libby. Goldberg's explanation of his findings were twofold. First, that the skewed distributions of cue weights perturb the regression weights and, second, that they also attenuate the correlation of predicted values with those from other models, and hence the value of the transformation.

Libby's reply makes the points that Goldberg used an inappropriate analysis (regression) on his (Libby's) results since his subjects were restricted to dichotomous or 6-point responses. This contrasts with the continuous and normal theory form of the linear regression model used by Goldberg. Also, Libby takes issue with the normalizing transformation/approximation used by Goldberg. This, he claims, transforms the model to a non-linear one and, because of the apparently non-linear nature of some of his subjects' judgments, it is scarcely surprising that the newly-transformed models out-performed the judges.

The matter is still undecided, although more recent studies, for example, Brehmer *et al.* (1980) and Camerer (1981), conclude in effect that linear (bootstrapped) models are at least as good as the judges on which their weights are based. Brehmer *et al.*'s subjects, for example were faced with a medical diagnostic task (they had to cope with a fictitious disease called Brunswik's Agony). Although subjects could cope with a variety of cue conditions, they were unable to work with interacting or configural cues even when given specific instructions about the nature of the configuration. Camerer provides a brief discussion of the more general conditions under which bootstrapping takes place. The main conclusion is that this happens under a variety of circumstances, particularly when the environment has been more or less completely specified by the judge himself.

Summary of work so far

The previous two sections have provided a brief survey of the main approaches to multiple cue perception. Beginning with Anderson and his followers, we covered work on the linear model as a description of the process of person perception. Next came the Oregon work which initially viewed such linear models as descriptors but, through the pressure exerted by their applied interests, quickly came to view them as models to replace man, that is, as a way of bootstrapping human judgment. The applied theme was continued through a consideration of the neo-Brunswikians, and the section ended with a brief mention of certain criticisms levelled against this latter work.

Other approaches: The Reverend Bayes and the theory of reasoned action

Bayes' theorem as a model for person perception

On the face of it, Bayes theorem,* that handy extension of the formula for conditional probability, would seem to offer a useful model for multiple cue studies. After all, describing it as the (optimal) revision of opinion about a collection of hypotheses in the face of new data would seem to capture the essence of most impression formation/revision experiments (see Slovic and Lichtenstein, 1971, for a classic statement of the achievement and promise of Bayes' theorem; the review also includes an attempted reconciliation with the regression approaches of Hoffman and Goldberg). Unfortunately, there have been few direct tests of the approach in person perception. (See Lovie and Davies (1970), for one of the more simplistic ones; see also McCauley and Jones (1979), for a fun one on presidential assassinations: the usual conservatism effect was found; that is, that people lagged behind the Bayesian revision.) In addition, the naive Bayesian model has come under near fatal attack as a general description of behaviour (Tversky and Kahneman, 1974; Lyon and Slovic, 1976; Nisbett and Ross, 1980).

The major use of Bayes' theorem in social psychology today, however, is in metatheory. It has been used, for example, by Ajzen and his colleagues to analyse predictions from attribution theory about causality and consistency. Here the value of Bayes' theorem is not that it provides a model for behaviour, but rather that its analysis of the choice situation helps to disentangle many of the conflicting findings in the area (Ajzen and Fishbein, 1975; Ajzen, 1977; Ajzen et al., 1979).

---

* Bayes' theorem shows how to infer *from* an existing distribution (e.g. of coin tossings) and a prior estimate of probabilities (heads/tails) *to* a new (or posterior) estimate of probability. It supposes, therefore, that a person's subjective estimate of probability will be recalculated – and may vary – after each new item of information is added. The actual formula is stated in Lovie and Davies (1970).

Theory of reasoned action

The final approach that I shall mention is the so-called Theory of Reasoned Action developed by Fishbein and Ajzen (Fishbein and Ajzen, 1975; Ajzen and Fishbein, 1977, 1980; Fishbein, 1980). The theory is of interest here because of its concern with how people combine their attitude towards a given behaviour (e.g. giving up smoking) with a subjective norm (e.g. society's perceived views on smoking) to arrive at an intention (whether to give up smoking). In Ajzen and Fishbein (1980) this combination rule is seen as a linear (regression) one, with a set of weights reflecting the degree of importance of the predictor variables (attitudes and norms) and the use of R^2 (the square of the multiple correlation coefficient) to assess the degree of agreement between these variables and the behavioural criterion. The explicit aim of the work is to demonstrate that action is in reasonable and consistent agreement with the weighted attitudes and norms of their subjects, and hence that it is predictable from them. Most of their recent effort has gone into demonstrating the value of this simple combination rule in many practical settings: it has been tested with family planning decisions, weight loss and dieting, voting behaviour in both American and British elections, and consumer choices (see Ajzen and Fishbein, 1980, for more examples and citations of other relevant work). They claim considerable empirical support for their theory.

Discussion

There is one major unresolved issue from previous sections: can people's behaviour be represented by a linear model? That is to say, does the highly reliable bootstrap effect undermine the results of integration theory? In some ways, of course, this is not a fair comparison to make since there are clear differences between the aims, methods and stimuli of the two approaches. However, bootstrapping does imply that a linear regression model derived from the subject's own responses performs better than the subject himself, and hence is not very descriptive of that particular judge. Unfortunately, since much of the bootstrapping evidence is based on correlational criteria, one cannot really conclude one way or the other over problems of model fit, as Anderson and Shanteau (1977) have properly pointed out.

Equally true, however, is the change in attitude towards the linear model by the Oregon group, who now view it as being too flexible and too slippery an entity to be a good descriptor of people. As I have maintained earlier, their contention now is that the linear model is the simplest and most parsimonious system which reliably out-performs their judges, and hence it is increasingly irrelevant to ask whether or not it is also a model of man. To this extent, therefore, the comparison is somewhat inappropriate.

Anderson and Shanteau, however, would not appear to agree with this position, since they differentiate between models as devices to predict (bootstrap) or to understand (integration theory) behaviour (1977, pp. 1155, 1168), and they seem to argue that the Oregon workers have a tendency to slip from one to the other without acknowledging the transition. This is, I feel, an unjust criticism, particularly as Dawes (1975) has argued that his linear models are 'models of the task' not of the person, and that his experiments and those by Goldberg and others are really concerned with teaching people how to use such 'models of the task'. Perhaps Anderson's criticisms amount in the end to a statement that Dawes and his colleagues have considered too small a class of models, unlike Anderson whose original integration treatment is now seen as only a small part of a more general system of cognitive algebra (Anderson, 1974). Alternatively, Anderson, with his more realistic philosophy of science, is either unwilling or unable to accept the instrumentalism of Dawes.

There are, however, other differences between the two approaches that might account for the discrepancies. For example, Anderson's work has primarily been with rather pallid, homogeneous items of information, mainly in tightly controlled laboratory settings with a generally homogeneous group of subjects. Dawes *et al.*'s work has been with much more realistic problems, with subjects whose day-to-day job it is to carry out the tasks on which the research was based. Einhorn *et al.* (1979) have even argued that a considerable amount of the bootstrapping effect could be accounted for by the information processing and cognitive demands that the various tasks make on their subjects, thus arguing that process-tracing studies might throw some light on such stressful activities. (Of course, for such cognitive insights to be of value we would need to know quite what people do when making clinical and graduate selection decisions. Dawes's pragmatic approach would not be of much use here except in that bootstrapping might give us more detailed information about where, when and how people need to be helped.)

The politics of applied work might also explain the differences between the results. For example, Dawes (1979) has pointed out that the necessity for positive discrimination for certain minorities could mean that the linear model's decisions would be overruled for those individuals, since a mechanical way of arriving at student selection without even an interview might be viewed as discriminatory. No such feelings of delicacy are likely to deter the subject in Anderson's laboratory when faced with a list of traits from making a decision about the likeability of the person described. Yet other differences might lie in the varied ways in which the information is presented. As was noted earlier, the Phelps and Shanteau (1978) study showed that, when pictures of gilts (female breeding pigs) were used instead of lists of their characteristics, the expert judges made use of far fewer dimensions and could, therefore, be less effective judges because they were more likely to miss discriminating clues. In other words, a regression equation based on a reduced set of predictors is likely to be less useful than one based on all the available ones, under a variety of predictor weight scenarios. Unfortunately, too few such intra-task studies have been performed for any firm conclusions to be drawn (see also Shanteau and Nagy, 1979).

I would like to pursue a little further the bootstrapping problem of how people and the linear model relate. Dawes and Corrigan (1974) suggest that people should select and code the variables, but not combine them except as a straight sum. Just how people should relate to such formal systems has in fact been pursued for some time, much of the work being stimulated by early work on Bayesian information processing systems (Sawyer, 1966; Einhorn, 1972; Hogarth, 1980). In general, people's roles in this work have been somewhat subordinate to the processes of mechanical combination (usually computer driven). However, since such models are likely to have a considerable value in generating good decisions, it will be important to ensure that access to such technology is as easy as possible. I have argued elsewhere (Lovie, 1978) that psychology could help by providing better aids to the understanding and use of what Bell (1976) has termed 'intellectual technology'. Work on bootstrapping should provide a good place to start on this particular road (see also Einhorn and Hogarth's recent review (1981) on the provision of such cognitive aids for decision making).

My final comments will be concerned more directly with the other chapters in the present book. In their influential work on attribution theory, Nisbett and Ross (1980) have used Dawes's bootstrapping results as partial support for their attacks on people's rationality. Clearly they view Kelley's consistency principle as implying a linear combination rule which Dawes's judges, equally clearly, did not employ. Although Anderson has also attacked the consistency principles behind balance and congruity theory (1971), his conclusions are not as negative as those of Nisbett and Ross. Perhaps one needs to look more closely at the differences between these two main approaches to see if such pessimism is justified.

References

Ajzen, I. (1977) Intuitive theories of events and the effects of base-rate information on prediction. *Journal of Personality and Social Psychology 35*: 303–14.

Ajzen, I. and Fishbein, M. (1975) A Bayesian analysis of attribution processes. *Psychological Bulletin 82*: 261–77.

Ajzen, I. and Fishbein, M. (1977) Attitude-behavior relations: a theoretical analysis and review of empirical research. *Psychological Bulletin 84*: 888–918.

Ajzen, I. and Fishbein, M. (1980) *Understanding Attitudes and Predicting Behavior*. Englewood Cliffs, N. J., Prentice-Hall.

Ajzen, I., Dalto, C. A. and Blyth, D. P. (1979) Consistency and bias in the attribution of attitudes. *Journal of Personality and Social Psychology 37*: 1871–6.

Anderson, N. H. (1961) Scales and statistics: parametric and nonparametric. *Psychological Bulletin 58*: 305–16.

Anderson. N. H. (1965) Averaging versus adding as a stimulus-combination rule in impression formation. *Journal of Experimental Psychology 70*: 394–400.

Anderson, N. H. (1967) Averaging model analysis of set size effect in impression formation. *Journal of Experimental Psychology 75*: 158–65.

Anderson, N. H. (1970) Functional measurement and psychophysical judgment. *Psychological Bulletin 77*: 153–70.

Anderson, N. H. (1971) Integration theory and attitude change. *Psychological Review 78*: 171–206.

Anderson, N. H. (1972) Looking for configurality in clinical judgment. *Psychological Bulletin 78*: 93–102.

Anderson, N. H. (1973a) Serial position curves in impression formation. *Journal of Experimental Psychology 97*: 8–12.

Anderson, N. H. (1973b) Comments on the articles of Hodges and of Schönemann, Cafferty and Rotton. *Psychological Review 80*: 88–92.

Anderson, N. H. (1974) Information integration theory: a brief survey. In D. H. Krantz *et al.* (eds) *Contemporary Developments in Mathematical Psychology*; vol. II. San Francisco, Calif.: Freeman.

Anderson, N. H. (1977) Some problems in using analysis of variance in balance theory. *Journal of Personality and Social Psychology 35*: 140–58.

Anderson. N. H. (1979) Indeterminate theory: reply to Gollob. *Journal of Personality and Social Psychology 37*: 950–2.

Anderson, N. H. and Shanteau, J. C. (1977) Weak inference with linear models. *Psychological Bulletin 84*: 1135–70.

Asch, S. E. (1946) Forming impressions of personality. *Journal of Abnormal and*

Social Psychology 41: 258–90.

Beach, B. H. and Beach, L. R. (1978) A note on judgments of situational favorableness and probability of success. *Organisational Behavior and Human Performance 22*: 69–74.

Beach, L. R., Mitchell, T. R., Deaton, M. D. and Prothero, J. (1978) Information relevance, content and source credibility in the revision of opinion. *Organizational Behavior and Human Performance 21*: 1–16.

Bell, D. (1976) *The Coming of Post-Industrial Society*. Harmondsworth, Middlesex: Penguin Books.

Birnbaum, M. H. and Stegner, S. E. (1979) Source credibility in social judgment: bias, expertise and the judge's point of view. *Journal of Personality and Social Psychology 37*: 48–74.

Brehmer, B. (1976) Social judgment theory and the analysis of interpersonal conflict. *Psychological Bulletin 83*: 985–1103.

Brehmer, B. (1979) Preliminaries to a psychology of inference. *Scandinavian Journal of Psychology 20*: 193–210.

Brehmer, B., Hagafors, R. and Johansson, R. (1980) Cognitive skills in judgment: subjects' ability to use information about weights, function forms and organizing principles. *Organizational Behavior and Human Performance 26*: 373–85.

Bruner, J. S., Shapiro, D. and Tagiuri, R. (1958) The meaning of traits in isolation and in combination. In R. Tagiuri and L. Petrullo (eds) *Person Perception and Interpersonal Behavior*. Stanford, Calif.: Stanford University Press.

Camerer, C. (1981) General conditions for the success of bootstrapping models. *Organizational Behavior and Human Performance 27*: 411–22.

Dawes, R. M. (1964) Social selection based on multidimensional criteria. *Journal of Abnormal and Social Psychology 68*: 104–9.

Dawes, R. M. (1971) A case study of graduate admissions: application of three principles of decision-making. *American Psychologist 26*: 180–8.

Dawes, R. M. (1975) The mind, the model and the task. In F. Restle *et al.* (eds) *Cognitive Theory*, vol. I. Hillsdale, N. J.: Lawrence Erlbaum Associates.

Dawes, R. M. (1976) Shallow psychology. In J. S. Carroll and J. W. Payne (eds) *Cognition and Social Behavior*. Hillsdale, N. J.: Lawrence Erlbaum Associates.

Dawes, R. M. (1979) The robust beauty of improper linear models. *American Psychologist 34*: 571–82.

Dawes, R. M. and Corrigan, B. (1974) Linear models in decision-making. *Psychological Bulletin 81*: 95–106.

Dreben, E. K., Fiske, S. T. and Hastie, R. (1979) The independence of evaluative and item information: impression and recall order effects in behavior-based impression formation. *Journal of Personality and Social Psychology 37*: 1758–68.

Einhorn, H. J. (1970) The use of nonlinear noncompensatory models in decision-making. *Psychological Bulletin 73*: 221-30.

Einhorn, H. J. (1971) The use of nonlinear, noncompensatory models as a function of task and amount of information. *Organizational Behavior and Human Performance 6*: 1-27.

Einhorn, H. J. (1972) Expert measurement and mechanical combination. *Organizational Behavior and Human Performance 7*: 86-106.

Einhorn, H. J., Kleinmuntz, B. N. and Kleinmuntz, B. (1979) Linear regression and process-tracing models of judgment. *Psychological Review 86*: 465-85.

Einhorn, H. J. and Hogarth, R. M. (1981) Behavioral decision theory: processes of judgment and choice. *Annual Review of Psychology 32*: 53-88.

Farkas, A. J. and Anderson, N. H. (1979) Multidimensional input in equity theory. *Journal of Personality and Social Psychology 37*: 879-96.

Fishbein, M. (1980) A theory of reasoned action: some applications and implications. In H. E. Howe (ed.) *Nebraska Symposium on Motivation, 1979*, vol. 27 Lincoln, Nebr.: University of Nebraska Press.

Fishbein, M. and Ajzen, I. (1975) *Belief, Attitude, Intention and Behavior: An Introduction to Theory and Research*. Reading, Mass.: Addison-Wesley.

Goldberg, L. R. (1965) Diagnosticians versus diagnostic signs: the diagnosis of psychosis versus neurosis from the MMPI. *Psychological Monographs 79(9)*, whole no. 602.

Goldberg, L. R. (1968) Simple models or simple processes? Some research on clinical judgment. *American Psychologist 23*: 483-96.

Goldberg, L. R. (1970) Man versus model of man: a rationale plus some evidence for a method of improving clinical inferences. *Psychological Bulletin 73*: 422-32.

Goldberg, L. R. (1976) Man versus model of man: just how conflicting is the evidence? *Organizational Behavior and Human Performance 16*: 13-22.

Gollob, H. F. (1979) A reply to Norman H. Anderson's critique of the subject-verb-object approach to social cognition. *Journal of Personality and Social Psychology 37*: 931-49.

Hammond, K. R. and Summers, D. A. (1972) Cognitive control. *Psychological Review 79*: 58-67.

Hammond, K. R. and Wascoe, N. E. (eds) (1980) *Realizations of Brunswik's Representative Design. New Directions for Methodology of Social and Behavioral Science*. San Francisco, Calif.: Jossey-Bass.

Hammond, K. R., Stewart, T. F., Brehmer, B. and Steinmann, D. O. (1975) Social judgment theory. In M. F. Kaplan and S. Schwartz (eds) *Human Judgment and Decision Processes*. New York: Academic Press.

Hodges, B. H. (1973) Adding and averaging models for information integration. *Psychological Review 80*: 80-4.

Hoffman, P. J. (1960) The paramorphic representation of clinical judgment. *Psychological Bulletin 57*: 116-31.

Hoffman, P. J., Slovic, P. and Rorer, L. G. (1968) An analysis of variance model for the assessment of configural and utilization in clinical judgment. *Psychological Bulletin 69*: 338–49.

Hogarth, R. M. (1980) *Judgement and Choice*. Chichester: Wiley.

Hovland, C. I. (ed.) (1957) *The Order of Presentation in Persuasion*. New Haven, Conn.: Yale University Press.

Hovland, C. I. (ed.) (1957) *The Order of Presentation in Persuasion*. New Haven,- Conn.: Yale University Press.

Krantz, D. H., Tversky, A. and Anderson, N. M. (1971) An exchange on functional and conjoint measurement. *Psychological Review 78*: 457–8.

Lampel, A. K. and Anderson, N. H. (1968) Combining visual and verbal information in an impression-formation task. *Journal of Personality and Social Psychology 9*: 1–6.

Libby, R. (1976a) Man versus model of man: some conflicting evidence. *Organizational Behavior and Human Performance 16*: 1–12.

Libby, R. (1976b) Man versus model of man: the need for a nonlinear model. *Organizational Behavior and Human Performance 16*: 23–6.

Lovie, A. D. (1978) Applied psychology in the post-industrial society. *Bulletin of the British Psychological Society 31*: 281–4.

Lovie, A. D. and Davies, A. D. M. (1970) An application of Bayes' theory to person perception: The effect of rate of revision and initial revision on the perception of another's age. *Acta Psychologica 34*: 322–7.

Lyon, D. and Slovic, P. (1976) Dominance of accuracy information and neglect of base rates in probability estimation. *Acta Psychologica 40*: 287–98.

McCauley, C. and Jones, S. (1979) The popularity of conspiracy theories of presidential assassination: a Bayesian analysis. *Journal of Personality and Social Psychology 37*: 637–44.

Meehl, P. E. (1954) *Clinical versus Statistical Prediction*. Minneapolis: University of Minnesota Press.

Mervis, C. B. and Rosch, E. (1981) Categorization of natural objects. *Annual Review of Psychology 32*: 89–115.

Nisbett, R. E. and Ross, L. (1980) *Human Inference: Strategies and Shortcomings in Social Judgment*. Englewood Cliffs, N. J.: Prentice-Hall.

Ostrom, T. M. and Davis, D. (1979) Idiosyncratic weighing of trait information in impression formation. *Journal of Personality and Social Psychology 36*: 2025–43.

Ostrom, T. M., Werner, C. and Saks, M. J. (1978) An integration theory analysis of juror presumption of guilt or innocence. *Journal of Personality and Social Psychology 36*: 436–50.

Phelps, R. H. and Shanteau, J. C. (1978) Livestock judges: how much information can an expert use? *Organizational Behavior and Human Performance 21*: 209–19.

Sawyer, J. (1966) Measurement and prediction, clinical and statistical. *Psychological Bulletin 66*: 178–200.

Schönemann, P. H., Cafferty, T. and Rotton, J. (1973) A note on additive functional measurement. *Psychological Review 80*: 85–7.

Shanteau, J. C. and Nagy, G. F. (1979) Probability of acceptance in dating choice. *Journal of Personality and Social Psychology 37*: 522–33.

Slovic, P. and Lichtenstein, S. (1971) Comparison of Bayesian and regression approaches to the study of information processing in judgment. *Organizational Behavior and Human Performance 6*: 649–744.

Tucker, L. R. (1964) A suggested alternative formulation in the developments by Hursch, Hammond and Hursch, and by Hammond, Hursch and Todd. *Psychological Review 71*: 528–30.

Tversky, A. and Kahneman, D. (1974) Judgment under uncertainty: heuristics and biases. *Science 185*: 1124–31.

Warr, P. B. and Knapper, C. (1968) *The Perception of People and Events*. Chichester: Wiley.

Yntema, D. B. and Torgerson, W. S. (1961) Man–computer cooperation in decisions involving commonsense. *IRE Transactions Human Factors in Electronics, HFE-2*: 20–6.

5 Problems of context and criterion in nonverbal communication: a new look at the accuracy issue

Dane Archer *and*
Robin M. Akert

Abstract

Four key problems which have impeded research on nonverbal communication are examined: (a) sampling and labeling nonverbal behavior, (b) preserving the context in which the behavior occurs, (c) generating a source of nonverbal behavior, and (d) determining the criterion of accurate interpretation. These problems are particularly acute for research on the recognition of emotion.

Seven distinct varieties of context are identified, and the degree to which research has been faithful to these contexts is discussed. The criterion problem is described, and it is argued that this problem is insoluble within the emotion recognition tradition.

The paper presents a 9-cell typology of research designs, and the relative merits and frequencies of these nine design types are described. Finally, a new concept in nonverbal communication research is presented. This concept, embodied in the Social Interpretations Task (SIT), provides a solution to some of the problems of context and criterion which have beset the field of nonverbal communication.

**Problems of context and criterion in nonverbal communication:
a new solution.**

In 1872, Charles Darwin set the agenda for the next century of
research on nonverbal communication. The publication of *The Expression of the Emotions in Man and Animals* in that year launched generations
of research on the degree to which specific nonverbal indicators of
various emotions could be 'decoded'. The originality and impact of
Darwin's contribution are unrivalled, and the questions he raised
about emotions – and even the methods he used – continue to pre-
occupy this domain of the social sciences. Darwin's influence on
nonverbal communication was clearly paradigmatic, just as his work
on the descent of species was paradigmatic for evolution and biology
generally.

A century of subsequent research, however, now makes it clear that
Darwin's influence has been something of a mixed legacy for nonverbal communication. Darwin's 1872 volume unwittingly launched
researchers of nonverbal behavior on the elusive trail of emotion.
Studies of the recognition of the emotions are valuable, of course, if
for no other reason than that emotion plays an important and much
discussed role in everyday life. The problem is that, since Darwin,
students of nonverbal communication have studied little else. As a
result of this topical monopoly, we know very little about how various
nonverbal 'channels' (e.g. the face) are used in the interpretation of
anything other than emotions.

This problem is particularly acute since research on the 'decoding'
of emotions is flawed by a number of unique, inherent constraints. It is
our position that these constraints constitute a ceiling on the prospects
of this research tradition. Although this chapter touches lightly on four
of these problem areas, our two primary concerns are with the issue of
context and with the problem we regard as intractable in emotion
research: the impossibility of an unambiguous criterion of interpretive
accuracy. For example, in a study using judgments about what emotion is in a photographed face, how does a researcher decide what the
right answer is?[1]

In this chapter, we describe a new solution to these classic problems
of context and criterion – a new solution which we hope will contribute to unlocking the current impasse in nonverbal communication
research. Finally, it is the argument of this chapter that the traditional
approach to the study of emotion in nonverbal communication

research has been largely mined. Recent years have seen the emergence of some extremely complex and comprehensive studies of nonverbal cues to the recognition of emotion (Ekman *et al.*, 1972; Rosenthal *et al.*, 1974a, b). It is now time, we believe, for at least some researchers to turn to the rich and largely untapped spectrum of interpretations about qualities other than emotion, and to the study of the interpretive process itself.

Problems in emotion recognition research: a concise catalogue

Because the study of the emotions has dominated nonverbal communication research, there have been several discussions of methodological dilemmas in this tradition. Some of the best known of these analyses are by Frijda (1969), Ekman *et al.*, (1972) and Ekman (1973). Since these treatments are both comprehensive and excellent, we shall only list in briefest catalogue fashion the four methodological issues which seem to us to warrant the greatest uneasiness: (a) measurement issues, (b) context and situation, (c) behavior sources, and (d) the criterion problem. Of all these concerns, it seems to us that the context issue is the most complex and that the criterion problem is insoluble within the emotion tradition.

Measurement issues: sampling and labeling

The sampling problem in emotion research can be conceptualized in several dimensions, although these dimensions have not always been reflected in research designs. The most obvious of these is the sampling of subjects – i.e. people to act as judges or 'decoders' of some nonverbal stimuli. Emotion research also implies two other major dimensions of sampling, however, whether or not a researcher attempts these systematically. The first concerns selecting emotions; the second concerns selecting the people to emote.

Selecting emotions requires a three-part or three-stage sampling of emotion types, emotion intensities and emotion instances. In a hypothetical study of judgments of photographed emotions, for example, a researcher could decide to include a photograph of the 'happiness' emotion type – because it occupies a niche in some theoretical schema, because it seems easy to photograph, because every other nonverbal researcher has included it, or for no considered reason at all. Each of these decisions, of course, is a form of sampling from some population, but many emotion researchers have either not recognized that sampling was involved or else have not considered their own sampling rationale important enough to report.

Even when emotion types have been sampled, our hypothetical investigator must still sample from some distribution of intensities. If the emotion of 'happiness' is selected, our hypothetical researcher could still conceivably photograph a quiet smile, the face of someone convulsed by a joke, or even the incongruously tear-streaked face of a person ecstatic and 'overcome' at having won a tension-filled contest. These three examples of 'happiness' are surely only three of a great many points on some (as yet uncharted) distribution of intensity. Even the apparently simple question 'Can happiness be judged from facial photographs?', therefore, is not meaningful without making clear the intensity of happiness to which one is referring.

Once an emotion type and intensity are somehow sampled – for example, 'happiness' in the form of a quiet smile – our hypothetical researcher must still decide how to sample instances of this emotion. Is the first picture taken the one to be used, or only one that somehow looks 'right'? Looking 'right' is itself a fascinating concept. For example, it may refer only to photographs of a certain intensity, to photographs of the peak of an emotion rather than its 'onset' or 'offset', or to expressions which conform to some stereotyped or pronounced version of an emotion. That such decisions are made, and that they reflect an uninvestigated form of sampling, is illustrated by studies in which a researcher reports having reshot photographs if they were 'unsatisfactory' (e.g. Gitter *et al.*, 1972). Even if a researcher uses a systematic sampling procedure – e.g. using a photograph only if judges consistently label it as showing the same emotion – there is still a risk of tautological argument (Cook, 1971). It seems circular, for example, to report that photographs of emotions produce a high rate of agreement – across judges, across sexes, or across cultures – if these photographs were chosen in the first place precisely because judges agreed on their emotional content.

Emotion researchers also sample, systematically or not, a population of potential 'encoders' – those who emote or transmit the emotions to be studied. Although this sampling also draws from a largely unknown population, it seems unlikely that this distribution is inconsequential. For example, Landis (1924) found that the same situations elicited markedly dissimilar nonverbal expressions in different people.

For this reason, Bruner and Tagiuri (1954) suggested nearly three decades ago that researchers control for the possibility of expressive idiosyncracies by sampling types of encoders. The prospect of variance across encoders is particularly worrisome in decoding studies which have used few encoders, or even one alone.[2] It is probably true, of course, that there is great variation across individuals in the ways they 'express' *all* qualities (age, education, social class, interpersonal relationships, etc.). But this variance is particularly unsettling in the case of emotion research because no firm criterion of the emotion exists. If individuals vary in their expressions of an emotion, it could well be because some of them are not experiencing the emotion – at any rate, it cannot be verified that they are.

In addition to the potential influence of sampling at many levels, a separate measurement issue concerns the use of verbal labels of emotion. For example, Schlosberg (1941) demonstrated long ago that the 'category width' used by a researcher to identify the 'right' answer could affect judges' performance levels – if rough synonyms are acceptable answers in an open-ended question format, judges will obviously do better. Even in a multiple-choice format, the similarity of the alternate answers clearly affects performance (Knapp, 1972).

A more radical criticism, however, challenges the whole enterprise of using verbal labels to study emotion. As somewhat remote abstractions, labels provide a filtering process which may distort the meaning of judges' performance levels. An emotion label may catalyze a judge's perceptual search for a 'typical' constellation of nonverbal cues. These 'typical' constellations, however, could well differ from judge to judge – as Kramer (1963, p. 413) said, researchers have often made 'the unwarranted assumption that a label such as "grief" or "joy" meant the same thing.'

In addition, the use of verbal labels seems faintly ironic since it has long been argued that we lack an adequate vocabulary for describing nonverbal behavior (Sapir, 1927; Kramer, 1963). Labels therefore invite judges to do precisely that which people are alleged to do poorly. Finally, some critics argued that people actually tend to think in terms of the emotional implications of specific situations, and not in terms of abstract emotion labels (Frijda, 1969, p. 169). In summary, the use of emotion labels may not only introduce systematic error, it also seems unfaithful to the naturalistic processes by which emotions are recognized in real life.

Context and situation

The second major concern about emotion research is that it has been uniquely affected by the tension between experimental control and mundane realism. In an effort to maximize control, many researchers have tried to capture isolated nonverbal cues which are implicated in a specific emotion. For example, a still photograph is more manageable than a film or videotape since it contains a smaller number of variables, 'bits' of information, and potential cues. There is no question, however, that all real emotions are embedded in the stream of behavior. A major criticism made by 'realists', therefore, is that fragmentary nonverbal 'excerpts' have little or nothing to do with the form in which nonverbal cues are encountered in everyday life.

The word 'context' appears frequently in discussions of nonverbal communication, and it is obviously a key concept. It seems to us, however, that there are seven varieties of context, and that these need to be differentiated in any discussion of the ways in which emotion research has lacked 'context'. Since notions of context also play a central role in the innovation to be discussed later in this chapter, each of these aspects of context will be discussed in turn. In our opinion, the seven most important varieties of context in natural nonverbal communication are the following:

(1) Channel isolation   In everyday life, we encounter a virtual 'banquet' of nonverbal channels. There are, of course, cases in which the number of channels is restricted – e.g. communicating with a deaf or mute person, telephone conversations, etc. In most face-to-face interaction, however, we can draw upon a complex array of nonverbal channels in trying to decode any aspect of a person's behavior. We may try to use these channels simultaneously, perhaps weighing the information in one channel against that in other channels. For example, in deciding whether someone is really 'angry', we may look for a tremulous voice, a tense or shaking body or a red face. We may insist on finding evidence in several channels before making the attribution that the person is *really* angry. Many studies of emotion have failed to resemble this aspect of natural context, however, by showing only one or two channels to judges – for example, a great many studies have used only still photographs.[3]

(2) Absence of verbal information   Judging from most published research, many investigators have forgotten that real nonverbal

behavior occurs in concert with verbal behavior. When we make judgments about a person's emotions or other qualities in real life, we undoubtedly process both these levels of information. The important point is that specific nonverbal clues may not have any independent 'meaning' in social interaction. Nonverbal cues may acquire meaning principally in terms of their reinforcement (or contradiction) of what a person says. This verbal context has been invisible in studies of nonverbal communication, and almost all emotion researchers have deliberately pruned all traces of words from the stimuli used in their studies. This has occasionally taken the form of presenting decoders with silent films of a speaking person – an extreme violation of the natural 'ecology' of communication.

(3) Prior experience   In decoding the everyday nonverbal behavior of people we know, we have on our side the tremendous interpretive advantage of history. From prior experience, we possess a 'catalogue' of the encoding characteristics of these people, and this serves as a background against which new behavior is judged. We can use this historical context in deciding, for example, whether a person is angry or upset, or whether the observed level of agitation is merely an enduring characteristic of this person. Whether or not prior experience actually makes us more accurate judges of the people we know, it still provides a context within which we assess their behavior. Prior experience is, not surprisingly, almost never operationalized in emotion research. Any study using standard samples of behavior – photographs, films, etc. – is, of course, generally unable to take advantage of encoder–decoder familiarity.

(4) Behavior streams   Static excerpts of nonverbal cues are unnatural in that they truncate the continuous quality of real life. Photographs are perhaps the worst offenders. Single photographs report only a cross-sectional slice of behavior, and are extremely unfaithful to the natural 'streams' of social interaction. Perhaps as a result, one often sees photographs that appear bizarre – like the grotesquely distorted face of an athlete photographed at the peak of performance. In real life, these unrepresentative slices of behavior are probably disattended on the basis of the ongoing behavior. The frozen, unlifelike nature of photographs prompted Bruner and Tagiuri to write (1954, p. 638): 'Historically speaking, we may have been done a disservice by the pioneering efforts of those who, like Darwin, took the human face in a

state of arrested animation as an adequate stimulus situation for studying how well we recognize human emotion.'

A specific gesture, facial expression or tone of voice is always embedded in a continuous, flowing context which we need to determine the meaning of behavior. Any research design which isolates individual nonverbal 'instants' from a stream of behavior, therefore, unnaturally prunes these expressions of a vital matrix. A verbal metaphor for this loss of context might be showing a person one line from a 10-page essay, and then asking him to guess what the essay was about.

(5) 'Real time' exposure lengths   Real nonverbal cues are extremely ephemeral. In social interaction, these cues race by us and disappear beyond recall. We only attach meaning to these cues, therefore, as they are presented to us in 'real time' – i.e. the exposure lengths we observe in real life. Most studies of nonverbal cues have been unnatural in that they have not resembled anything like 'real time'. In judgment studies, for example, judges usually examine photographs at lengths greatly in excess of 'real time' – for either a fixed interval or for as long as the judges wish. In the early days of emotion research, the reasons for this artificiality were purely technological – still photographs were the only visual means of capturing nonverbal behavior. Even now that film and videotape are readily available, however, many researchers continue to use photographs rather than 'real time' exposures. As technology develops, it has even become possible to capture nonverbal cues in less than 'real time' – e.g. using slow motion, one frame of a 16-mm film, one stop-motion 'scan' of a videotape, or the almost imperceptible exposures possible with a tachistoscope. All these approaches, however, fail to present judges with cues in natural exposure lengths and, therefore, fail to create experimentally an approximation of natural decoding. Only film, videotape and audiotape present nonverbal cues as they occur in 'real time'.

(6) Situational antecedents   One of the most important types of context is the setting in which a nonverbal act occurs. If a person looks sad, for example, is it at the loss of a chess game or at the loss of a spouse? If a person looks happy, is it in response to a joke someone has just told, or does it reflect satisfaction at a job accomplished yesterday? If a person looks nervous, is it the foreboding of facing an exam tomorrow or the immediate anxiety of a person speaking before a large audience? In all

these cases, even if a judge could recognize gross features of an expression, it is clear that a more qualitative assessment depends upon contextual information. For this reason, Frijda (1969, p. 192) described emotion recognition as a two-stage process consisting first of an assessment of the pattern of an expression itself and, second, specification of this pattern according to situational cues. A famous demonstration of the effects of situational antecedents was given by the film-maker Eisenstein. Using the same equivocal facial expression, Eisenstein found that audiences attributed horror, love or concentration to the expression, depending on whether it was juxtaposed with a 'shot' of a corpse, a baby or a machine (Miller, 1972, p. 370). It is clear that appropriate verbal and nonverbal behavior differs radically across situations (e.g. greeting, working, leaving, loving, etc.), and Hall (1977, p. 132) has even suggested the existence of 'situational dialects' – scripts for language and behavior which are unique to each situation and 'known' by members of the same culture.

The situational antecedents of nonverbal behavior are complicated, and include elements like the number of people involved in interaction, their relative status, the presence of interpersonal bonds like kinship or marriage, the past history of the interactants, the immediate history of the interaction, and the physical setting in which interaction takes place. As just a simple example, a smile can be a reaction to the playfulness of one's two-year-old son, or a response to a joke told by one's employer. The smiles in these two situations will surely differ in quality. Research which excerpts nonverbal acts from situations clearly deprives judges of indispensable cues to the qualitative meaning of these acts.

(7) Recognition versus interpretation   Most researchers have studied whether judges can recognize an emotion which the encoder makes no effort to disguise. In everyday life, we often need to interpret both overt and covert cues to emotion – i.e. we need to go beyond a person's manifest 'performance' of an emotion to see whether this performance conceals greater emotional complexity. For example, is a defeated athlete's hearty congratulation of the winner genuinely good-natured, or does it conceal bitter disappointment – and how do we tell the difference? This distinction between manifest and 'backstage' emotion is an important dimension of realism since face-to-face interactants frequently strive to disguise their real feelings (Jorgensen and Howell, 1969). Studies which do not capture expression *in vivo*,

therefore, are much more one-dimensional than real life.

There is another sense in which 'recognition' and 'interpretation' are very different enterprises. The recognition tradition reflects a conception that nonverbal cues are linear transmissions. Even the language of this tradition (e.g. 'encoding', 'decoding', 'message', etc.) indicates an orientation in which a single nonverbal cue is intentionally sent or telegraphed to someone who receives and then unscrambles the message. This transmission metaphor has clearly affected emotion recognition research. Most studies have in fact shown a single, deliberate, nonverbal cue out of context to a judge who then ponders its translation. This paradigm is hardly lifelike.

Real-life social interpretation is both more complex and more subtle. The interpretations we make in everyday life are based on a weighing of many different levels and intensities of cues. These cues flow by us in a great many simultaneous channels, including words, and they may be in mutual concert or apparent conflict. These cues are in part a response to the situation in which they occur, and they are influenced by the relationship among the interactants. Real social interpretation, therefore, consists of processing, combining and reducing a large array of contexted cues. The linear, unlifelike nature of most nonverbal research prompted Hastorf *et al.* (1970) to conclude:

> such cues do not exist in isolation; if content of the conversation can influence the meaning of an eye glance, then context can influence the meaning of the shrug of a shoulder. The central issue must change from an expansion of the list of cues to a concern with *the inference process by which those cues are added together to arrive at a perception*. There must be factors that lead to the emphasizing of one cue or the discounting of another. The next important step, we think, will be more direct explanation of the processes by which cues are combined to form the total impression. (p. 25, emphasis added)

Behavior sources

Although all researchers have tried to capture nonverbal behavior, they have pursued it in quite different directions. We believe that there are three readily distinguishable types of sources for specimens of nonverbal communication: (a) posed, (b) induced and (c) naturalistic.

The most popular source has been posed behavior. Some of the photographs in Darwin's 1872 volume are of people posing various emotions, and Feleky (1914) began the modern enthusiasm for this approach. She photographed herself over a period of a year and selected from hundreds of pictures those she considered – by some standard – sufficiently expressive. Since then, there have been hundreds of studies using posed nonverbal stimuli. Posed behavior has, however, prompted considerable criticism. For one thing, posed behavior does not reflect real-life efforts to manage, control or suppress the surfacing of genuine emotions in social interaction. Since posing involves a deliberate and self-conscious attempt at 'transmission', there has also been a concern that posed emotions may be more conventional and exaggerated than *in vivo* affects. For example, Frijda (1969, p. 173) found that posed expressions were more 'typical' and 'pronounced' than spontaneous expressions. Posed expressions may also differ from unposed affects in other ways – their duration, whether the encoder has eye contact with other people, whether posed facial expressions are unaccompanied by important reinforcing cues in other channels, whether posed expressions vary across encoders as much as spontaneous expressions do, and so on.

Induced nonverbal cues are experimentally created expressions which are unintentional on the part of the encoder. These have been less frequently researched than posed expressions, although both expression types share a Darwinian connection. In addition to posed photographs, Darwin's 1872 volume also included some pictures which one might call induced, taken by an anatomist named Duchenne, which show a man's facial muscles being directly stimulated by electricity. This direct 'firing' of muscles is, however, atypical. Most efforts to induce expressions have tried to catalyze various emotions by exposing encoders to unexpected stimuli – e.g. by showing pleasant or disturbing pictures. In general, however, induced behavior has not been pursued as energetically as posed behavior. For one thing, inducing expressions is more cumbersome than asking people to pose them. A second obstacle is that only a narrow range of induced affects is investigable for obvious ethical reasons. In early emotion research, however, the induced method was sometimes used broadly and with ethical abandon (Knapp, 1972, p. 124). Finally, it seems possible that efforts to induce emotions could easily elicit reactive artifacts – expressions which combine an emotion and the subject's knowledge that inducing an emotion is the experimenter's goal.

From a perspective of experimental realism, the most attractive behavior source is, of course, 'naturalistic' nonverbal expressions. Natural expressive behavior is immune to the criticism of inauthenticity – unlike posed behavior – and is also less reactive than induced behavior. The principal attraction of naturalistic nonverbal behavior, of course, is that it is, of the three behavior sources, the least likely to be an idiosyncratic product of the research process itself. For this reason, naturalistic nonverbal behavior seems likely to resemble best the types, range and intensities of nonverbal behaviors most common in everyday life.

There are two distinguishable varieties of naturalistic behavior. The first of these is behavior recorded without the awareness of the people observed. This 'candid camera' approach includes covert photography, filming, videotape recording, audiotape recording, and also any other unobtrusive strategy of discerning nonverbal acts – e.g. after an interview, measuring the distance between the interviewer's and interviewee's chairs to obtain a crude proxemic index of the interviewee's anxiety. The obvious attractions of this nonreactive approach appear, however, to be in conflict with current conceptions of a researcher's ethical obligations to the researched.

The second method of capturing naturalistic behavior does not require the unwitting participation of the observed. Instead, this second method involves recording ongoing interactions with the consent of those studied. It can be argued, of course, that behavior recorded in this way is not as naturalistic as behavior stealthily purloined using the candid camera method. Although this appears to be true by definition, there are a number of ways to assuage concerns about the naturalism of behavior recorded from knowing encoders. The first is to compare behavior late in a recording with early behavior – perhaps by obtaining blind ratings – in an effort to detect anxiety, reactivity, or 'unnaturalness'. If any differences occur, late-recorded behavior could be used in preference to earlier behavior. In general, researchers report finding that self-consciousness and reactivity to recording devices diminish with exposure – i.e. longer recording sessions appear preferable to short sessions. The second way to address concerns about the naturalism of recorded behavior is to publish or make available records of the nonverbal behavior captured in this manner. This has the unequalled advantage of allowing others to gauge for themselves the realism or naturalism of the behavior.

The criterion problem

The final and most intractable problem concerns the criterion of accuracy. This problem has been called the 'most critical' issue in perception research (Bruner and Tagiuri, 1954, p. 641). In research on the recognition of emotion, the criterion is the standard by which the 'correctness' of interpretations are judged. For example, once one has isolated a sample of expressive behavior for a judgment study, one must somehow decide upon the 'true' content of this sample. Without a criterion of the correct answer, it is obviously impossible to draw conclusions about the accuracy with which an emotion can be judged, the relative accuracy of different groups of decoders, whether decoding accuracy correlates with intelligence – or any other accuracy-related issue.

The most popular choice of criterion has been the use of expert opinion or ratings (i.e. samples of nonverbal behavior are examined and labeled either by an 'expert' or using the pooled judgments of a panel of raters). For example, in an early and famous study of photographs of facial expressions of emotion, 'the expressions were allowed to be defined solely by the agreement of observers' (Frois-Wittmann, 1930). Since it was noted earlier that the most popular source of nonverbal behavior has been posed expressions, the most common research design in the emotion recognition tradition can be described in terms of these two factors. This popular design uses posed nonverbal behavior as stimuli and expert opinion or ratings as the criterion of response accuracy. An illustrative list of thirty-two studies using this design type is shown in chronological order in Table 5.1.

Despite the evident popularity of this design type, there has been considerable criticism of the use of expert opinion or ratings as the criterion of accuracy. The main criticism has been that this criterion is no more than a fallible estimate and, even worse, that it is inherently incapable of verification. Even if an expert is informed and experienced, or even if raters agree with one another about what an expression 'means', there is no bedrock position to which these opinions can be anchored. The 'right' answer is only nominally 'right' by agreement. As early as 1933, Vernon voiced this concern: 'The criterion which determines the correctness of the judgments should be objective, as far as possible, avoiding the ambiguity and bias of ratings' (1933, p. 45). Two decades later, this criticism was elaborated by Bruner and Tagiuri: 'The criteria employed have been too often of a consensual kind: accuracy is mostly defined as agreement with others. . . . Accuracy may mean simply that

Table 5.1   Studies using posed behavior and expert opinion or ratings as the criterion of accurate judgment

Darwin (1872)	Thompson and Meltzer (1964)
Feleky (1914)	Machotka (1965)
Langfeld (1918)	Addington (1968)
Buzby (1924)	Shapiro, Foster and Powell (1968)
Frois-Wittmann (1930)	Boucher (1969)
Vernon (1933)	Bugental, Kaswan, Love and Fox (1970)
Taylor (1934)	Mehrabian (1970)
Estes (1938)	Izard (1971)
Dusenbury and Knower (1939)	Beier an Zautra (1972)
Fay and Middleton (1940a)	Creek and Watkins (1972)
Schlosberg (1941)	Cuceloglu (1972)
Sarbin and Hardyck (1955)	Ekman, Friesen and Ellsworth (1972)
Beldoch (1964)	Gitter, Kozel and Mostofsky (1972)
Kramer (1964)	Mehrabian (1972)
Levy (1964)	Burns and Beier (1973)
Markel, Meisels and	Rosenthal, Archer, Koivumaki,
Houck (1964)	DiMatteo and Rogers (1974a, b)

a particular judge shares the most common bias found among its fellow judges' (p. 646). It also seems ironic that some studies using posed expressions have used panels of raters to determine the 'genuineness' of the performances – this seems like an internal contradiction since the researcher *knows* that the encoder was not experiencing the emotion for which 'genuineness' ratings are obtained.

Expert opinion and ratings are not, however, the only possible type of criterion. For example, Cook (1971, p. 83) lists several others which we think can be combined to form three general but quite distinct types: (a) face validity or 'expressor's' intent, (b) expert opinion or ratings, and (c) objective or biographic information. The third type is the most rigorous in that it alone provides an unambiguous benchmark of response accuracy. A researcher can determine the correctness of a decoder's judgments unequivocally if and only if the criterion is an objective or biographic fact known about the encoder or the encoding situation. For this reason, objective or biographic facts have been described as the 'ideal criterion' (Cook, 1971, p. 83).

This ideal criterion, however, has seldom been used in decoding research and is, in fact, impossible within the emotion recognition tradition. There is no factual or unambiguous way to verify the accuracy of judgments about emotions *per se*. This dilemma has been recognized for some time. For example, Osgood and Heyer (1950) observed that 'independent criteria of actual emotional states are typically lacking.' This criterion problem was also neatly summarized in an emotion recognition study by Soskin and Kauffman (1961):

> Analyzing [judgments of emotions from the voice] presents certain difficulties. The 'accuracy' of these judgments cannot be determined because there is no unequivocal way of establishing that a speaker was experiencing 'anxiety' or 'anger' or 'depression' in the situation from which the stimulus recording was taken.

The criterion problem, therefore, is insoluble within the emotion recognition paradigm. It is impossible to use the optimal type of objective or biographic criterion in a study of emotion decoding, and it seems to us that this places a constraint or ceiling on the validity of emotion recognition research. Judgment studies in which the correct answer is indeterminate are like a mathematics examination in which the right answers are a matter of opinion. No matter what methodological elegance a researcher brings to bear upon nonverbal samples of emotion, the recognition enterprise is fatally flawed if the 'real' content of the samples is by definition unknown and unknowable.

A typology of decoding research designs

As mentioned earlier, decoding studies have used three different sources of nonverbal behavior: posed, induced and naturalistic. These three sources can be thought of as categories of nonverbal stimuli; just as the three criterion types just described (face validity or expressor's intent, expert opinion or ratings, objective or biographic information) can be thought of as categories for assessing responses. These two factors can be combined to form a typology of research designs. This typology contains nine cells, one for each possible design type in decoding research. This typology is indicated in Table 5.2, again with illustrative studies listed in chronological order.

It is now clear that the most popular design – using posed stimuli and expert opinion or ratings as the response criterion, as in the thirty-two studies listed in Table 5.1 – is only one of nine possible types of designs. This common design is the 'Type 2' design in terms of the 9-cell typology, and we have identified more Type 2 studies than any other type. The distribution of studies across the nine cells

Table 5.2 A typology of decoding studies in nonverbal communication

Source of nonverbal behavior	Criterion of accurate judgment		
	Face validity or expressor's intent	Expert opinion or ratings	Objective or biographic information
Posed	Type 1	Type 2	Type 3
	Kline and Johannsen (1935) Dickey and Knower (1941) Fay and Middleton (1941) Triandis and Lambert (1958) Davitz and Davitz (1959) Davitz (1964) Hunt and Lin (1967) Jorgensen and Howell (1969) Mehrabian (1971) Gitter, Black and Mostofsky (1972) Rosenthal, Archer, Koivumaki, DiMatteo and Rogers (1974a, b)	See Table 4.1	Vernon (1933) Allport and Cantril (1934) Wolff (1943) Ellis (1967) Ekman and Friesen (1974)
Induced	Type 4	Type 5	Type 6
		Landis (1924)	Fay and Middleton (1940b) Lanzetta and Kleck (1970) Ekman and Friesen (1974)
Naturalistic	Type 7	Type 8	Type 9
		Munn (1940) Vinacke and Fong (1955) Starkweather (1956) Dittman, Parloff and Boomer (1965) Shapiro (1966) Milmoe, Rosenthal, Blane, Chafetz and Wolf (1967) Shapiro, Foster and Powell (1968) Beakel and Mehrabian (1969) Ekman and Friesen (1969) Bugental, Love and Gianetto (1971)	Pear (1931) Vernon (1933) Archer and Akert (1977)

provides a crude reflection of the degree to which various approaches have been 'mined'.[4] The top row of the typology is thickly populated, and includes all the studies in Table 5.1 – this indicates the popularity of posed nonverbal stimuli. The middle column of the typology is also thickly populated and this reflects the dominance of expert opinion and ratings as the response criterion.

Some of the studies in Table 5.2 have used objective or biographic information as the response criterion. These have studied the decoding of qualities other than emotion *per se* since, as discussed earlier, use of this 'ideal' criterion is impossible within the emotion recognition tradition. For example, Ellis (1967) studied the degree to which objective aspects of socioeconomic status (education, etc.) could be decoded from the voice. Similarly, Lanzetta and Kleck (1970) studied whether judges could decode an objective situation – judges saw videotaped encoders and had to guess whether or not each encoder was bracing for an expected shock. Both these studies are classified in the third column of Table 5.2 because both used an unambiguous standard of judgment accuracy.

The impossibility of verifying judgments about emotions is one explanation for the popularity of 'softer' criteria – e.g. opinion and ratings. Even in emotion recognition research, however, there has been a baffling tendency for researchers to overlook relatively powerful criteria in favor of more abstract, 'softer' criteria like ratings. A classic instance of this tendency was the well-known study by Munn (1940). Munn examined news magazines for photographs of people in emotional situations (e.g. reacting to a drowning, etc.). Munn could have used an objective criterion (i.e. he could have asked judges to guess which of several situations had produced the expressions in the photograph, for example, he could have asked judges, 'Is the person in this photograph reacting to a joke, a drowning, losing a game, or a movie?' If he had used this objective criterion, his study would have been classified as a Type 9 design in Table 5.2.

For some reason, however, he chose a 'softer', unverifiable criterion and merely asked judges their opinion of the emotion shown in the photographs. Several other studies have also shown a surprising preference for 'soft' criteria of accuracy when an objective criterion could have been used. For example, Bugental *et al.* (1971) collected ratings of the qualitative behavior of parents of 'disturbed' and 'normal' children, but did not use the more objective criterion of asking judges to identify which adults were the parents of the 'disturbed' children. Even Frijda (1969, p. 175), despite his great sensitivity to the criterion problem, asked subjects in his own research to rate specimens of induced emotion, rather than to recognize the objective situations which had produced the emotion. In several of the studies listed in Table 5.2, researchers could have used an objective criterion of accuracy, but did not. If they had, their studies would have been classified in different cells in Table 5.2.

This failure to take advantage of an objective criterion is unfortunate for both methodological and theoretical reasons. Methodologically, ratings and other 'soft' response types are inherently less desirable than objective criteria. Even in terms of theoretical precision, however, the use of ratings is an unnecessary abstraction from the behavior itself. If a researcher has used some method to induce expressive behavior, or knows the circumstances surrounding a naturalistic segment of behavior, the most direct and theoretically parsimonious choice of a decoding task is simply to ask judges to try to recognize these objective conditions. The widespread use of 'softer', unverifiable response measures may reflect Darwin's prototypal influence, or even just an epistemological habit. So many decoding studies have used ratings, judgments on semantic differential scales, and abstract labels of emotion that there may be a tendency to choose these non-factual response types, even when an objective criterion could have been used.

The distribution of illustrative studies in Table 5.2 shows that some design types have been used less frequently than others. For example, Type 4 and Type 7 designs are virtually untried. Type 4 designs are induced, and only manipulations as vivid as those used by Landis (1924) seem to warrant use of a face validity criterion. The expressor's intent is irrelevant in an induced study, of course, except as it inhibits a person's response to the inducing situation. We found no Type 7 studies, although the design does not seem impossible, for example, a researcher could covertly film people in natural interaction, and then construct a criterion by interviewing them about the emotions, if any, they had been experiencing or had intended to display. We suspect that Type 7 designs have remained untapped because naturalistic affects are quite flat and banal most of the time, and researchers have, for the most part, been drawn to the more dramatic or high-intensity emotions.

Of all the decoding designs in Table 5.2, Type 9 designs deserves special attention. As discussed earlier, the most desirable source for specimens of nonverbal stimuli is naturalistic behavior. In addition, objective or biographic information is the most rigorous and unambiguous type of response criterion. The Type 9 research design in Table 5.2 is the unique intersection of these two optimal design features. This design maximizes the naturalism and contextual quality of specimens of nonverbal behavior, and it also maximizes the methodological rigor of assessing the accuracy of judgments about this behavior.

Despite its unique and unrivalled strengths, the Type 9 design has seldom been used. For one thing, collecting specimens of naturalistic behavior in context is more difficult than, for example, collecting posed behavior. Also, it has not been possible in the past to use an objective criterion in emotion research since this tradition has concerned the recognition of emotion *per se*. These two obstacles have caused the Type 9 design to be underutilized. For the past few years, however, we have been working on a new method for studying the process of interpretation, and the Archer and Akert (1977) reference in cell 9 of Table 5.2 is the first study to result from this new approach.

The social interpretations task: a new approach to studying the process of interpretation

For the past three years we have been developing a naturalistic method to use in studying the process of interpretation. This method is a Type 9 design, in terms of the typology in Table 5.2, because it relies on naturalistic sequences of behavior in context, and because it uses an objective criterion of accurate interpretation. The basis of this approach is a 30-minute videotape we have named the Social Interpretations Task (SIT). The tape itself consists of twenty natural sequences of behavior, each 30–60 seconds in length. These twenty scenes were edited from relatively long (i.e. 5–15-minutes) videotape records of each interaction. On the SIT videotape, each scene is followed by a brief interval to allow decoders to indicate their answers.

Each scene of the SIT shows one, two, three or more people in unposed situations. Viewers of the SIT try to answer a different interpretative question about the people in each scene or their relationships. The SIT tape is accompanied by an answer sheet with twenty questions in a multiple-choice format. The SIT is intended as a device for studying the process of interpretation rather than as a test of individual differences in decoding ability. The unit of analysis, therefore, is the scene rather than the decoder, and the concern is with how many decoders get each scene right rather than with how many scenes each decoder gets right.

The design of the SIT is perhaps best indicated by describing some of the twenty scenes included. The first scene on the SIT tape, for example, consists of two women playing with a 7-month-old baby. After the scene is finished, viewers are asked to identify which woman is the baby's mother. Scene 5 shows a young woman talking on the telephone; viewers are then asked to decide whether she is talking to a man or to a woman. In Scene 8, two men discuss a game of basketball they have just played; viewers are then asked to decide which man won the game. The content of the other scenes is indicated briefly in Table 5.3.[5] This table also lists the chance accuracy on each scene (based on the number of multiple-choice alternatives), as well as the actual performance on each SIT scene of 1388 college-age decoders.

Table 5.3 The social interpretations task: accuracy scores of 1388 college-age decoders

The 20 SIT interpretation questions (scenes)	Chance level accuracy[a]	Mean accuracy of college-age decoders (n = 1388)
1 Who is the mother? (two women and a baby)	0.33[b]	0.64
2 Which man is not married? (three men)	0.33	0.40
3 Which woman has no children? (three men)	0.33	0.50
4 Who will pick up the dropped groceries? (three bystanders outside a market)	0.33	0.21
5 Is she speaking to a man or a woman? (one woman on the 'phone)	0.50	0.90
6 Friends, acquaintances or strangers? (one man and one woman)	0.33	0.60
7 Which conversation is with a student? (woman talks with student; professor)	0.50	0.65

8	Who won the basketball game? (two men)	0.33[b]	0.57
9	Which man is 30, married, a veteran? (three men)	0.33	0.56
10	Which couple says they're in love? (two men and two women)	0.33[b]	0.28
11	Speaking to mother, father, friend? (one woman on telephone)	0.33	0.55
12	Which woman is married to the man? (three women and one man)	0.33	0.34
13	Who owns the guitar? (two men play the guitar)	0.33[b]	0.28
14	Which woman is older? (two women)	0.50	0.55
15	Who is talking? (one voice; three women interacting)	0.33	0.34
16	Which man is not wearing pants? (Two men, shown from waist up)	0.50	0.62
17	Is man father of boy on left, right, both? (one man, two boys and one woman)	0.33	0.47
18	Which is a reaction to a gory photograph? (woman looks at three pho- tographs)	0.33	0.38
19	Who won the tennis game? (two men)	0.33[b]	0.30
20	Who won the poker game? (three men)	0.33	0.55
Total accuracy on 20 SIT scenes		7.33	9.69
Standard deviation			2.32

[a]Chance levels reflect the number of multiple choice answers; these levels also have been verified empirically.
[b]For these questions, a third alternative was included, e.g. neither, the game was tied, etc.

The SIT differs radically from previous decoding research in its approach to emotion. In each of the scenes, emotion can be a vehicle to accurate interpretation, but emotion is not itself the criterion of accuracy. For example, the three scenes described above may all have emotional implications – the sentiments of the baby's mother, the woman's emotional response to the person on the other end of the telephone, the emotions of victorious and defeated basketball players – but the decoder is not asked to recognize these emotions *per se*. Instead, the decoder is asked to reach an objective interpretation, which may or may not reflect the decoder's 'reading' of emotional cues in the SIT scenes.

The SIT also differs from the traditional approach to decoding emotions in that emotions are only one of many potential vehicles for interpretation. There are many other types of cues in addition to emotion cues (e.g. eye contact, hesitations, words, gestures, proxemics, interaction, etc. just as there are in real life. The SIT, therefore, restores emotional cues to their natural context, as one aspect of a complex array or 'banquet' of communications in a great many channels. Although emotion cues are an important ingredient in this communications banquet, they are far from the entire menu.

Since the SIT is a new approach to studying the process of interpretation, it is incumbent upon us to examine the SIT critically in the light of our earlier discussion of the four major dilemmas of decoding research. The first of these consisted of the measurement issues of sampling and labeling. It is clear that the construction of the SIT involved some forms of sampling. Where most decoding studies have sampled categories of emotion, the SIT is a sample of interpretable situations. Although we know of no described population or universe of such interpretations, we have tried to maximize realism by including interpretations like those made in everyday life. We, of course, avoided obviously artificial situations (e.g. people receiving the ubiquitous laboratory electric shock), but we also tried to include: (a) common *relationships* – parent–child interactions, male–female relationships, love and marital bonds, status differences, friendships, etc.; (b) common *situations* – competitive games, helping, embarrassment, music, etc.; and (c) common inferences about other people's *background* – marital status, age, childhood memories, etc. The only interpretations we consciously avoided were those we felt might bring unwelcome attention or possible stigma to the people in the SIT scenes (e.g. which of two people has been treated for alcoholism, etc.). While it is true that we have sampled rather than exhausted the range of possible interpretations, we feel we have sampled reasonably broadly, if informally.

The construction of the SIT involved other types of sampling as well. Since we were not trying to capture emotions, we did not, of course, sample specific intensities in the way emotion recognition researchers have. The SIT scenes were edited from raw videotapes according to two simple conventions: (a) since we did not want a simple test of hearing, we avoided explicit mentions of the correct answer (e.g. 'I won the game because . . .'), this only occurred once or twice in all the raw videotape footage; and (b) we tried to select sequences in which all the people in a scene participated. In addition, the SIT involves a total of forty-nine encoders, and it seems very unlikely, therefore, that we have sampled encoders who are in some way narrowly idiosyncratic. Finally, in terms of the labeling issue, the SIT involves no explicit labels of emotions. Instead, judges are asked to recognize relationships, situations and aspects of individual background.

The second major issue concerned the problem of context and situation, and seven dimensions of this problem were identified. The SIT appears to restore six of these to the process of interpretation in that the SIT (i) contains a full communications repertoire, with information presented naturalistically in all major nonverbal channels;[6] (ii) includes the verbal channel; (iii) uses continuous streams of behavior, rather than truncated and brief stimuli; (iv) shows behavior in 'real time' rather than artificial exposure lengths; (v) indicates the situational antecedents of nonverbal acts rather than isolated acts alone; and (vi) requires interpretation and not merely recognition (i.e. cues to the right answer are complex rather than one-dimensional and explicit). The one aspect of context the SIT does not include is prior experience with the encoder – it seems likely that no standardized method will reflect this component of natural interpretation.

The third major issue concerned the source of behavior used in nonverbal communication research. The SIT contains naturalistic behavior, and the SIT scenes consist of unposed interaction and spontaneous conversation.[7] The candid camera approach, however, was only used in one scene; the people in the other nineteen scenes were aware that they were being videotaped. To reduce reactivity, the cameras were allowed to run for some time before the actual

30–60-second segment used in the final scene.

The fourth and final issue concerned the criterion problem. It is in this area that the SIT constitutes a particularly abrupt departure from most previous decoding research. The SIT uses the 'ideal' criterion of objective and biographic information. In Scene 1, for example, one of the two women *is* in fact the child's mother; in Scene 5, the woman *is* in fact talking to either a man or a woman; and in Scene 8, one of the two men *did* in fact win the basketball game. All twenty scenes have an objective criterion of accuracy, and the 'right' answers to the SIT items are therefore beyond dispute.

The SIT videotape is not, of course, without any shortcomings of its own. For example, we could have wished for some improvement in the technical quality of the sound and lighting we obtained in some scenes. The twenty scenes in the SIT videotape, however, are primarily intended as a model of the SIT concept, and not the definitive or ultimate version of this approach. It would be relatively simple to generate new scenes which contained the essential design features of the SIT.

The most distinctive aspects of the SIT – in our opinion – are its use of naturalistic, 'contexted' behavior in all communication channels as stimuli, and its use of objective information as the incontrovertible criterion of interpretive accuracy. In these two important areas, the SIT offers an alternative to the mainstream direction of past research in nonverbal communication.

The first study made possible by the SIT has already been published (Archer and Akert, 1977). This study, called 'Words and everything else', demonstrated that nonverbal cues are indispensable to accurate social interpretation, and that they greatly enhance the accuracy of judgments based on verbal cues alone.

Future work with the SIT will center on the process of interpretation itself. We have completed data collection in several areas, including a study of the degree to which decoders can articulate the cues they 'process' in arriving at an interpretation. We have also completed data collection in several studies of the apparent contributions of different nonverbal channels to interpretive accuracy, and carried out analyses of sex differences in aggregate accuracy on the SIT and accuracy differences on individual scenes. We are also interested in the difference between 'easy' and 'difficult' scenes. A cursory inspection of Table 5.3 reveals considerable variance in accuracy across the twenty SIT scenes. While this difference is not unexpected

(i.e. it seems reasonable that real social interpretations vary in difficulty), it is still intriguing, and we are trying to characterize the
'information structure' that differentiates easy scenes from difficult
ones.

In summary, the study of nonverbal communication has been beset
by four enduring dilemmas: (i) issues of measurement like the
sampling and labeling of specimens of behavior; (ii) a widespread
tendency to excerpt nonverbal behavior from the seven distinct types
of context in which it is naturally embedded; (iii) inherent and
incomparable differences among the three sources of nonverbal
behavior – posed, induced and naturalistic; and (iv) the seeming
impossibility of finding an indisputable criterion of what constitutes
an accurate interpretation of any given specimen of nonverbal
behavior.

The most frequently encountered research design in the field of
nonverbal communication has studied only the recognition of emotion, and has been characterized by unspecified or unwitting sampling
procedures, by slices of nonverbal acts stripped of all forms of context,
by posed behavior which seems most unlikely to resemble the range
and intensity of real-life encounters, and by criteria for judging
response accuracy which seem 'soft' and are at any rate impossible to
verify. These design weaknesses have combined to erode both the
internal rigor and the external validity of much of the research in this
field.

No single innovation can be a panacea for all these design dilemmas
and instrument ills. What does appear to be necessary, however, is a
fresh conception of the ways in which nonverbal communication
might best be studied. In undertaking a reassessment of this nature, it
seems of paramount theoretical importance to ensure that the rigorous
study of nonverbal communication preserve the subtle, many-
channeled, fully-contexted, continuous quality of nonverbal behavior
which – after all – made it attractive to researchers in the first place.
This chapter describes one alternative to the mainstream of past
nonverbal communication research. This alternative conception is
embodied in the Social Interpretations Task. The most distinctive
features of the SIT are its use of natural sequences of unposed verbal
and nonverbal behavior in context, and its insistence on rigorous and
unambiguous criteria for determining whether interpretations of this
behavior are accurate.

Notes

1 Another popular domain of research, the study of nonverbal cues to aspects of personality, also suffers from the impossibility of an unambiguous criterion and much of our discussion applies to this field as well. Some criticisms of this literature can be found in McHenry (1971).

2 If a researcher's goal, however, is merely to provide a test of individual differences in decoding accuracy, use of a single encoder may be appropriate, i.e. an individual's decoding ability may be reliable or stable across encoders. At any rate, this is an empirical question.

3 An exception is the program of research using the Profile of Nonverbal Sensitivity (PONS) film by Rosenthal *et al.* (1974a, b). The PONS film contains five pure nonverbal channels and six paired combinations of these channels, for a total of eleven different channels.

4 This list is meant to be illustrative and not exhaustive, and classification was in some cases difficult. Some studies have used more than one source of nonverbal stimuli or more than one type of response criterion, and these studies are therefore listed in more than one cell of Table 5.2.

5 It should be mentioned that these twenty scenes are meant only as instances of the SIT concept; they are not intended as the definitive or only possible version of it, and other scenes could easily be created which have both naturalistic stimuli and objective response criteria. We believe the important thing about the SIT is the concept behind it rather than the twenty specific scenes it contains.

6 Channels like olfaction and thermal cues could not, of course, be included in this videotape method.

7 In one scene, however, three people were all asked to claim that they had won a card game when only one of them was actually the winner. Even in this scene, however, no scripts were used and the dialogue was spontaneous.

Acknowledgements

This research was supported by Faculty Research Funds granted by the University of California. Sincere appreciation is due to Paul Ekman and Maureen O'Sullivan for advice and suggestions, and to Roger Brown and Robert Rosenthal for comments and observations. Ruth Tebbets and Michael Beller helped with different phases of the project.

Correspondence concerning this work should be sent to: Professor Dane Archer, Stevenson College, University of California, Santa Cruz, California 95064, USA.

References

Addington, D. W. (1968) The relationship of selected vocal characteristics to personality perception. *Speech Monographs 35*: 492–503.

Allport, G. W. and Cantril, H. (1934) Judging personality from voice. *Journal of Social Psychology 5*: 37–55.

Archer, D. and Akert, R. M. (1977) Words and everything else: Verbal and nonverbal cues in social interaction. *Journal of Personality and Social Psychology 35*: 443–9.

Argyle, M. (1969) *Social Interaction*. London: Methuen.

Beakel, N. G. and Mehrabian, A. (1969) Inconsistent communications and psychopathology. *Journal of Abnormal Psychology 74*: 126–30.

Beier, E. G. and Zautra, A. J. (1972) The identification of vocal communication of emotion across cultures. *Journal of Consulting and Clinical Psychology 39*: 166.

Beldoch, M. (1964) Sensitivity to expression of emotional meaning in three modes of communication. In J. R. Davitz (ed.) *The Communication of Emotional Meaning*. New York: McGraw-Hill.

Boucher, J. D. (1969) Facial displays of fear, sadness, and pain. *Perceptual and Motor Skills 28*: 239–42.

Bruner, J. S. and Tagiuri, R. (1954) The perception of people. In G. Lindzey (ed.) *The Handbook of Social Psychology*. Reading, Mass.: Addison-Wesley.

Brunswik, E. (1956) *Perception and the Representative Design of Psychological Experiments*. Berkeley, Calif.: University of California Press.

Buck, R. W., Savin, V. J., Miller, R. E. and Caul, W. F. (1972) Communication of effect through facial expressions in humans. *Journal of Personality and Social Psychology 23*: 362–71.

Bugental, D. E., Kaswan, J. W., Love, L. R. and Fox, M. N. (1970) Child versus adult perception of evaluative messages in verbal, vocal and visual channels. *Developmental Psychology 2*: 367–75.

Bugental, D. E., Love, L. R. and Gianetto, R. M. (1971) Perfidious feminine faces. *Journal of Personality and Social Psychology 17*: 314–18.

Burns, K. L. and Beier, E. G. (1973) Significance of vocal and visual channels in the decoding of emotional meaning. *Journal of Communication 23*: 118–30.

Buzby, D. E. (1924) The interpretation of facial expression. *American Journal of Psychology 35*: 602–4.

Coleman, J. C. (1949) Facial expression of emotion. *Psychological Monographs 63*.

Cook, M. (1971) *Interpersonal Perception*. Baltimore, Md: Penguin Books.

Creek, L. V. and Watkins, J. T. (1972) Responses to incongruent verbal and nonverbal emotional cues. *Journal of Communication 22*: 311–16.

Cuceloglu, D. (1972) Facial code in affective communication. *Comparative Group Studies 3*: 395–408.

Darwin, C. (1872) *The Expression of the Emotions in Man and Animals*. London: John Murray.

Davitz, J. R. (ed.) (1964) *The Communication of Emotional Meaning*. New York: McGraw-Hill.

Davitz, J. R. and Davitz, L. (1959) Correlates of accuracy in the communication of feelings. *Journal of Communication* 9: 110–17.

Dickey, E. C., and Knower, F. H. (1941) A note on some ethnological differences in recognition of simulated expressions of the emotions. *American Journal of Sociology* 47: 190–3.

Dittman, A. T., Parloff, M. B. and Boomer, D. S. (1965) Facial and bodily expression: a study of receptivity of emotional cues. *Psychiatry* 28: 239–44.

Dunlap, K. (1927) The role of eye muscles and mouth muscles in the expression of the emotions. *Genetic Psychology Monographs* 2: 199–233.

Dusenbury, D. and Knower, F. (1939) Experimental studies of the symbolism of action and voice–II: A study of the specificity of meaning in abstract tonal symbols. *Quarterly Journal of Speech* 25: 67–75.

Ekman, P. (1973) Cross-cultural studies of facial expression. In P. Ekman (ed.) *Darwin and Facial Expression*. New York: Academic Press.

Ekman, P. and Friesen, W. V. (1969) Nonverbal leakage and clues to deception. *Psychiatry* 32: 88–105.

Ekman, P., and Friesen, W. V. (1974) Detecting deception from the body or face. *Journal of Personality and Social Psychology* 29: 288–98.

Ekman, P. and Friesen, W. V. (1975) *Unmasking The Face*. Englewood Cliffs, N. J.: Prentice-Hall.

Ekman, P., Friesen, W. V. and Ellsworth, P. (1972) *Emotion in The Human Face: Guidelines for Research and an Integration of Findings*. New York: Pergamon Press.

Ellis, D. S. (1967) Speech and social status in America. *Social Forces* 45: 431–7.

Estes, S. G. (1938) Judging personality from expressive behavior. *Journal of Abnormal and Social Psychology* 33: 217–36.

Fay, P. J. and Middleton, W. C. (1940a) Judgment of Kretschmerian body types from the voice as transmitted over a public address system. *Journal of Social Psychology* 12: 151–62.

Fay, P. J. and Middleton, W. C. (1940b) The ability to judge the rested or tired condition of a speaker from his voice as transmitted over a public address system. *Journal of Applied Psychology* 24: 645–50.

Fay, P. J. and Middleton, W. C. (1941) The ability to judge truth telling or lying, from the voice as transmitted over a public address system. *Journal of General Psychology* 24: 211–15.

Feleky, A. M. (1914) The expression of the emotions. *Psychological Review* 21: 33–41.

Frijda, N. A. (1969) Recognition of emotion. In L. Berkowitz (ed.) *Advances in Experimental Social Psychology*, vol. 4. New York: Academic Press.

Frois-Wittmann, J. (1930) The judgment of facial expression. *Journal of Experimental Psychology 13*: 113–51.

Gates, G. S. (1923) An experimental study of the growth of social perception. *Journal of Educational Psychology 14*: 449–61.

Gitin, S. R. (1970) A dimensional analysis of manual expression. *Journal of Personality and Social Psychology 15*: 271–7.

Gitter, A. G., Black, H. and Mostofsky, D. (1972) Race and sex in the perception of emotion. *Journal of Social Issues 28*: 63–78.

Gitter, A. G., Kozel, N. J. and Mostofsky, D. I. (1972) Perception of emotion: the role of race, sex and presentation mode. *Journal of Social Psychology 88*: 213–22.

Hall, E. T. (1977) *Beyond Culture*. New York: Anchor-Doubleday.

Harms, L. S. (1961) Listener judgments of status cues in speech. *Quarterly Journal of Speech 47*: 164–8.

Hastorf, A., Schneider, D. and Polefka, J. (1970) *Person Perception*. Reading, Mass.: Addison-Wesley.

Heider, F. and Simmel, M. (1944) An experimental study of apparent behavior. *American Journal of Psychology 57*; 243–59.

Hunt, R. G. and Lin, T. K. (1967) Accuracy of judgments of personal attributes from speech. *Journal of Personality and Social Psychology 6*: 450–3.

Huntley, C. W. (1940) Judgments of self based upon records of expressive behavior. *Journal of Abnormal and Social Psychology 35*: 398–427.

Izard, C. E. (1971) *The Face of Emotion*. New York: Appleton.

Jorgensen, E. C. and Howell, R. J. (1969) Judging unposed emotional behavior. *Psychotherapy: Theory, Research, and Practice 6*: 161–5.

Kline, L. W. and Johannsen, D. E. (1935) Comparative role of face and of the face–body–hands as aids in identifying emotions. *Journal of Abnormal and Social Psychology 29*: 415–26.

Knapp, M. L. (1972) *Nonverbal Communication in Human Interaction*. New York: Holt, Rinehart & Winston.

Kramer, E. (1963) Judgment of personal characteristics and emotions from nonverbal properties of speech. *Psychological Bulletin 60*: 408–20.

Kramer, E. (1964) Elimination of verbal cues in judgments of emotion from voice. *Journal of Abnormal and Social Psychology 68*: 390–6.

Lambert, W. E., Frankel, H. and Tucker, G. R. (1966) Judging personality through speech: a French–Canadian example. *Journal of Communication 16*: 305–21.

Landis, C. (1924) Studies of emotional reactions: II. General behavior and facial expression, *Journal of Comparative Psychology 4*: 447–509.

Langfeld, H. S. (1918) The judgment of facial expression and suggestion. *Psychological Review 25*: 488–94.

Lanzetta, J. T. and Kleck, R. E. (1970) Encoding and decoding of nonverbal affect in humans. *Journal of Personality and Social Psychology 16*: 12–19.

Levy, P. K. (1964) The ability to express and perceive vocal communication of feeling. In J. R. Davitz (ed.) *The Communication of Emotional Meaning*. New York: McGraw-Hill.

Machotka, P. (1965) Body movement as communication. *Dialogues: Behavioral Science Research 2*: 33–66.

Markel, N. M., Meisels, M. and Houck, J. E. (1964) Judging personality from voice quality. *Journal of Abnormal and Social Psychology 69*: 458–63.

McHenry, R. (1971) New methods of assessing the accuracy of interpersonal perception. *Journal for the Theory of Social Behavior 1*: 109–19.

Mehrabian, A. (1970) When are feelings communicated inconsistently? *Journal of Experimental Research in Personality 4*: 198–212.

Mehrabian, A. (1971) Nonverbal betrayal of feeling. *Journal of Experimental Research in Personality 5*: 64–73.

Mehrabian, A. (1972) *Nonverbal Communication*. New York: Aldine-Atherton.

Miller, J. (1972) Plays and players. In R. A. Hinde (ed.) *Non-Verbal Communication*. New York. Cambridge University Press.

Milmoe, S., Rosenthal, R., Blane, H. T., Chafetz, M. E. and Wolf, I. (1967) The doctor's voice: postdictor of successful referral of alcoholic patients. *Journal of Abnormal Psychology 72*: 78–84.

Munn, N. L. (1940) The effect of knowledge of the situation upon judgment of emotion from facial expression. *Journal of Abnormal and Social Psychology 35*: 324–38.

Osgood, C. E. and Heyer, A. W., Jr (1950) Objective studies in meaning. II. The validity of posed facial expressions as gestural signs in interpersonal communications. *American Psychologist 5*: 298.

Pear, T. H. (1931) *Voice and Personality*. London: Chapman & Hall.

Rosenthal, R., Archer, D., Koivumaki, J. H., DiMatteo, M. R. and Rogers, P. (1974a) Assessing sensitivity to nonverbal communication: The PONS Test. *Division 8 Newsletter (APA)*, January: 1–3.

Rosenthal, R., Archer, D., Koivumaki, J. H., DiMatteo, M. R. and Rogers, P. (1974b) The language without words. *Psychology Today* September: 44–50.

Sapir, E. (1927) Speech as a personality trait. *American Journal of Sociology 32*: 892–905.

Sarbin, T. R., and Hardyck, C. D. (1955) Conformance in role perception as a personality variable. *Journal of Consulting Psychology 19*: 109–11.

Schlosberg, H. (1941) A scale for judgment of facial expression. *Journal of Experimental Psychology 29*: 497–510.

Shapiro, J. G. (1966) Consistency in the expression of emotion. *Dissertation Abstracts 26*: 6878–9.

Shapiro, J. G., Foster, C. P. and Powell, T. (1968) Facial and bodily cues of genuineness, empathy, and warmth. *Journal of Clinical Psychology 24*: 233–6.

Soskin, W. F. and Kauffman, P. E. (1961) Judgment of emotions in word-free voice samples. *Journal of Communication 11*: 73–81.

Starkweather, J. A. (1956) The communication value of content-free speech. *American Journal of Psychology 69*: 121–3.

Stritch, T. and Secord, P. (1956) Interaction effects in the perception of faces. *Journal of Personality 24*: 272–84.

Taylor, H. C. (1934) Social agreements on personality traits as judged from speech. *Journal of Social Psychology 5*: 244–8.

Thompson, D. F. and Meltzer, L. (1964) Communication of emotional intent by facial expression. *Journal of Abnormal and Social Psychology 68*: 129–35.

Triandis, H. C., and Lambert, W. W. (1958) A restatement and test of Schlosberg's theory of emotion with two kinds of subjects from Greece. *Journal of Abnormal and Social Psychology 56*: 321–8.

Vernon, P. E. (1933) Some characteristics of the good judge of personality. *Journal of Social Psychology 4*: 42–57.

Vinacke, W. E. and Fong, R. W. (1955) The judgment of facial expressions by three national-racial groups in Hawaii: II. Oriental faces. *Journal of Social Psychology 41*: 185–95.

Weitz, S. (ed.) (1974) *Nonverbal Communication*. New York: Oxford.

Wolff, W. (1943) *The Expression of Personality: Experimental Depth Psychology*. New York: Harper & Brothers.

6 The good judge of others' personality: methodological problems and their resolution

Mark Cook

Historical background

In 1906 Pearson published research on family resemblance in intelligence, using a 7-point rating scale. At much the same time the world's first intelligence test appeared – the Binet–Simon scale. Before long researchers began comparing the two types of measure, and numerous studies of the correctness of 'subjective estimates' of intelligence followed (even though the Binet scale was partly validated against teachers' ratings of intelligence). Research was extended to judgements of personality traits, but the corresponding uncertainty over whether tests validated 'subjective estimates' or 'subjective estimates' validated tests took longer to resolve, and still persists today for many inventories are partly validated against peer ratings or rankings. (Hampson, in see Chapter 1, argues that this is a false dichotomy, and that tests and subjective estimates together 'construct' personality; neither has a prior claim to define it.) During the late 1930s and 1940s, and into the early 1950s, numerous studies on the accuracy of judging personality and ability by laymen and experts were published (see reviews in Taft, 1955). Interest was maintained until the mid-1950s, when a series of damning, but difficult to follow and not always perfectly understood, critiques by Cronbach (Cronbach, 1955; Gage and Cronbach, 1955) dampened enthusiasm. Since then research has proceeded haltingly, except for the steady stream of papers on the validity of personnel selection, and on clinical judgement.

Personnel departments, psychiatrists, clinical psychologists and counsellors continue to be interested in accuracy, for the simple reason that they must daily try to make accurate judgements of other people, even though their academic colleagues may tell them they cannot, and should not try. Sociologists are fond of arguing that all opinions of others tend to become self-fulfilling prophecies, or are devices for the social control of troublesome minorities. Some even – in common with certain philosophers – argue the absurdity of the very notion of what someone is really like differing from what people think he is like. Psychologists tend to focus more narrowly on the complex methodological problems of studying accuracy, and to conclude that they are so nearly insuperable as to make research in the area impossible. Vernon (1964) asked, 'Might we not question whether the whole area has not been shown to be so complicated that it is hardly possible to interpret the true psychological significance of any experimental findings?'

Others disagree. Adinolfi (1971) says, 'There is probably little doubt among clinicians who daily struggle with the problem of comprehending the individual case that the problem is essentially one of accurate person perception.' (For 'clinician', read 'occupational psychologist', or even – when selecting the ablest students – 'academic psychologist'.) Allport (Allport and Odbert, 1936) remarked many years ago how the very people who argue that traits don't exist use them to describe people in references and everyday conversation.

Whether people can or can not, or should or should not, pass judgements on each other's personalities, the fact is that they do, and many such verdicts have far-reaching effects. The psychologist must say something about the accuracy of these judgements, because if the psychologist doesn't, no one else will. And to state such an opinion, the psychologist needs an experimental technique for studying the accuracy of person perception. Dane Archer and Robin Akert's chapter offers an excellent account of research on expressive behaviour using questions like 'Can people see who is boss?', or 'Who are friends?', or 'Who is winning?', and provides a snag-free method for studying them. This chapter discusses research on accuracy of judgements of personality and ability, and examines the problems that arise with ratings, multiple choice and ranking.

Ratings and their problems

Ratings have a long history. A form of rating scale was devised by the philosopher and utopian reformer Robert Owen as early as 1825 (Ellson and Ellson, 1953). Children in the New Harmony Colony in Indiana were rated on ten 100–point scales, such as 'courage', 'imagination' or 'excitability'. The scale didn't use paper and pencil, but was made of solid brass, with sliding brass pointers, a very early example of 'brass instrument' psychology. The first large personality rating study was done by Heymans and Wiersma in the Netherlands, who collected ratings of 2523 persons made by some 400 family doctors. Studies of rating personality thereafter proliferated (see Eysenck (1970) for a good review of early research, while being wary of his tendency to read extraversion and neuroticism into every set of results). Most early research took ratings as a valid measure of personality, without questioning their accuracy. As ratings came to be used more widely, several defects were noticed. Ratings of a single characteristic show 'leniency effect' where the rater gives generally good ratings to everyone he rates, or 'central tendency' when he avoids using the extremes of the scale. Ratings of several characteristics show 'halo effect' (Thorndike, 1920; see also Cooper, 1981) where the rater gives consistently favourable ratings across conceptually distinct traits, or 'logical error' (Newcomb, 1931) where the rater wrongly assumes particular traits correlate.

Several early studies compared ratings and intelligence test data (Brigham, 1914; Webb, 1915; Rugg, 1921; Magson, 1926). The first comparison of personality ratings and test data seems to date from 1929, when McDonough found a 0.39 correlation between teacher ratings of stability and scores on the Woodworth-Cady neuroticism questionnaire indicating that ratings agreed with the subject's own self-description. The main body of research on ratings of personal characteristics owes its inspiration to the 1938 study of Estes, which compared ratings of subjects' 'needs', with criterion ratings provided by Murray's (1938) Harvard Psychological Clinic assessment team. Numerous studies followed. Sometimes subjects rated traits based on personality theories such as Murray's needs, sometimes on particular personality measures, such as the 16PF (Christensen, 1970) or the

MMPI (Crow and Hammond, 1957). Alternatively subjects rate targets' likes and feelings; Suchman's (1956) subjects predicted targets' ratings of self-confidence, etc. following a group discussion. Ryle (Ryle and Lunghi, 1971) used an adaptation of the Role Repertory Grid Test, the 'dyad grid', in which a psychotherapist predicted a patient's ratings of propositions like 'my wife dominates me', the intention being to measure how well the therapist could judge the patient's attitudes to his personal relationships. Steiner and Dodge's (1957) subjects rated a curious mixture of traits, including interest in classical music, religiosity and behavioural consistency.

The rating method has its disadvantages. Many people find it difficult to choose an arbitrary number to represent someone's extraversion or intelligence, so experimenters commonly find rating scales evoke puzzlement or hostility in their subjects. But it is the *scoring* of ratings to yield accuracy scores that presents the biggest problem. Some researchers analyse ratings in crude inefficient ways, such as scoring 'hits' when predicted and criterion ratings coincide (Ausubel and Schiff, 1955), or by comparing group mean ratings (Quarantelli and Cooper, 1966). An index of the *size* of *individual* errors is obviously what is needed; Estes (1938) devised the index of squared differences – D^2 – where D is the absolute difference between criterion rating and estimated rating. The smaller the index, the more accurate (apparently) the subject. This system of scoring, in various forms, was used in most subsequent rating research, until its deficiencies were noted by Cronbach (1955). Some investigators (e.g. Dymond, 1950; Steiner and Dodge, 1957; and more recently DePaulo and Rosenthal, 1979), used raw, i.e. unsquared, difference scores; but the same problems arise.

Cronbach's critique of difference scores

Cronbach (1955) argued that difference scores are statistically complex, and not necessarily good measures of a person's accuracy of rating others. Table 6.1 illustrates his argument, using three sets of estimated ratings, and a set of criterion ratings – all fictitious.

Three subjects have each rated ten targets, A-J, for narrowmindedness on a 9-point scale. The first subject, Mr Level, has a raw difference score of 20, and so is apparently the 'worst' judge. Inspection of Table 6.1 shows that all his ratings are 2 scale points below the criterion rating; if this constant error were eliminated, his difference

Table 6.1   Imaginary data, representing the ratings by three judges of ten subjects, on a single trait

	A	B	C	D	E	F	G	H	I	J	
					Subjects						
Criterion rating	5	6	5	4	5	7	4	5	4	5	
Judge 1	3	4	3	2	3	5	2	3	2	3	difference score – 20
Judge 2	5	8	5	2	5	9	2	5	2	5	difference score – 10
Judge 3	5	5	5	5	5	5	5	5	5	5	difference score – 6

score would be zero, and his judgement perfect. Cronbach calls such constant errors differences in 'level'. Their true significance is uncertain; Mr Level may actually be underestimating the narrowmindedness of the ten targets, he may be subject to a 'leniency' effect, or he may be uncertain how to use the rating scale, and in some sense mean the same by a rating of 3 as the criterion rater means by a rating of 5. Since the scale is arbitrary, it is impossible to distinguish between these three possibilities, and hence it is impossible to be certain that disagreement between Mr Level and the criterion truly indicates Mr Level's judgement of character is at fault.

Mr Spread scores 11, and is thus the second best judge of narrowmindedness. He has correctly identified the mean score as 5, and correctly perceived that targets A, C, E, H and J score at the mean. He has also correctly perceived that targets B and F score above the mean, and targets D, G and I below. Mr Spread's only error lies in consistently overestimating the size of deviation from the mean by 2 or 3 scale points. Cronbach calls this an error of 'spread'. As with error of level, it is impossible to say whether Mr Spread disagrees with the criterion about the true range of narrowmindedess in the ten targets, or merely about the choice of an arbitrary number to represent it.

Mr Profile scores a difference score of only 6, and is thus, according to difference scores, the best judge of narrowmindedness. But inspection of Table 6.1 shows that he has achieved his high accuracy in a very odd way – by giving every target exactly the same rating. The other two judges, Mr Level and Mr Spread, had at least accurately perceived which target differed from the average, and in which direction. Mr Profile fails to do either. Cronbach calls this an error of 'correlation' or profile.

There is obviously something wrong with a scoring system that favours Mr Profile over Mr Level and Mr Spread, and this is the central defect of difference scores. Anyone who correctly estimates the average of the criterion ratings, or who just happens to adopt the same mean in his ratings, is automatically at an enormous advantage.

Cronbach actually analysed a difference score based on a number of targets, *and a number of traits*, and extracted *seven* components, not three; trait rating studies at the time usually derived a single overall accuracy score from ratings of a number of target persons on a number of traits (Taft, 1956; Crow and Hammond, 1957). (A difference score based on only ten ratings, as in Table 6.1, would probably prove statistically unreliable. On the other hand, one based on a number of different traits is less meaningful. It would be better to increase the number of targets if reliability is a problem.) In choosing to consider the multitarget multitrait difference score, Cronbach complicated the analysis considerably, and probably helped many readers fail to understand his argument. Table 6.2 presents ratings by one subject of five traits (I-V), in six targets (A-F), and a corresponding set of criterion ratings – all fictitious as before.

Table 6.2   One subject's ratings, of six subjects, on five traits, with corresponding criterion ratings in parentheses.

| | | Subjects | | | | | | |
		A	B	C	D	E	F	
Traits	I	5	7	5	8	2	5	32
		(3)	(4)	(3)	(5)	(1)	(3)	(19)
	II	6	8	6	9	3	6	38
		(8)	(9)	(8)	(9)	(5)	(8)	(47)
	III	4	6	3	6	1	4	24
		(4)	(6)	(3)	(6)	(1)	(4)	(24)
	IV	3	5	2	5	1	3	19
		(3)	(5)	(2)	(1)	(6)	(9)	(28)
	V	5	5	5	5	5	5	30
		(7)	(5)	(3)	(4)	(3)	(1)	(23)
	Total	23	31	21	33	12	23	143
		(27)	(29)	(19)	(25)	(16)	(25)	(141)

The seven components are:

(1) Elevation   The difference between the grand mean of all ratings, for all targets on all traits, and the corresponding grand mean of the criterion ratings.

(2–3) Differential elevation, spread and correlation   Are derived from the means of all ratings made across all traits, for a particular target, i.e. the column means in Table 6.2. It has a *spread* component, based on the variation between the means, and a *correlation* component derived from comparing the profile of the predicted column means with the profile of the criterion column means.

(4–5) Stereotype accuracy, spread and correlation   Are derived from the means of all the ratings across all targets, on a particular trait, i.e. the row means in Table 6.2. It too has *spread* and *correlation* components, the former based on the spread of the means, and the latter derived from comparing the profile of the predicted row means with the profile of the criterion row means.

(6–7) Differential accuracy, spread and correlation   Are derived from the ratings of each target on each trait, not those pooled across traits nor across targets. It too has *spread* and *correlation* components, based on the variation of the predicted ratings, and similarity of their profile to the criterion ratings.

Cronbach and others (Crow and Hammond, 1957; Sechrest and Jackson, 1960) see stereotype accuracy as the ability to judge people in general, arguably a very useful ability for politicians, chairmen or advertising executives, but in rating studies stereotype accuracy could signify nothing more interesting than the coincidence of the subject's mean rating and the criterion mean.

Differential elevation is derived from the mean of a target's scores on a number of different traits. Cronbach (1955) argues that it can measure accuracy of perception of the target's morale, where all traits being rated reflect a sense of well-being. But this is indistinguishable from a 'halo', where the rater gives generally favourable ratings across a range of conceptually different scales.

Cronbach's message has not yet reached – and presumably after twenty-five years never will reach – all parts of the psychological world; studies using ratings and difference scores still appear. Two studies using ratings in Repertory Grid format (Watson, 1970; Ryle and Lunghi, 1971) also appear to have used difference scores, although it is difficult to be sure since their account merely names the computer program used to score the data. Some research on perception in married couples, for example Murstein and Beck (1972), still uses ratings and difference scores. Recent studies on correlates of 'self-monitoring' (Tunnell, 1980) and empathy (Mills and Hogan, 1978) have used difference scores to compare self-ratings with peer ratings; Tunnell acknowledges the possible difficulties and also presents a profile analysis, but Mills and Hogan do not, and do not refer to Cronbach's critique.

The significance of Cronbach's critique

Cronbach's components may be no more than undesirable artifacts of ratings, which need only to be eliminated; or they may be real and important parts of judging others' personality. Smith (1966) likens them to Thurstone's (1938) analysis of intelligence – the realization that an apparently monolithic ability is really a set of related sub-abilities. But Cronbach's components derive only from multitrait multitarget ratings, so their generality is limited. (British commentators tend to view Thurstone's account of intelligence with some scepticism.)

Cronbach's observations are very useful when considering judgements that must use ratings. Examinations, and 'marks' in general, are a case in point, for they are a form of rating (in Britain generally a very badly designed one). Most psychologists have found themselves trying at one time or another – usually unsuccessfully – to explain to innumerate examining boards that differences in *level* adopted by Drs A and B mean students choosing Dr A's course will get better degrees because Dr A marks leniently; while differences in *spread* mean that Dr C's marks, which hardly vary from one student to the next, might as well not be included, whereas Dr D's, which use the full range of the scale, have a disproportionate say in the final list.

Ratings are also widely used in personnel work, at least in North America (Landy and Farr, 1980). Numerous attempts have been made to find better rating formats, or to train management to make better ratings (Borman, 1979), with mixed results. Borman trained his raters to produce less 'halo', but didn't improve their accuracy. Bernardin and Pence (1980) found that training designed to reduce 'halo' and leniency made ratings *less* accurate, and invented a new response set; after training, the raters saw *too little* correlation between the thirteen scales used, instead of *too much*. Borman and Bernardin both used sets of videotaped or written examples of good, bad and average behaviour as stimuli, and the intended quality of the performance as criterion, backed up by expert ratings.

Cronbach's analysis is less relevant if one's main interest is studying accuracy of judging personality; if ratings create methodological problems, the answer is to use a technique that doesn't. The difficulties Cronbach described were not unknown. Guilford's 1936 text, *Psychometric Methods*, refers to the problems of 'leniency' or *level*, and 'central tendency' or lack of *spread*, as do most pre-war texts on personality assessment. Vernon (1953) summarizes the problems in a single sentence: 'the outstanding defect of this type of scale is the variations in standards and distributions adopted by different raters.'

Avoiding rating artifacts   The researcher who doesn't consider Cronbach's components interesting in their own right, and who wants only a single meaningful measure of accuracy from his trait ratings, can do several things:

(i) Analyse the ratings of each trait separately, thus creating three components not seven. This is an inherently desirable strategy, but may require the number of targets to be increased, to ensure a reliable score.

(ii) Use standard scores, to ensure the predicted and criterion ratings have the same *level* and the same *spread*. This effectively abolishes two of Cronbach's three components – *level* and *spread* – and leaves only *correlation* or profile. Since individual differences in level and spread may reflect only idiosyncrasies in the use of the scale, their abolition is arguably no loss.

Cronbach (1955) and Boyd (1964) proposed scoring systems based on deviations from overall rating means – essentially standard score analyses. Cline and Richards (1960) devised an Interpersonal Accuracy (IA) score, with two components, one of which (IAr) is calculated by correlating the subject's ratings with the criterion ratings for each trait, and transforming to Fisher's Z. Christensen (1970) devised a 'refined difference score' (RD) in which the subject's rating of each target is expressed as a deviation from that subject's rating of the 'typical male white college student' (assuming all targets were white male college students). Criterion ratings are expressed in the same way, and differences squared and summed.

(iii) Correlate predicted and criterion ratings. This eliminates differences in *level*, and takes account of differences in *spread*, because the lazy rater, like 'Mr Profile', will get a zero correlation. (Absence of spread on one variable necessarily produces a zero correlation.) Correlation has been used by early researchers such as Valentine (1929), and recent researchers (Gabennesch and Hunt, 1971). Exline (1957) ranked his ratings first and calculated a rank order correlation. He noted that this had 'the advantage of eliminating the possibility that low error scores merely reflect the judges' willingness to use the extremes, or ability to judge deviations of others from a central tendency.' Exline's example possibly inspired a number of recent researchers who have correlated peer with self-ratings (Funder, 1980; Kenrick and Stringfield, 1980; Tunnell, 1980), without always acknowledging any debt to Exline, or indeed to Cronbach. (Funder was using self and peer ratings, not to test accuracy of peers' perception of target, but accuracy of target's perception of self, using peer ratings as criterion – another example of one researcher's criterion being another researcher's variable. Various studies of this type, reviewed by Schrauger and Schöneman (1979), find people generally poor at seeing themselves as others see them.)

Multiple choice methods and their problems

McHenry (1971) describes the rater's task as 'guess the amount of the trait'. The other favourite approach to measuring accuracy of perceiving personality tells the subject – in McHenry's words – to 'guess what he would write'. The subject predicts which response the target made, or chooses the answer that describes him best.

Recent research (Schroder, 1972) uses film or videotape of the target making a series of choices; the film stops at the crucial moment, and subjects predict the target's choice. Archer and Akert, in Chapter 5, discuss this type of research in detail, and describe their own 'Social Interpretations Test'. In these studies the subject's task is to predict specific outcomes, rather than characterize the target's personality. In Cline's 'Behavior Postdiction Test' (Cline, 1964) subjects 'postdict' the target's typical behaviour: 'When . . . in a violent argument he/becomes very sarcastic/uses profanity and obscene words/leaves the room or area/strikes his opponent with his fists.' The criterion, according to Cline, is how the target reacts, as reported by himself and verified by two close friends; Cline's critics (McHenry, 1971) argue that this supposes a degree of consistency in the target's behaviour, across different arguments with different people about different things, which is implausible.

Another variation on the multiple choice theme is the 'programmed case' (Fancher, 1969), in which the target's biography is turned into a set of multiple choice questions: 'At the outbreak of World War 2 he [an American] joined the US Marines/started a Master's degree in political science/went to London as war correspondent.' '*Programmed*', because the subject learns after each choice the correct answer, so that his image of the target is continuously corrected; this makes his judgement improve during the task. The criterion in the 'programmed case', as in Schroeder's and Archer's films, is the choice the target actually made.

The most common multiple choice technique is the so-called 'empathy' paradigm, in which the subject predicts how the target answers a number of questions. The questions are taken from a personality questionnaire, so the results – apparently – reveal the accuracy of perception of whatever trait(s) the questionnaire measures. The criterion is what the target's answer actually was. This is a very attractive paradigm, especially to academic psychologists with large captive audiences; one distributes copies of the selected questionnaire(s), instructs the class first to complete it in the usual way, then to complete as many more as time or the class's patience will permit, in the way designated individuals (best friends, worst enemies, total strangers) complete it. A comparison of target's own completion with predicted completion(s) yields an accuracy score; the inventory, as completed by the subject himself, describes the personality of the good, bad or indifferent judge of others.

The first empathy study seems to be Cartwright and French's (1939), whose two subjects (Cartwright and French themselves) predicted the responses of one target to 'A Survey of Public Opinion on some Religious and Economic Issues', the Allport–Vernon 'Study of Values' and miscellaneous 'items diagnostic of personality traits and social attitudes'. Cartwright and French's paper is yet another example of one researcher's criterion being another's variable, for they presented their results as a check on the validity of the questionnaire method, using the experimenters' predictions as the criterion. Remmers (1950) reversed his perspective and regarded the target's completion as the criterion, and the subject's ability to predict it as an index of his 'empathy'. He reported a study of labour leaders' 'empathy' with management – i.e. ability to predict their responses to a questionnaire about supervisors – and concluded by quoting Burns on the gift 'To see oursilves as ithers see us!'

The combination of an easy experimental procedure and a significant issue made the 'empathy' paradigm highly popular, and numerous studies appeared in the late 1940s and early 1950s, coinciding with the 'boom' in trait rating studies. The slump came too at the same time, and from the same source – critiques by Cronbach (Gage and Cronbach, 1955). The 'empathy' paradigm turned out to have just as many hidden snags as ratings, so its results were just as likely to be uninterpretable. These critiques identified three main artifacts in empathy studies: stereotype accuracy, response sets and assumed similarity.

Stereotype accuracy   In a rating study anyone who guesses the average rating maximizes his 'accuracy' score, because the average rating is likely to be the most common rating given. Similarly in an 'empathy' study, anyone who knows, or guesses, the likeliest answer is on the way to maximizing his 'accuracy' score. Hence British students wouldn't find predicting each others' answers to the Wilson Conservatism Scale very difficult, because students, in the author's experience of class use of the scale, never score over 50, even though the scale's range is 0–100. Few if any students approve of capital or corporal punishment; few favour racial segregation or disapprove of coloured immigration. Hence it is easy for one student to predict another's answer to most items on the scale; Gage (1952) showed many years ago that predictions made for 'the typical student', on the Kuder Interests Test, fitted individual students better than the same judge's attempts to predict for that target after seeing him.

It is easy to predict the typical person's responses to questions like 'My mother is/was a good woman,' or 'I sometimes feel as if I am floating six inches off the ground', precisely because these questions were included in their respective inventories to detect rare classes of person – psychotics and inattentive/facetious respondents. The subject stops trying to detect differences between people and starts judging questionnaire items. Several studies (Dymond, 1954; Stelmachers and McHugh, 1964; McHenry, 1971) suggest people can only achieve above-chance accuracy on empathy tasks by stereotype accuracy, and cannot perceive individual differences in response. Dymond (1954) eliminated from her 'empathy' task all MMPI items where most people gave the same answer, and made two interesting discoveries. First, that she had to discard sixty of her original 115, and secondly that her subjects (happily or unhappily married couples) could barely exceed chance prediction on the remaining fifty-five. McHenry's study, using the Maudsley Personality Inventory, confirmed this.

Stereotype accuracy artifacts are not exclusive to 'empathy' studies, but arise in any multiple choice task – a fact often overlooked. For example, in Schroder's (1972) filmed choice test, it is possible that one choice is more inherently likely than another, and that subjects can see this or, in some less rational way, profit from it. Stereotype accuracy could, in theory, be a problem even in the programmed case method; if one of the choices is more likely, or a more common response, subjects could respond to the stereotype, not the individual. Cline (1964) tested a group who completed his Behavior Postdiction Test for 'the typical college male', and reports they did worse than subjects who had seen the films; he doesn't say whether they scored at chance level, which would definitely prove they weren't profiting from stereotypes. Stereotype accuracy can be controlled by ensuring every answer is equally probable, as Dymond (1954) did, but this cannot be done where something uncommon (suicide, psychosis, bank fraud) is being predicted. Stereotype accuracy's presence can be checked by predictions of the typical subject, as in Gage (1952) or Cline (1964); or the experimenter can change the judgement task, to prevent subjects' profiting from stereotype accuracy.

Response set artifacts   People completing questionnaires sometimes tend to answer 'yes' in preference to 'no' (acquiescence set); they sometimes try to present themselves in a favourable light (social desirability set). These are 'response sets', and when questionnaires are used in an 'empathy' study, they cause 'response set artifacts'. For example, if the targets tend to prefer to answer 'yes', and the subjects completing the inventory share the same preference, their answers will be the same, not because the subjects have correctly perceived the targets, but because they are subject to the same response set.

Assumed similarity   Scodel and Mussen (1953) reported that authoritarian subjects were – apparently – poorer judges of people, a finding that makes intuitive sense as an example of the non-psychological-mindedness of the authoritarian. But close inspection of the data showed the authoritarian subjects poor at judging authoritarianism only (and no worse than average at predicting MMPI responses); they made wrong predictions because they assumed the target was as authoritarian as themselves (when, in fact, Scodel and Mussen's design paired high and low authoritarian subjects). 'Assumed similarity' in Scodel's study guaranteed incorrect predictions. Other designs will work in the opposite direction, and guarantee 'accuracy' to subjects who 'assume similarity'. Opinion varies about the extent of 'assumed similarity' artifacts. Not all subjects assume similarity; Scodel's low authoritarians did not. Corsini (1956) reported low and generally insignificant correlations between 'accuracy' and true similarity of judge and target, which implies his subjects were assuming at best a very limited similarity.

A more recent empathy study (Stelmachers and McHugh, 1964) analysed expert and lay predictions of four targets' MMPI responses, and obtained very depressing results. They found that both classes of subject would have made better predictions for three of the four targets if they had *either* assumed complete similarity (i.e. given their own answer every time and made no attempt to predict the target's); *or* chosen the socially desirable answer every time, even though two of the targets were a conversion hysteric and a juvenile delinquent; *or* chosen the more common answer every time (i.e. used *stereotype accuracy*).

Since Stelmacher and McHugh's study few 'empathy' studies have been reported; the last recorded sighting appears to be Cloyd (1977). The empathy task seems basically impossible, unless subjects 'cheat' by ignoring the target person and concentrating on the question.

Rank order and its problems

Correlating predicted and criterion ratings has the virtue of eliminating unwanted components like *level* and *spread*, but also poses the questions: Why use ratings in the first place? Why not instruct the subjects to rank order the targets, and compare this rank with the criterion ratings? Or why not obtain the criterion data also in rank order form?

The rank order method was used in early studies of judging intelligence (Hollingworth, 1916; Chassell and Chassell, 1921; Adams, 1927), but was supplanted by rating and multiple choice methods, including the 'empathy' paradigm. Ranking has been used to a limited extent in sociometric research (Greer *et al.*, 1954; Tagiuri, 1958), and in research on marriage (Levinger and Breedlove, 1966; Clements, 1967). Higgins *et al.* (1980) use rank orders of preferences for food, etc. in a study of children's ability to say what people of various ages will like most. Berlew and Williams (1964) used *paired comparisons*, in a study of the effects of ambition on person perception (a paired comparison is a rank order of two targets). The validation of personality inventories often uses *peer nominations*, in which subjects select the most dominant and/or least dominant of their peers; this too is a variation on the group ranking theme (Goúgh, 1975). Most studies have required their subjects to place the targets in order of possession of a particular trait(s); Bronfenbrenner *et al.*'s (1958) subjects rank ordered a number of traits for each target, saying, for example, that a particular target was more extravert than intelligent.

Disadvantages of ranking methods   The use of rank order has a number of problems, some real, some apparent.

(i) A rank order cannot represent unequal differences nor, if used strictly, can it represent ties. The subject must say the same about a very bright target and a very dim target as about two almost identical persons – one is more intelligent than the other. And if two targets are genuinely equally intelligent, requiring the subject to rank them forces him to distort his opinion to fit the experiment's system of measurement.

In theory, a rating scale allows subjects to describe such cases more accurately, matching the similarity of the ratings to the similarity of the targets, but the whole point of Cronbach's critique is that the way subjects rate others is as likely to reflect idiosyncrasies in their use of the scale as real variations in the targets being judged. (In theory repeated ranking could offer a solution. If the subject is forced to make distinctions he can't really see, he is likely to change his mind the second time round, whereas if the distinction is clear to him, he will make it consistently.)

(ii) Ranking also requires the subjects to see all the targets before forming an opinion, or else to change earlier opinions in the light of later ones, whereas ratings can be made immediately. This is a particular problem when subjects rank order targets seen in filmed interviews. Unpublished work by the author found differing orders of presentation changed the average rank assigned to one target by two rank positions in seven; these order effects seemed to be contrast effects, where targets of average extraversion are seen as more extravert when they follow a very introvert target. Order effects were greatly reduced if brief extracts of the interviews were shown again in different order at the end of the main presentation. Subjects who rank order targets they already know well, or who are all present in a group, don't face this problem (Cook and Smith, 1974). (In practice, subjects often can't use rating scales with any confidence until they have seen several targets. Most examiners look at a sample of scripts to establish a level before starting marking.)

Advantages of rank order methods.   The rank order method also has major advantages:

(i) It avoids *level* and *spread* problems.

(ii) It is acceptable to subjects (Cook and Smith, 1974), perhaps because it is familiar from horse races, athletics, beauty contests, school end of term reports, and the like.

(iii) It avoids stereotype accuracy and 'response set artifacts'. In a rating study, the subject whose mean rating coincides with the criterion mean ratings is automatically at an advantage; such 'coincidence' is often far from coincidental. 'Response sets' cause ratings to cluster in certain parts of the scale. Cohen (1953) noted that ratings typically show a 'central tendency'; the subject whose ratings use the same 'central tendency' will score more 'hits' – like 'Mr Profile' – and his mistakes will be smaller. Sometimes ratings are skewed by 'social desirability sets'. Lindgren and Robinson (1953), in a critique of Dymond's (1949) work, note that most targets described themselves as 'fairly friendly' (point 4 of a 5-point scale); the subject who adopts this as his mean rating is again at an advantage. Moreover the subject who does this may not be making a conscious judgement about how most people use Dymond's scale; he may be following a norm (that one should say fairly nice things about others) that happens to match the norm the targets were following (that one should be fairly friendly to other people).

The rank order method eliminates response set artifacts, because such artifacts cause targets to make one response more frequently than the other(s), i.e. rate others 'fairly friendly'; in a rank order each response can be made once only. Matching, in which subjects match handwriting samples to their authors, or sorting, in which subjects sort the targets into groups of specified size (e.g. 12 Catholics, 12 Jews, 12 Protestants; Toch *et al.*, 1962), similarly prevent response set artifacts by restricting the number of times each response may be used.

Cook and Smith (1974) used a group ranking technique, and found subjects could rank each other for extraversion; predicted ranks correlated on average 0.452 with a criterion rank derived from the Eysenck Personality Inventory (EPI). Attempts to rank order subjects on intelligence proved less successful, probably because the student samples used had a limited spread; earlier studies had shown subjects could rank order targets for intelligence. Cook and Smith's authoritarianism data also pointed to the importance of a wide spread of criterion scores. Some groups could rank each other for authoritarianism, and agree significantly with the criterion inventory, but others could not. The former had a good spread of authoritarianism scores, while the latter didn't. Attempts to rank order groups for neuroticism using the EPI as criterion were entirely unsuccessful, several groups actually generating significant negative correlations between predicted and criterion orders. Later unpublished research by Cook and Buckley suggested this happened because subjects assumed a near perfect correlation between introversion and neuroticism, which does not exist; whether subjects really think this, or simply made the assumption because they found it impossible to judge neuroticism, is uncertain. Cook and Smith's study points to one limitation of the rank order technique – the need for an adequate range of subjects – and suggests another – that subjects will use implicit personality theories; the method seems nevertheless to have enough value to merit its further use.

Towards a rebirth of accuracy research?

Academic social psychologists have professed a disinterest in research on accuracy of perceiving personality since Cronbach's critiques. Attribution theory (see chapter 1) has been the 'great white hope' of person perception researchers since 1965 or so. In the course of developing attribution theory from its modest beginnings to its present elaborated state, some attribution theorists have unwittingly illustrated the truth of the complaint that social psychology is a circular science not a cumulative one, by rediscovering familiar issues under new names. Ross *et al.* (1977) solved the problem of why people ignore 'consensus information' by rediscovering assumed similarity. Attribution theory says that information that everyone behaves in a particular way ought to 'discount' the inference that someone meant to do something, because he's that sort of person. People do reason that if everyone (i.e. the 'consensus') does something, then doing it doesn't tell you what a person is like, but they may not use real consensus information, nor even the consensus information supplied by the experimenter; they may use a 'false consensus'. People who support women's liberation expect everyone else to – presently still a 'false consensus' apparently – so they don't think this support tells them anything about a person. Which is another way of saying people assume similarity when guessing other people's opinions – a fact well known since at least 1952.

Having rediscovered 'assumed similarity', attribution theorists now seem poised to rediscover accuracy. Many papers since 1971 have discussed 'fundamental attribution error' – the apparently pervasive tendency of observers to overrate the influence of personality traits on other peoples' behaviour. But to describe something as an error implies there is a correct answer; Harvey *et al.* (1981) note that this requires the researcher to be able to distinguish between accurate and inaccurate judgements of other people's personality, which means in turn we need a method of studying the accuracy of naive judgement of personality. . . . At least attribution theorists rediscovered the artifacts before rediscovering the issue itself.

References

Adams, H. F. (1927) The good judge of personality. *Journal of Abnormal and Social Psychology 22*: 172–81.

Adinolfi, A. A. (1971) The relevance of person perception research to clinical psychology. *Journal of Consulting and Clinical Psychology 37*: 167–76.

Allport, G. W. and Odbert, S. (1936) Trait names: a psycho-lexical study. *Psychological Monographs 47*: no. 221.

Argyle, M. (1957) *The Scientific Study of Social Behaviour*. London: Methuen.

Ausubel, D. P. and Schiff, L. M. (1955) Some intrapersonal and interpersonal determinants of individual differences in socioempathic ability among adolescents. *Journal of Social Psychology 41*: 39–56.

Bannister, D. (1962) The nature and measurement of schizophrenic thought disorder. *Journal of Mental Science 108*: 825–42.

Berlew, D. F. and Williams, A. F. (1964) Interpersonal sensitivity under motive arousing conditions. *Journal of Abnormal and Social Psychology 68*: 150–9.

Bernardin, H. J. and Pence, E. C. (1980) Effects of rater training: creation of new response sets and decreasing accuracy. *Journal of Applied Psychology 65*: 60–6.

Borman, W. C. (1979) Format and training effects on rating accuracy and rater errors. *Journal of Applied Psychology 64*: 410–21.

Boyd, J. B. (1964) Person perception accuracy as a function of increasing familiarity, target characteristics and sex of perceiver. Unpublished doctoral dissertation, University of Mississippi, Hattiesburg.

Brigham C. C. (1914) An experimental critique of the Binet–Simon scale. *Journal of Educational Psychology 5*: 439–48.

Bronfenbrenner, U., Harding, J. and Gallwey, M. (1958). The measurement of skill in social perception. In D. C. McClelland (ed.) *Talent and Society*. New York: Van Nostrand.

Cartwright, D. and French, J. R. P. (1939) The reliability of life-history studies. *Character and Personality 8*: 110–19.

Chassell, C. F. and Chassell, L. M. (1921) A survey of the first three grades of the Horace Mann School by means of psychological tests and teachers estimates. *Journal of Educational Psychology 12*: 72–81.

Christensen, L. (1970) Validity of person-perception accuracy scores. *Perceptual and Motor Skills 30*: 671–7.

Clements, W. H. (1967) Marital interaction and marital stability: a point of view and a descriptive comparison of stable and unstable marriage. *Journal of Marriage and the Family 29*: 697–702.

Cline, V. B. (1964) Interpersonal perception. In B. A. Maher (ed.) *Progress in Experimental Personality Research,* vol. 1. New York: Academic Press.

Cline, V. B. and Richards, J. M. (1960) Accuracy of person perception – a general trait? *Journal of Abnormal and Social Psychology 60*: 1–7.

Cloyd, L. (1977) Effects of acquaintanceship on accuracy of person perception. *Perceptual and Motor Skills 44*: 819–26.

Cohen, E. (1953) The methodology of Notcutt & Silva's 'Knowledge of other people: a critique'. *Journal of Abnormal and Social Psychology 48*: 155.

Cook, M. and Smith, J. M. C. (1974) Group ranking techniques in the study of the accuracy of person perception. *British Journal of Psychology 65*: 427–35.

Cooper, W. H. (1981) Ubiquitous halo. *Psychological Bulletin 90*: 218–44.

Corsini, R. J. (1956) Understanding and similarity in marriage. *Journal of Abnormal and Social Psychology 52*: 327–32.

Cronbach, L. J. (1955) Processes affecting scores on 'understanding of others' and 'assumed similarity'. *Psychological Bulletin 52*: 177–93.

Crow, W. J. and Hammond, K. R. (1957) The generality of accuracy and response sets in person perception. *Journal of Abnormal and Social Psychology 54*: 384–90.

DePaulo, B. M. and Rosenthal, R. (1979) Telling lies. *Journal of Personality and Social Psychology 37*: 1713–22.

Dymond, R. F. (1949) A scale for the measurement of empathic ability. *Journal of Consulting Psychology 13*: 127–33.

Dymond, R. F. (1950) Personality and empathy. *Journal of Consulting Psychology 14*: 343–50.

Dymond, R. F. (1954) Interpersonal perception and marital happiness. *Canadian Journal of Psychology 8*: 164–171.

Ellson, D. G. and Ellson, E. C. (1953) Historical note on the rating scale. *Psychological Bulletin 50*: 383–4.

Estes, S. C. (1938) Judging personality from expressive behaviour. *Journal of Abnormal and Social Psychology 33*: 217–36.

Exline, R. V. (1957) Group climate as a factor in the relevance and accuracy of social perception. *Journal of Abnormal and Social Psychology 55*: 382–8.

Eysenck, H. J. (1970) *The Structure of Human Personality*, 3rd edn. London: Methuen.

Fancher, R. E. (1969) Group and individual accuracy in person perception. *Journal of Consulting Psychology 33*: 127.

Funder, D. C. (1980) On seeing ourselves as others see us: self other agreement and discrepancy in personality ratings. *Journal of Personality 48*: 473–93.

Gabennesch, H. and Hunt, L. L. (1971) The relative accuracy of interpersonal perception of high and low authoritarians. *Journal of Experimental Research on Personality 5*: 43–8.

Gage, N. L. (1952) Judging interests from expressive behavior. *Psychological Monographs 66* (18), whole no. 350.

Gage, N. L. and Cronbach, L. J. (1955) Conceptual and methodological problems in interpersonal perception. *Psychological Review 62*: 411–22.

Gough, H. (1975) *Manual of the California Psychological Inventory*. Palo Alto, Calif.: Consulting Psychologists Press.

Greer, F. L., Galanter, E. H. and Nordlie, P. G. (1954) Interpersonal knowledge and individual and group effectiveness. *Journal of Abnormal and Social Psychology 49*: 411–14.

Guilford, J. P. (1936) *Psychometric Methods*. New York: McGraw-Hill.

Harvey, J. H., Town, J. P. and Yarkin, K. L. (1981) How fundamental is The Fundamental Attribution Error? *Journal of Personality and Social Psychology 40*: 346–9.

Higgins, E. T., Feldman, N. S. and Ruble, D. N. (1980) Accuracy and differentiation in social prediction: a developmental perspective. *Journal of Personality 48*: 520–40.

Hollingworth, H. L. (1916) *Vocational Psychology*. New York: Appleton.

Kenrick, D. T. and Stringfield, D. O. (1980) Personality traits and the eye of the beholder: crossing some traditional philosophical boundaries in the search for consistency in all of the people. *Psychological Review 81*: 88–104.

Landy, F. J. and Farr, J. L. (1980) Performance rating. *Psychological Bulletin 87*: 72–107.

Levinger, G. and Breedlove, J. (1966) Interpersonal attraction and agreement: a study of marriage partners. *Journal of Personality and Social Psychology 3*: 367–72.

Lindgren, H. C. and Robinson, J. (1953) An evaluation of Dymond's test of insight and empathy. *Journal of Consulting Psychology 17*: 172–6.

Magson, E. H. (1926) How we judge intelligence. *British Journal of Psychology Monograph Supplement 3* (9).

McDonough, M. R. (1929) The empirical study of character. *Catholic University of America Studies in Psychology and Psychiatry 2*: 3.

McHenry. R. (1971) New methods of assessing the accuracy of interpersonal perception. *Journal for the Theory of Social Behaviour 1*: 109–19.

Mills, C. and Hogan, R. (1978) A role theoretical interpretation of personality scale item responses. *Journal of Personality 46*: 578–85.

Murray, H. A. (1938) *Explorations in Personality*. New York: Oxford University Press.

Murstein, B. I. and Beck, G. D. (1972) Person perception, marriage adjustment and social desirability. *Journal of Consulting and Clinical Psychology 39*: 396–403.

Newcomb, T. (1931) An experiment designed to test the validity of a rating scale technique. *Journal of Educational Psychology 22*: 279–89.

Quarantelli, E. L. and Cooper, J. (1966) Self conceptions and others: a further test of Meadean hypotheses. *Sociological Quarterly 7*: 281–97.

Remmers, H. H. (1950) A quantitative index of social–psychological empathy. *American Journal of Orthopsychiatry 20*: 161–5.

Ross, L., Greene, D. and House, P. (1977) The 'false consensus effect': an egocentric bias in social perception and attribution processes. *Journal of Experimental Social Psychology 13*: 299–301.

Rugg, H. (1921) Is rating of human character practicable? *Journal of Educational Psychology 12*: 425–38, 485–501.

Ryle, A. and Lunghi, M. (1971) A therapist's prediction of a patient's dyad grid. *British Journal of Psychiatry 118*: 555–60.

Schrauger, J. S. and Schöneman, T. J. (1979) Symbolic interactionist view of self concept: through the looking glass darkly. *Psychological Bulletin 86*: 549–73.

Schroder, H. E. (1972) Use of feedback in clinical practice. *Journal of Consulting and Clinical Psychology 38*: 265–9.

Scodel, A. and Mussen, P. (1953) Social perceptions of authoritarians and nonauthoritarians. *Journal of Abnormal and Social Psychology 48*: 181–4.

Sechrest, L. and Jackson, D. N. (1960) Social intelligence and accuracy of interpersonal predictions. *Journal of Personality 29*: 167–81.

Smith, H. C. (1966) *Sensitivity to People*. New York: McGraw-Hill.

Steiner, I. D. and Dodge, J. S. (1957) A comparison of two techniques employed in the study of interpersonal perception. *Sociometry 20*: 1–7.

Stelmachers, Z. T. and McHugh, R. B. (1964) Contribution of stereotypes and individualised information to predictive accuracy. *Journal of Consulting Psychology 28*: 234–42.

Suchman, J. R. (1956) Social sensitivity in the small task-oriented group. *Journal of Abnormal and Social Psychology 52*: 75–83.

Taft, R. (1955) The ability to judge people. *Psychological Bulletin 52*: 1–23.

Taft, R. (1956) Some characteristics of good judges of others. *British Journal of Psychology 47*: 19–29.

Tagiuri, R. (1958) Social preference and its perception. In R. Tagiuri and L. Petrullo (eds) *Person Perception and Interpersonal Behaviour*. Stanford, Calif: Stanford University Press.

Thorndike, E. L. (1920) A constant error in psychological ratings. *Journal of Applied Psychology 4*: 5–9.

Thurstone, L. L. (1938) *Primary Mental Abilities*. Chicago: University of Chicago Press.

Toch, H. H., Rabin, A. I. and Wilkins, D. M. (1962) Factors entering into ethnic identifications: an experimental study. *Sociometry 25*: 297–312.

Tunnell, G. (1980) Intraindividual consistency in personality assessment: the effect of self-monitoring. *Journal of Personality 48*: 220–32.

Valentine, C. W. (1929) The relative ability of men and women in intuitive judgements of character. *British Journal of Psychology 19*: 213–88.

Vernon, P. E. (1953) *Personality Tests and Assessments*. London: Methuen.

Vernon, P. E. (1964) *Personality Assessment*. London: Methuen.

Watson, J. P. (1970) A measure of therapist–patient understanding. *British Journal of Psychiatry 117: 319–21*.

Webb, E. (1915) Character and intelligence. *British Journal of Psychology*, Monograph Supplement 1 (3).

7 Implicit personality theory and the employment interview

Mitchell Rothstein *and*
Douglas N. Jackson

Introduction

Our aim in this chapter is to gain further insight into the processes of person perception by integrating two streams of current psychological research, investigations of implicit personality theories of trait covariation and psychological studies of the employment interview. We believe that the utility of such an integration will be demonstrated by the contribution made both to knowledge of implicit personality theory and to an understanding of a critical function of the employment interview. The two streams of research are by themselves very broad topics consisting of numerous and varied theoretical developments and empirical contributions. Consequently, we must limit our discussion of these individual topics to studies of the employment interview which contribute to an understanding of how personality traits are perceived in others. We shall review selected published research and present some of our own empirical studies in support of this approach to the study of person perception. Readers seeking a more comprehensive review of the implicit personality theory literature are referred to Jackson and Paunonen (1980), Schneider (1973) and Schneider *et al.*, (1979). A thorough review of the psychological research on the employment interview may be found in the present volume (Arvey and Campion, Chapter 8).

Psychological studies of the employment interview

Arvey and Campion in this volume, point out that the employment interview has been the focus of research by industrial and organizational psychologists for over sixty years. During this time several excellent reviews have been published summarizing the results of this research (Wagner, 1949; Mayfield, 1964; Ulrich and Trumbo, 1965; Wright, 1969; Schmitt, 1976; Arvey, 1979; Arvey and Campion, 1984). A perusal of these reviews confronts the reader with the staggering number of variables investigated for their effects on the process and outcome of the employment interview. Arvey and Campion (Chapter 8) and Schmitt (1975) have developed models illustrating how these variables may impact decisions made in the interview. In general, there are three types of variables specified in these models: (a) characteristics of the interviewee (sex, race, physical appearance, intelligence, motivation, etc.), (b) characteristics of the interviewer (attitudes, experience, expectations, stereotypes, etc.) and (c) characteristics of the situation (job information available, degree of structure, number of interviews, order effects, etc.).

An examination of these papers strongly suggests that studies of the employment interview follow a consistent theme. Several characteristics (either interviewer, interviewee and/or situational) are identified as having important consequences for the process or outcome of an interview-based decision, and these characteristics are either systematically varied in an experimental analogue or, occasionally, observed in a real-life interview, and the predicted consequences are usually confirmed. Such research has made a very important contribution to the personnel selection literature. For example, researchers have made great progress in coming to understand the multiplicity of factors that affect human perception, information processing, and decision-making. Personnel practitioners have also greatly benefited from this research in that they have been sensitized to the potential effect those factors may have on their decisions in an employment interview. However, it must be said that the overall effect of this research on the role of the interview in personnel selection has been to derogate its utility. Researchers and reviewers of the literature in this area have repeatedly concluded that the results of their investigations demonstrated the lack of reliability and validity of judgments made in the employment interview. For example, in one of the more recent reviews, Schmitt (1976) concludes:

> There is not much in the research of the last dozen years to bolster the confidence of a personnel interviewer concerned with the reliability and validity of his decisions. There is a good deal of evidence concerning the influence of variables which may make his decision both less reliable and valid.

With all this criticism, the question must arise as to why personnel managers continue to interview their job applicants. Before directly addressing this question, two broader issues should first be considered with regard to this research. The first issue was realized by Schmitt when he observed that most of the studies in his review tended to stress what is *wrong* with interview decisions. We believe that this statement could be applied to the great majority of studies in this area. Interview research has generally been preoccupied with identifying sources of error and bias in judgments of applicant suitability. Secondly, the criteria of applicant suitability for the jobs in question for so many of these studies have been globally desirable characteristics that would be preferred in an applicant for almost any job. Thus, it is difficult to accept at face value all the negative conclusions regarding the utility of the employment interview, when the emphasis on sources of judgmental error has pre-empted the investigation of what the interview might measure better. Also, the use of globally desirable applicant characteristics does not allow differential judgments of suitability for different jobs – often a very important part of the interviewer's task. Furthermore most interview research ignores one important role of the employment interview – one clearly recognized by personnel managers, and considered by us in the next section.

Who do we interview?

The interview is unquestionably the most widely used and popular method of selecting employees in business and industry (Bellows and Estep, 1954; Spriegel and James, 1958; Ulrich and Trumbo, 1965; Landy and Trumbo, 1980; Latham *et al.*, 1980). This remains true despite continual criticism of its apparent failure to demonstrate adequate levels of reliability and validity, and of its susceptibility to a variety of judgmental errors and biases (Mayfield, 1964; Webster, 1964; Ulrich and Trumbo, 1965; Wright, 1969; Schmitt, 1976; Dunnette and Borman, 1979). If the interview is such a poor assessment device, it is curious that it is so widely used by personnel managers who, much more than researchers, must be very pragmatic and sensitive to the issue of the utility of the methods available to them for selecting employees. So why is the interview so appealing to personnel managers? A review of interview practitioners' and personnel administrators' literature reveals that they see the employment interview providing important information about an applicant that cannot be obtained from other selection procedures.

First, it should be noted that no mystical properties are attributed to the interview by professional employment interviewers. The interview is not regarded as some magical process by which the best applicant for the job is somehow revealed. Nor is the interview considered so mysterious that it cannot be understood or evaluated. On the contrary, the interview is seen quite clearly as merely a measuring tool and, as such, its utility is evaluated by its ability to meet a simple test – it must predict future job behavior (Lopez, 1975). There are numerous manuals and practitioners' guides listing the type of questions to ask an applicant to elicit responses relevant to the prediction of future job performance (e.g. Black, 1970; Peskin, 1971; Fear, 1978). These manuals attribute poor reliability and validity of interview judgments to inexperienced or unqualified interviewers (Lopez, 1975), although this interpretation has not been empirically verified (Bernstein et al., 1975). In addition, Peskin (1971) has argued that efforts to validate interview judgments are misleading because employment interviewers are often required to make sub-optimal decisions due to a variety of pressures to fill job vacancies, such as personnel shortages, non-competitive salary scales, poor company image, accelerated expansion and growth, and high turnover rates. There may be, however, a more parsimonious explanation. Careful review of interview research indicates that, except for some recent exploratory studies (i.e. Jackson et al., 1980; Rothstein and Jackson, 1980), one primary role of the interview, as seen by interview practitioners and personnel administrators, has never been examined.

Practitioners argue that tests and other methods of assessment determine what a person *can* do, but not what a person *will* do (Peskin, 1971; Fear, 1978). Most methods of employee selection attempt to predict effective job performance with some measure of relevant ability, aptitude and experience. However, these variables are not the only things that predict successful job performance (Lopez, 1975). There is general agreement among interview practitioners that certain jobs require specific traits of personality, motivation and character (Black, 1970; Peskin, 1971; Lopez, 1975; Fear, 1978); and these traits can only be measured by the employment interview. While this latter point is not *necessarily* true (i.e. a job description may specify traits which can be measured by an existing standard inventory), there is no question that interviewers believe that it is true and, moreover, they behave as if it were true.

It is important to note here that interviewers are not using the term 'traits' to refer to global, socially-desirable characteristics that might be judged as preferable for any job. While such judgments might be made in an interview, the primary concern is the differential evaluation of traits that are deemed important, and even necessary, for different job requirements. Lopez (1975), for example, is quite clear in this regard when he states that 'no matter how socially desirable or undesirable a personal trait may be, it is of no significance unless it affects job performance' (p. 131). Peskin (1971) also refers to specific job-relevant personality traits that are predictive of performance criteria. He gives as an example 'the applicant who strongly resents carelessness, who insists on perfection in himself and others, and who is methodical and meticulous in attention to detail [who] may be excellent at record keeping, report work, meeting deadlines, and maintaining documentation' (p. 236).

Many other examples of this type are given in the interview practitioner literature. It seems clear from this literature that interviewers regard personality traits in much the same way as psychologists now do. Whereas psychologists generally regard traits as some type of predisposition determining in part the probability of occurrence of a certain class of behaviors, interviewers are concerned with traits that predict the probability of a very specific class of behaviors, those that are relevant to job performance. Furthermore, interviewers are aware of the concept of trait covariation. Although they may use such terms as trait constellations (Fear, 1978), or the incidence of certain traits in certain types of applicants (Peskin, 1971), interviewers are none the less implying the concept of trait covariation. This becomes apparent in their discussions of the interrelationships among traits within people and how the presence of a number of related traits may be inferred from a single act or statement made during the course of the interview (see Fear, 1978, pp. 142–57). This inference process is very functional for interviewers who, in a short period of time, must assess the characteristics of an applicant and judge his relevance for the job. Thus, it is *not* surprising that interviewers have developed their own implicit theories of personality to aid in the prediction of effective job performance. What *is* surprising is that these theories of trait inference, the assumed relationships between traits and job performance criteria, and the reliability and validity of interview-based judgments of personality, have so seldom been subjected to empirical test or theoretical scrutiny by interview researchers!

Later in this chapter we report some results from our research on the reliability and accuracy of interview-based judgments of personality, and on the trait inferential networks obtained from impressions of personality in the interview. But what of the 'assumed' relationships between personality traits and job performance criteria that must form the basis upon which personnel managers make their decisions? The existence of these relationships has been a very controversial issue in industrial/organizational psychology (Guion and Gottier, 1965). Because this issue is critical to the present topic, it warrants more detailed discussion. Before doing so, however, bear in mind that, regardless of whether or not specific personality traits are related to specific performance criteria, this is not the only relationship that personnel managers believe is crucial in determining whether or not an applicant's personality traits would be suitable for a particular job. For example, job applicants are often interviewed by the supervisor under whom they will be working. In such circumstances a major concern of the supervisor will be the nature of the interpersonal working relationship with the potential employee. Similarly, interviewers are often concerned with whether or not a job applicant will be able to interact effectively on an interpersonal level with his/her co-workers. When this type of interpersonal interaction, between co-workers, or between a supervisor and worker, is an essential component of a job, personnel managers will evaluate a job applicant's personality traits very carefully to determine their suitability for this aspect of the job.

Applicant personality traits may also be assessed with regard to their fit with a particular organizational climate. Organizational climate has been defined as a function of both individual and organizational characteristics (Tom, 1971; James and Jones, 1974). Delineation of organizational characteristics has led to descriptions of organizations that are strikingly similar to terms used to designate personality traits. For example, organizations may be described as fostering autonomy and independence, as requiring considerable affiliation with co-workers and colleagues, or as demanding perseverance and endurance with job duties. Organizational climate is clearly perceived by individuals both within and outside an organization. Furthermore, it has also been demonstrated that different climates are preferred by different individuals (Vroom, 1966; Tom, 1971; Feldman and Arnold, 1978). Thus, personnel managers may be concerned with the degree of fit between a potential employee and an organization's climate and the effect of this fit on future turnover, job satisfaction and productivity. It is also possible that personality traits are not valid as direct predictors of specific performance criteria for a given job, but may nevertheless act as moderating variables between such common predictors as ability and experience, and standard performance criteria. Such a relationship has been proposed by Hackman and Oldham (1976) with respect to a personality variable they call 'growth need strength'. According to Hackman and Oldham, individuals high on this trait will exhibit higher levels of motivation, quality of job performance, and job satisfaction when their jobs are enriched, compared to individuals low on 'growth need strength'. Although Hackman and Oldham's proposal is inadequate for describing the multidimensional nature of personality and the enormous variety of job performance criteria, it is a modest beginning to an appreciation of the role of personality in work behaviour. It seems, therefore, that while the precise nature of the relationship between personality traits and job performance criteria needs to be explicated in the eyes of many researchers, personnel managers have long recognized the importance of personality traits on the job. Furthermore, it is quite clear from the professional personnel literature that the assessment of applicant personality traits is regarded as an important function of the interview.

Personality and job performance

We mentioned previously that the relationship between personality traits and job performance criteria is a controversial topic in industrial/organizational psychology. Although there is a long history of predicting job performance from measures of personality (e.g. Wiggins, 1973), Guion and Gottier (1965), examining the validity of personality measures in personnel selection, concluded that such measures have not demonstrated general usefulness for this purpose. This paper has been widely cited as evidence that personality is not predictive of job performance criteria (e.g. Campbell *et al.*, 1970; Gough, 1976; Guion 1976; Korman, 1977; Landy and Trumbo, 1980). Since the basic assumption underlying the assessment of applicant personality traits in the employment interview is that these traits are relevant to future job performance, it is important to discuss briefly Guion and Gottier's paper.

Guion and Gottier examined the research on the validity of personality measures in personnel selection, published from 1952 to 1963, in two journals, the *Journal of Applied Psychology* and *Personnel Psychology*. Several rather severe restrictions were put on the criteria used for choosing studies to be included in their review. The most restrictive was that for a personality test or measure to be included in the review, it must have been used in at least *three* research studies, all reported in the two specified journals. A few exceptions to this rule were allowed for 'home-made' tests developed by specific organizations for specific needs, and for some projective measures. The intention of these restrictions was clearly to ensure a certain level of quality in the studies to be assessed. However, such a procedure also put strict limitations on the generalizability of Guion and Gottier's conclusions. For example, if a particular personality test or measure was found to be a valid predictor of job performance criteria, but was only reported in one published study, it was not included in the review. Guion and Gottier give no indication of the number of studies rejected for this reason, but a review of the more recent literature reveals examples of such studies that are methodologically sound and highly conclusive (e.g. Ghiselli, 1969; Azen *et al.*, 1973; Landy, 1976; Edwards, 1977). Furthermore, once a test has been found to be a valid predictor on one occasion, journal editors' concern for unique contributions, as well as space limitations, are likely to exclude cross-validation studies. Guion and Gottier's strategy for choosing studies to review would thus appear to be far too conservative, and too likely to result in a substantial underestimation of the effects of personality on job behavior.

Not only did Guion and Gottier err in their choice of studies to exclude from their review, they apparently also erred in their choice of studies to include. Of the 134 research articles discussed, a total of only fifty-nine (44 per cent) can truly be considered studies that examine the relationship between *personality* and job performance. The other seventy-five studies (56 per cent) involve tests which either cannot be considered to be tests of personality or are inappropriate for use in personnel selection. For example, seventeen of the studies employed 'tests' that were actually personal history data forms. A further forty-two studies made use of vocational interest tests to predict job performance, a purpose for which they were never designed or constructed. Vocational interest tests are intended to identify interests that are in common with various occupational criterion groups. At best they have been shown to predict job satisfaction, but there is little rational or theoretical justification for their use as a predictor of job performance. Another sixteen studies used projective tests (Rorschach, Sentence Completion) and tests of psychopathology (MMPI), which again were never intended for use in predicting job-related criteria, and which furthermore have not demonstrated acceptable levels of reliability and validity.

The restriction that studies would only be chosen from two journals must also be questioned. These journals are pre-eminent in their field, but are by no means the only journals to publish studies in personnel selection. By selectively reviewing only studies that appeared in these two journals, Guion and Gottier undoubtedly missed a considerable amount of research which might have significantly altered their conclusions. In addition, personnel selection research is often carried out by organizations 'in house', a major proportion of which is not published (Campbell *et al.*, 1970). A few such research projects which have successfully used personality tests as predictors of job performance have recently come to our attention. They include the use of personality measures to predict performance in a wide variety of state civil service commission jobs (Cheloha *et al.*, 1977). Other unpublished research projects of this type are discussed by Campbell *et al.* (1970). Guion and Gottier cannot, of course, be faulted for overlooking research that was inaccessible to them or not available at the time. However, the fact that such research exists once again limits the present generalizability of their conclusions.

Finally, Guion and Gottier did not take into account the potential contribution made by personality measures to other predictors of job performance. Studies were chosen which considered personality as the *sole* predictor of performance criteria. Studies which used personality measures with a battery of other tests were not included in the review. Such studies would have been extremely important to the discussion since they would have demonstrated the increment in predictive validity provided by personality measures in a selection situation. Ignoring these studies substantially undervalues the true role of personality in predicting job performance. In general, then, Guion and Gottier set inappropriate criteria for choosing studies to be reviewed, so their conclusions that personality measures have no utility for personnel selection clearly cannot be accepted. Moreover, there is considerable evidence both that personality is related to specific job performance criteria (Ghiselli, 1969; Azen *et al.*, 1973; Wiggins, 1973; Landy, 1976; Cheloha *et al.*, 1977; Edwards, 1977), and that personnel managers advocate the inclusion of personality information in the employee selection process. Hence an investigation of the utility of assessing applicant personality traits in the employment interview is most certainly warranted.

Personality assessment in the employment interview

If we assume that applicants' pesonality traits are at least potentially important in the personnel selection process, we should at this point briefly discuss why personnel managers believe that the interview is the most appropriate place to assess such traits. One reason may be the belief that personality constructs relevant to job behavior are not measured by published tests and scales. There are a limited number of personality inventories available that have acceptable levels of reliability and validity and are not confounded with response biases (Wiggins, 1973). This limits the number of personality constructs available for use in selection, and implies a low probability that these constructs will meet the varied requirements of an infinite number of jobs. Personnel managers may have simply given up looking for published measures of the personality constructs they require, and hence become dependent on the interview as the preferred method of assessing these traits. Indeed, many industrial/organizational psychologists no doubt reinforced this belief with their contention that published personality inventories are not effective for personnel selection (Guion and Gottier, 1965).

Another reason for assessing applicant personality traits in the interview is the absence of trait-oriented information in most job descriptions. Although common job analysis procedures (Blum and Naylor, 1968) could easily be adapted to determine the personality characteristics required for a given job, this rarely occurs. Thus pesonnel managers and interviewers, faced with a job description containing a rather sterile list of the knowledge, skills, behaviors and task requirements necessary for a job, are left to make up their own minds which personality traits would be important for the job in question. Since most of the characteristics found in the average job description are measured best by empirically validated tests and personal data forms, personnel managers would logically conclude that the interview could be used most efficiently to assess personality traits and other personal characteristics.

If job descriptions do not commonly include personality traits relevant for a given job, personnel managers and interviewers must have some implicit notions of which traits are suitable for different jobs. This would be a fundamental prerequisite to making a decision on the basis of an assessment of an applicant's personality traits. The existence of stable *implicit personality theories* has been well documented (Bruner and Taguiri, 1954; Lay and Jackson, 1969), but these implicit theories must be relevant to the world of work if interviewers are to make use of them to select employees. This means that personality characteristics must be differentially judged appropriate for different jobs. Although interviewers hold common conceptions of generally desirable personality attributes of a good job applicant (Wright *et al.*, 1967; Hakel and Schuh, 1971; Shaw, 1972; Keenan, 1976), evidence has been lacking about the ways in which personality characteristics are perceived as being differentially relevant for widely different occupations.

Recently, Jackson *et al.* (1982) examined this issue by surveying professional employment interviewers to determine how they perceived the suitability of a number of personality characteristics for a series of different occupations. A sample of 132 recruitment interviewers (representing a 45 per cent return rate) from 138 companies in Canada and the United States were asked to imagine a typical person employed in each of fifteen occupations and to judge how characteristic or uncharacteristic (on a 9-point scale) a series of personality traits would be of that person. The fifteen occupations, sampling a wide variety of occupational groups, have been shown to be relatively independent of each other (Siess and Jackson, 1970). Each occupation was followed by a one-paragraph job description and a list of twenty conceptually distinct personality traits taken from Jackson's (1974) Personality Research Form (PRF). The PRF trait definitions were presented on a separate sheet for easy reference.

Each judge's ratings were conceived of as representing a set of perceived interpoint distances between each occupation and each personality trait. Using a modification of *multidimensional successive intervals scaling* and *singular value   decomposition*, the personality scales were reduced to a more parsimonious set of dimensions. This scaling procedure permitted each occupation to be represented as a set of projections on these dimensions. Eight dimensions, each showing very strong evidence of stability and replicability and accounting for 97.36 per cent of the variance, were extracted and interpreted.

Table 7.1   Projections of occupations on reference axes defined by personality traits

	Dimension							
	I	II	III	IV	V	VI	VII	VIII
Carpenter	-0.76	-0.77	0.40	-1.23	-2.03	-0.12	-0.40	0.68
Veterinarian	-0.83	-0.23	1.15	0.97	0.30	-0.91	-2.10	0.68
Life insurance salesperson	0.37	0.91	1.53	0.85	-1.16	1.16	-0.35	1.08
Orchestral librarian	-1.18	-1.89	0.16	-0.03	-0.80	-0.58	0.58	-1.15
Personnel manager	0.13	0.02	-0.17	0.64	0.67	1.13	-1.19	-1.53
Accountant	-1.30	0.84	0.83	-0.26	0.25	1.06	2.26	0.11
Advertising person	2.69	-1.52	0.39	-0.92	-0.15	0.03	0.31	-0.52
Architect	0.25	-1.18	0.23	-0.28	2.22	1.14	0.26	1.80
Computer programmer	-0.74	0.34	-1.28	-0.79	0.55	-1.08	0.58	0.54
Mathsolidus/science teacher	-0.14	-0.02	0.96	1.39	1.11	-1.45	0.77	-1.37
Purchasing agent	-0.01	0.88	0.05	-1.24	-0.30	0.76	-0.17	-1.23
Industrial supervisor	0.41	1.57	-0.65	-0.34	0.14	0.56	-0.61	-0.90
Coach	1.54	1.12	-0.29	0.98	-0.81	-1.52	1.00	0.89
Secretary	-0.24	-0.73	-2.58	1.74	-0.72	0.98	0.03	0.38
Mechanical engineer	-0.21	0.66	-0.74	-1.49	0.73	-1.15	-0.98	0.54

Note: Trait dimensions were defined by the following salients: 1 (+) thrill-seeking, impulsivity, changeable, attention-seeking, fun-loving, aggressive, sociable, ambitious, dominant, independent, (–) meek, seeks definiteness, orderly; II (+) dominant, ambitious, aggressive, persistent, (–) aesthetic, meek; III (+) persistent, (–) seeks help and advice; IV (+) supporting, sociable; V (+) intellectually curious; VI (+) approval-seeking; VII (+) defensive; VIII (+) ambitious, independent.

Table 7.1 illustrates the reduced rank transformation of the personality scales. The projections of the occupations on these axes reflect the degree to which occupations were judged by employment interviewers to be identified with certain prototypic personality constellations. Figure 7.1 illustrates the occupations plotted within the first two trait-defined dimensions. The first trait-defined personality dimension (Impulse Expression vs. Impulse Control) contrasts *advertising person* and *accountant*. Thus, an advertising person was seen as thrill-seeking, impulsive, changeable, attention seeking and fun-loving, while an accountant was perceived as meek, seeking definiteness and orderly. These results are highly consistent with those of Siess and Jackson (1970), who obtained self-report measures of personality and vocational interests, and also found a dimension defined at one pole by the PRF scales of impulsivity, change and autonomy and the occupation of advertising person, and at the other pole by the PRF scales of order and cognitive structure and the occupation of accountant. Also of note in the Jackson *et al.* (1982) results is that *computer programmers* were judged to be on the impulse control pole of the first dimension. This is also consistent with data reported by Woodruff (1980), who identified the PRF scale of cognitive structure as among the highest for 202 data processing personnel.

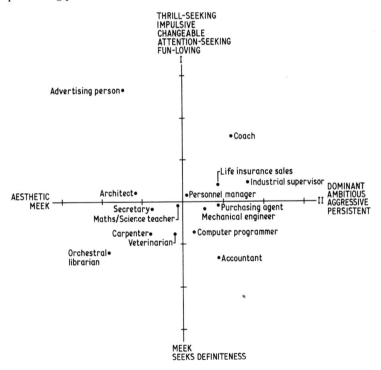

Fig. 7.1 Occupational locations in trait-defined space based on multidimensional scaling of employment interviewers' judgments: Dimension I – impulse expression vs. impulse control; Dimension II – aggressive leadership.

The second trait-defined personality dimension (aggressive leadership) contrasts personality traits for dominance, ambition, aggression and persistence with those of aesthetic and meek. The occupations defining the positive pole (*industrial supervisor, coach*) have a strong element of interpersonal influence, where the influence frequently involves direct, dominant behavior. The occupations defining the negative pole (*orchestral librarian, architect*), while sharing some interpersonal requirements, are notable for the absence of dominant, aggressive content. Again, the judgments of employment interviewers were similar to data derived from the objective findings of Siess and Jackson, who identified a similar dimension marked by PRF scales for dominance and aggression versus abasement.

The results of the Jackson *et al.* study clearly suggest that professional employment interviewers have highly differentiated and reliable implicit notions of the personality traits suitable for a number of different occupations. These implicit theories exist despite the fact that the personality traits are not articulated in the job descriptions. It is important to note as well that the interviewers in this study were not simply employing stereotypes of the appropriate traits for these occupations. Stereotypes are generally regarded as both oversimplified and inaccurate (e.g Katz and Braly, 1933). In the present study, the number of dimensions obtained by the interviewers' judgments imply a good deal of differentiation, rather than simplification. In addition, although we need to check whether personality traits *seen* to be characteristic of the various occupations really are characteristic of them (see Woodruff, 1980, for one example), the fact that the ratings obtained in this study were very consistent with the empirical results of Siess and Jackson (1970) is very encouraging.

While Jackson *et al.*'s (1982) results strongly suggest that employment interviewers hold stable implicit theories of the covariation between certain personality characteristics and their suitability for a number of different occupations, these results do not indicate how interviewers judge personality traits in a selection interview, or whether such judgments may be used as a basis for suitability and selection decisions for a given job. It is just these latter type of judgments that personnel managers and professional interviewers claim are such an important part of the employment interview. Thus, the interview appears to be an ideal arena for studying personality inferences and implicit personality theory. Because the judging of applicant personality characteristics is highly purposeful, interviewers will be very motivated to make their judgments as accurate as possible, and as meaningful to the job in question as possible.

In order to study these judgmental processes, and to determine their potential impact on personnel selection practices, we have recently undertaken a number of experimental investigations of personality assessment in the employment interview. Laboratory studies seem to be the preferred method of investigating decision-making processes in the interview for a number of important reasons. Peskin (1971) points out that employment interviewers are often required to make sub-optimal decisions due to the variety of pressures we have already listed. If sub-optimal decisions are being made in the interview for any of these reasons, then field studies of these decisions are bound to be non-productive. An additional problem with field studies of the interview is that the predictive validity of interview-based decisions is most often confounded with the overall selection decision. Since such selection decisions are based on a variety of information about the applicant, such as test scores, biographical data, letters of reference and application blanks, as well as an interview, it would be difficult or impossible to distinguish the effects of the various influences. Other difficulties that have plagued field research in this area have been interviewers' probable unfamiliarity with actual job-related activities, and the undependability of estimates of validity when criterion measures are fallible, and the fact that criterion data are not available on all applicants, particularly rejected ones.

All these problems have led many researchers to recommend undertaking experimental analyses of the interview. Dunnette and Borman (1979) have explicitly suggested that such analyses would profit from attention to the person perception literature in understanding how interviewers develop accurate perceptions of applicants. Moreover, experimental subjects appear to make judgments similar to those obtained from professional interviewers in terms of variability in judgments, inter-rater reliabilities, and main effects due to independent variables (Bernstein et al., 1975; Dunnette and Borman, 1979). This means data generated from experimental studies of the interview can be used to make concrete practical suggestions for personnel interviewers (Schmitt, 1976). In our view, since personnel managers and professional interviewers have emphasized the need to evaluate applicant personality characteristics in the employment interview, this type of assessment is a prime subject for experimental study. Laboratory studies of personality assessment in a simulated employment interview may be especially helpful in determining the parameters which affect the reliability and validity of judgments of this type. The results from one of our first experiments of this type (Rothstein and Jackson, 1980) strongly suggest that stable and reliable implicit notions of trait covariation may be utilized in the employment interview, and that the interview may indeed be an effective method of accurately assessing applicant personality characteristics, and judging their suitability for a given job.

Rothstein and Jackson used the inferential accuracy model of social perception (Jackson, 1972) in a simulated employment interview to investigate how interviewers perceive and evaluate the personality characteristics of job applicants for two specific jobs. Inferential accuracy is defined in terms of the interviewer's ability, given limited information about a target person, to judge other pertinent characteristics about that person correctly and to identify behavioral exemplars as part of a pattern of behavioral consistencies. The model postulates that two distinct processes underlie conceptions of behavioral covariation, and that individuals vary with respect to these processes. The first process, *sensitivity*, refers to individual differences in awareness of the shared implicit network of behavioral consistencies. The second process, *threshold*, refers to individual differences in readiness to attribute behaviors to others based on the implicative relations among behaviors.

Sensitivity is estimated by the correlations between an individual's judgments of the inferential relations between behaviors with regard to a target and some criterion that also assesses the target's characteristics. The criterion most often employed, if the target's self-reported characteristics are unavailable, is the group consensus regarding the order of behaviors within the target person, since the consensus of a large number of judges has been shown to relate to actual behavior covariation (Lay and Jackson, 1969; Lay *et al.*, 1973; Reed and Jackson, 1975; Jackson *et al.*, 1979). Thus, in Figure 7.2 the judged average scale scores for a given target are: Scale A – 1.0, Scale B – 3.0, Scale C – 5.0, Scale D – 7.0 and Scale E – 9.0. Judge 1 has rated the target in this example with scale scores of 1.0, 3.0, 5.0, 7.0 and 9.0, and Judge 2 has given ratings of 3.0 for each scale. Since Judge 1 mirrors the group consensus exactly, this judge would be highly *sensitive* to the consensus regarding the behavior covariation in the target. Judge 2, however, appears to pattern the ratings independently of the group consensus, thus providing evidence of lack of *sensitivity*.

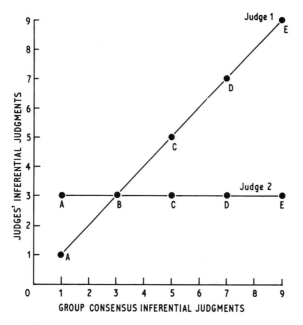

Fig. 7.2 Inferential judgments of two hypothetical judges differing in sensitivity on five traits, A–E.

Threshold is estimated by the average rating given targets by each judge. Because a low mean rating indicates a reluctance to attribute traits, the mean value must be reflected around the midpoint of the 9-point scale used to make the ratings, so that the magnitude of the resulting threshold estimate will be consistent with the definition of threshold. Thus, in the example given above, Judge 1 is more willing to attribute traits to the target on Scales C, D and E than Judge 2, and therefore Judge 1 has a lower threshold for attributing traits related to these scales. Similarly, both judges have an equal threshold for traits related to Scale B, and Judge 1 has a higher threshold for traits related to Scale A.

In the Rothstein and Jackson experiment subjects were asked to role play an employment interviewer seeking to hire either an engineer or an accountant. The job description given to subjects was either the job label (engineer or accountant), or the job label plus a short description of the type of person stated to be well suited for that job. These descriptions were based on the definitions of the personality traits used to create the target applicants (described below). Subjects listened to excerpts from a (simulated) employment interview, then made several decisions about the suitability of the applicant for the job for which he was ostensibly being interviewed. In addition, subjects were instructed to estimate, on the basis of what they had learned about the applicant they had heard being interviewed on the audiotape, the likelihood that the applicant would respond 'true' to a number of items from a modified form of the Personality Research Form (Jackson, 1974). These judgments were used to obtain *sensitivity* and *threshold* levels for each subject, and to determine the reliability and accuracy of the subjects' perceptions of the applicants' personality characteristics.

Information about the applicants was given to the subjects in the form of a number of self-referent statements made during the course of the interview. These statements were created from the definitions of specified scales of the Personality Research Form (PRF) and were chosen on the basis of an earlier empirical study (Siess and Jackson, 1970). Siess and Jackson factor analyzed the PRF and the Strong Vocational Interest Blank (SVIB) and identified seven bipolar dimensions representing common variance underlying vocational interests and personality. Two of these dimensions (illustrated in Figure 7.3) were characterized by the occupational interest scales for engineer and accountant. The PRF scales, which also loaded highly on these dimensions, were used to create the two target applicants who were evaluated in the interview. This personality information has no demonstrated criterion validity for the occupations of engineer and accountant, but this was not problematic for the main purposes of the Rothstein and Jackson experiment, which was to investigate the *process* by which interviewers form an impression of a job applicant. In sum, Rothstein and Jackson systematically varied:

(a) the job applicant target (i.e. the personality traits congruent with the occupational interest scales for engineer and accountant);

(b) the job for which the applicant was presumably applying (engineer or accountant); and

(c) the amount of job information given to subjects.

The purpose of the experiment was to investigate the potential of the interview for evaluating accurately the personality characteristics of job applicants.

The results suggest reliable and accurate assessments of applicants' personality can be made in the employment interview. First, the reliability of the personality judgments is measured, by calculating a

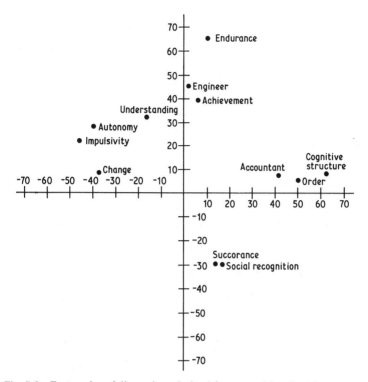

Fig. 7.3 Factor plot of dimensions derived from a multimethod factor analysis of the PRF and SVIB (Siess and Jackson, 1970). Factor I – technically oriented achievement; Factor III – impulse control versus expression.

profile of judged scale scores for each applicant. Then subjects were randomly split into groups, for each applicant target, and judgmental profiles for each group were intercorrelated. The split-half inter-rater reliability coefficients were 0.99 for both targets. To determine whether these extremely high reliabilities for judgments of personality were perhaps confounded with some type of global desirability judgment, the judgmental profiles for each group were also correlated with a vector of desirability scale scores for each scale of the PRF (Jackson, 1974, p. 12) and the results clearly exclude the desirability stereotype interpretation. The profile generated for the first target was relatively uncorrelated with that for the second target, (0.44–0.49), whereas the intra-target correlations were high, indicating that the two profiles were perceived as substantively unique and not based on global

desirability judgments. In addition, neither profile correlated to any
great degree with the desirability scale scores (0.24–0.29). In fact
when desirability was partialed out of the reliability coefficients, they
both remained at 0.99.

Another index of the reliability of the personality judgments in this
experiment derives from analysis of *sensitivity* scores. Figure 7.4 illustrates the frequency distributions of sensitivity scores for the four
conditions in which subjects were exposed to a common target and
common instructions. The large number of subjects with high

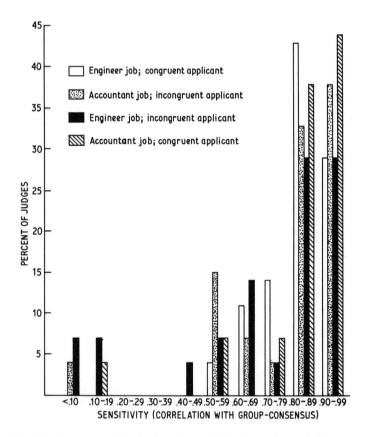

Fig. 7.4 Frequency distribution of sensitivity for each condition, as estimated by the correlation between group consensus judgments and an individual's judgments of the likelihood that targets would manifest certain behaviours.

sensitivity scores shows the majority were highly knowledgeable about, and able to use in their judgments, the consensus about the covariation of traits in the target applicants. A few low scores indicate there were a few individuals who made quite different judgments from those of the group consensus.

Accuracy of the personality judgments was determined by the analysis of *threshold* scores. These were calculated for each subject by averaging their rating on items for each scale of the PRF. Averaged over subjects the mean threshold levels for each target are shown in Table 7.2. These average thresholds reflect the degree to which traits underlying each scale were attributed to targets. For each of the 'marker' scales used to create targets, subjects attributed significantly different traits to the appropriate target. Moreover, the pattern of these attributions accurately reflected the information given in the audiotape of the simulated interview. Another very important aspect of these attributions, which reveals the extensiveness of subjects' knowledge of the implicative relations among traits in the targets, is also illustrated in Table 7.2. The direction of the differences between the original PRF factor loadings obtained by Siess and Jackson (1970) for the two dimensions highlighted by the engineer and accountant scales of the SVIB is identical to the direction of the differences between the mean threshold levels obtained by subjects for the two targets. This is the case for *all* of the PRF scales in which the mean threshold levels were significantly different, *even though five of these scales were not marker scales for either target*. Thus, subjects not only accurately judged the salient personality characteristics of the applicants, but in addition were able to make use of their implicit conceptions of trait covariation to attribute a further pattern of characteristics in the applicants which accurately matched the empirical covariation of these characteristics found by Siess and Jackson.

A further indication of the potential utility of the employment interview for assessing applicant personality characteristics was found in the subjects' judgments of applicant suitability for the job. A multivariate analysis of variance of suitability judgments resulted in a significant multivariate F only for the Applicant Target × Job Category, $F(4,99) = 11.38$, $p < 0.00001$, and the Applicant Target × Job Category × Amount of Job Information, $F(4,99) = 3.69$, $p < 0.01$, interactions. Subsequent univariate F tests on these interactions for each dependent measure showed a pattern similar to the multivariate analysis, for each measure except 'certainty of decision' where F values were nonsignificant.

Table 7.2 Comparison of mean threshold levels obtained in social perception task with factor loadings obtained empirically by Siess and Jackson

	Mean threshold levels		Significance of t-test between mean threshold levels	Siess and Jackson factor loadings	
	Engineer target	Accountant target		Technically oriented achievement	Impulse control v. expression
Abasement	3.89	4.23	n.s.	0.05	−0.16
Achievement[1]	7.35	6.47	0.0001	0.39	0.06
Affiliation	3.98	4.47	0.03	−0.13	0.14
Aggression	5.13	4.79	n.s.	0.00	0.03
Autonomy[2]	6.45	4.38	0.0001	0.28	−0.40
Change[2]	6.15	3.15	0.0001	0.08	0.38
Cognitive structure[2]	5.89	7.44	0.0001	0.08	0.62
Defendence	5.15	5.38	n.s.	−0.16	−0.09
Dominance	5.93	4.80	0.0001	0.03	−0.04
Endurance[1]	6.98	6.33	0.004	0.65	0.10
Exhibition	4.96	3.87	0.0001	−0.19	−0.32
Harm avoidance	4.68	6.95	0.0001	−0.18	0.12
Impulsivity[2]	3.30	2.51	0.001	0.22	0.46
Nurturance	3.75	4.39	0.001	0.04	0.07
Order[2]	6.69	7.63	0.0001	0.05	0.50
Play	3.68	3.26	n.s.	0.01	0.04
Sentience	4.38	4.63	n.s.	−0.04	−0.02
Social recognition[1]	3.01	5.62	0.0001	−0.30	0.16
Succorance[1]	3.05	4.90	0.0001	−0.30	0.14
Understanding[1]	6.73	5.27	0.0001	0.32	−0.17
Engineer	—	—	—	0.45	0.02
Accountant	—	—	—	0.07	0.41

[1] Marker scales for engineer target.

[2] Marker scales for accountant target.

The mean differences between conditions in the Applicant Target × Job Category interaction on the three significant dependent measures indicated that when subjects were instructed to evaluate the applicant for a job as an engineer (or accountant), and when the applicant displayed personality characteristics congruent with the occupation, then subjects rated the target as more suitable, more likely to be satisfied with his work, and more likely to be hired. These mean differences were all significant at the 0.05 level, or better.

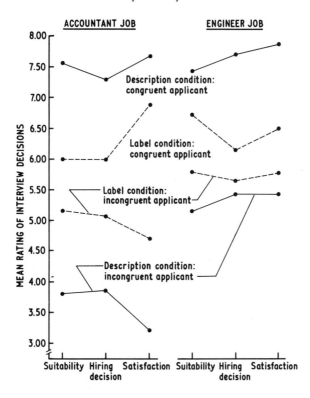

Fig. 7.5 Mean selection decisions in the applicant target × job category × amount of job information interaction.

The Applicant Target × Job Category × Amount of Job Information interaction (Figure 7.5) demonstrates that subjects rated the target whose personality characteristics were congruent with the occupation higher on all three dependent measures when they were given more detailed criterion information regarding a suitable applicant. These results are consistent with other interview research which has reported significant increases in the reliability and accuracy of interviewers' judgments about an applicant as more relevant job information is made available (Langdale and Weitz, 1973; Weiner and Schneiderman, 1974; Peters and Terborg, 1975).

In sum, Rothstein and Jackson (1980) demonstrated that judgments of personality characteristics of two applicants were highly reliable, were not based on a global desirability stereotype, and were substantively unique to each target. A majority of subjects were highly aware of, and able to use in their judgments, the consensus regarding the covariation of traits relevant to the two applicants, although some subjects were less aware of this consensus. Subjects attributed a pattern of perceived and inferred personality characteristics to the applicants which accurately reflected the brief information subjects could distill from the audio recording of the interview, and which closely matched the empirical covariation of these traits found by Siess and Jackson (1970). Finally, subjects were clearly able to judge accurately the suitability of a job applicant for the job in question, especially when the job description was 'worker-oriented' (Landy and Trumbo, 1980) and included personality traits regarded as important for the job.

The results of this experiment are very encouraging, both to researchers interested in implicit personality theory and to personnel practitioners who have long argued for the utility of the employment interview. Subjects in this study were able to use their implicit notions of trait covariation to aid them in a practical, decision-making task, probably not unlike a professional employment interviewer. Of course, the criterion validity of the judgments of applicant personality requires confirmation. Nevertheless, the results of this study clearly suggest that personality characteristics of job applicants may be reliably and accurately assessed in the employment interview, just as personnel managers and interviewers have long stated.

The role of desirability of self-presentation and work experience

A number of other experiments have subsequently been undertaken in our laboratory to investigate other potential factors that may affect interviewer judgments of applicant personality traits and to determine the generalizability of these findings to other occupational groups, personality traits and subjects (judges). Jackson *et al.*, (1980) reported three studies of the effects of the desirability of a job applicant's style of self-presentation and relevant previous work experience on interviewers' and other judges' ratings of suitability. These studies used basically the same experimental paradigm as Rothstein and Jackson (1980). Several different occupations were chosen for study, each one representing a pole from one of the vocational interest and personality dimensions found by Siess and Jackson (1970). Job applicants' educational level was held constant for all three studies. Experience was held constant for the first two studies but was varied systematically in the third. Unlike the Rothstein and Jackson study, Jackson *et al.* presented information to the subjects in the form of written transcripts of the interview. Also, the statements reflecting personality characteristics made by the job applicants in the interview transcripts were actual PRF items selected to indicate the particular personality traits related to each occupation. This procedure was used to control more rigorously for the desirability of the applicants' statements. Each transcript was followed by a set of rating scales in which judgments were made of employee suitability and predicted on-the-job performance.

In the first study, four occupations were selected from opposite poles of two of the Siess and Jackson (1970) dimensions. *Accountant*, associated with personality scales of cognitive structure and order, was contrasted with *advertising person*, associated with personality scales for autonomy, change and impulsivity. *Industrial supervisor*, associated with personality scales of aggression and dominance, was contrasted with the occupation of *orchestral librarian*, associated with personality scales of abasement and harm avoidance. Two interview transcripts were prepared for each occupation, one which was positively congruent (i.e. the applicant's statements reflected the personality traits associated with the occupation as indicated by Siess and Jackson), and the other which was negatively congruent (i.e. the applicant's statements reflected the personality traits associated with the occupation on the opposite pole of the dimension). Subjects were assigned randomly to positive and negative congruence conditions, and given a booklet containing job descriptions and four interview transcripts in random order. A 2 × 4 (congruence × occupation) repeated measures analysis of variance was computed for each dependent measure; main effects for both congruence and occupation were obtained (the interaction was not significant) for each dependent variable. The large and highly significant differences between the positive and negative congruent conditions indicate that when personality information in the interview transcript was consistent with Siess and Jackson's (1970) findings, judges were more likely to find the applicant suitable, and predicted higher on-the-job performance than when the information was negatively congruent. Also, the main effect for occupation suggests that judges made differential use of personality information in evaluating applicant characteristics for different occupations. Thus, in this first study the positive congruence of personality information to job clearly exerted a strong positive effect on the rating of suitability of job applicants.

In their second study, Jackson *et al.* examined the effects of 'neutral' personality characteristics (i.e. traits falling in the neutral range of the occupational dimensions obtained by Siess and Jackson), and the desirability of self-referent statements made in the interview, on subsequent suitability judgments. To extend ecological validity, professional employment interviewers were used as judges in this study. Four occupations (*engineer, guidance counsellor, writer of radio advertising copy* and *statistician*) were used, each representing a different Siess and Jackson orthogonal factor from those used in the first study. Interview transcripts for each of the four jobs were prepared for three congruence conditions: positive, neutral or negative. PRF items embedded in the interview also varied in desirability (high or low). The design was a $4 \times 3 \times 2$ (occupation $\times$ congruence $\times$ desirability) analysis of variance, with subjects nested within congruence $\times$ desirability. In addition to the dependent measures used in the first study, a 9-point rating of 'How suitable would this applicant be as an employee in any job?' was obtained.

For the suitability rating, there were significant main effects found for all three factors; the congruence $\times$ occupation, desirability $\times$ occupation, and congruence $\times$ desirability $\times$ occupation interactions were all significant (but not the congruence $\times$ desirability interaction). The most important finding was that, in general, the mean suitability rating based on neutral information fell between those for positively and negatively congruent information, which clearly suggests a continuum of personality information varying in congruence with the occupation. In addition, job applicants described in the high desirability transcripts were for the most part (the one exception was the neutral transcript for statistician) chosen as being more suitable than applicants having transcripts constructed from items low in desirability. These findings were identical for the results of the analysis of predicted performance on the job.

The significant desirability $\times$ job interaction suggests that self-presentation desirability is differentially relevant to different occupations. Certain jobs require different amounts of contact with clients and co-workers, and for it to have any influence, desirability must be relevant to the job. A guidance counselor would have far more interpersonal interactions than a statistician, for example, and interpersonal skills would more freqently be called on, so the desirability of a candidate's self-presentation would be more relevant to the first occupation than to the second. This interpretation is supported in the Siess and Jackson (1970) study by the high loading for the PRF desirability scale on the dimension on which guidance counselor was also salient. It makes sense, therefore, for interviewers to be sensitive to desirability of self-presentation style. Compare the plots of the interactions of personality congruence and desirability for engineer and guidance counselor, shown in Figure 7.7. For engineer, the effects of desirability operate within the context of the powerful effects of the relevance or congruence of the personality information; for guidance counselor, although there is a marked effect of congruence for the high desirability condition, this effect was obliterated under the low desirability conditions. However congruent the personality may be to the job, selection interviewers see little merit in an applicant for the position of guidance counselor who is self-deprecating in recounting personally important events, or who is maladroit in putting his or her best foot forward.

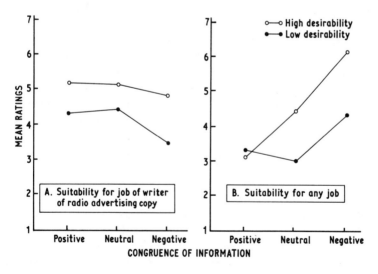

Fig. 7.6 Congruence of information × desirability interaction for ratings of suitability.

Regarding the rating 'How suitable would this applicant be as an employee for any job?', the data reveal a strong effect for the desirability of self-presentation manipulation and for occupation, but not for congruence. The main effect for occupation suggests that whether an applicant's mode of self-presentation was seen as being desirable or not for any job was influenced by the particular job for which he or she was applying. Further, the significant congruence × desirability interaction suggests that the influence of personality congruence on the ratings of suitability for any job was job-specific as well. In any case, there does not seem to be the same consistent effect of congruence on ratings of general desirability of self-presentation, as was obtained for the suitability and on-the-job performance ratings (i.e. the irrelevant data were seen as neutral). This observation is in accord with the non-significance of the congruence main effect on the general desirability ratings.

The distinction between the differential evaluations made for a specific occupation and a general evaluation for any job may be best illustrated by a comparison of the respective ratings for the occupation *writer of radio advertising copy* (Figure 7.6). The Siess and Jackson study suggested that advertising was high on impulsivity, change and autonomy, and low on order and cognitive structure. Advertisers thus appear to share characteristics somewhat below average in judged desirability, based on PRF standardization data (Jackson, 1974). But Figure 7.6A indicates that congruent personality information (i.e. personality traits implying impulse expression) tends to yield higher ratings for suitability for advertising writers. The situation is dramatically reversed when the rating is for the suitability of the candidate for any job (Figure 7.6B), in which case the incongruent personality information (implying impulse control) is markedly preferred. Clearly, for the average job, traits preferred for advertising persons are anathema.

In their third experiment, Jackson *et al.* replicated the basic design of the first study (i.e. the occupation and congruence factors were identical), but in addition applicant experience (0 or 3 years of job related experience) was included as a factor. Once again, the main effects for occupation and congruence were significant for both ratings of suitability and predicted job performance, that is, previous results were replicated. Surprisingly, there was no effect of level of applicant experience, and no significant interactions. Apparently, judges in this study perceived congruence between personality and job to be more critical in predicting suitability and expected job performance than actual past experience. It is also possible, of course, that even three

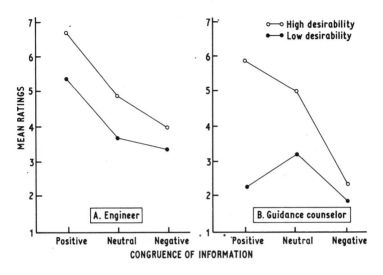

Fig. 7.7 Congruence of information × desirability interaction.

years' experience is not sufficient to affect interviewers' judgments. Also, experience may have been discounted by judges because no information about success was provided.

In sum, Rothestein and Jackson's (1980) and Jackson *et al.*'s (1980) studies clearly suggest that implicit personality theory plays a functional role in the employment interview. Interviewers are exposed to only a small subset of applicant behavior and from this limited information inferences regarding broader constructs, as well as appropriate decisions, must be made. With regard to applicant personality information, our research program strongly indicates that these inferences and decisions are highly reliable and appropriate. Applicant personality characteristics were assessed with a high degree of reliability and accuracy, and judgments of job suitability and predicted performance were made which were highly consistent with results derived empirically from occupational interest personality scale data. These findings were obtained across a number of different occupations and personality trait and were apparently more important to subjects' judgments than applicant experience or the general desirability of the self-referent statements made. Clearly, such results support the idea that there are stable implicit conceptions of personality (Bruner and Taguiri, 1954; Lay and Jackson, 1969), and that these implicit personality theories have reference to the world of work.

It is important to note that the research does not prove that the differential judgments of job suitability based on personality information are necessarily valid. That is, there are no data as yet which demonstrate that the personality characteristics judged to be suitable for a given job are in fact predictive of successful job performance. Indeed, the literature shows a remarkable dearth of studies of the discriminant validity of personality information derived from an employment interview. Such data, however, would be extremely difficult to obtain because of the problems of small sample sizes, restricted range of attributes represented by employees already on the job, and variability in job duties and performance criteria across positions which have the same job label. But even in the absence of criterion validity data, the results from our research program provide a unique understanding of the employment interview decision process and the factors which may affect an interviewer's perception and evaluation of a job applicant. Moreover, given the widespread use of the employment interview (Landy and Trumbo, 1980; Latham *et al.*, 1980), and the explicit recommendation by professionals in the field that one of the primary functions of the interview is to assess applicant personality (Black, 1970; Peskin, 1971; Lopez, 1975; Fear, 1978), our data clearly suggest that the interview is more useful than its critics (Wagner, 1949; Mayfield, 1964; Ulrich and Trumbo, 1965) suppose.

As previously noted, critics of the interview have uniformly condemned it as lacking acceptable levels of reliability and validity (Mayfield, 1964; Webster, 1964; Ulrich and Trumbo, 1965; Wright, 1969; Schmitt, 1976; Dunnette and Borman, 1979). Yet, in our research, we have found that personality may be reliably and accurately assessed by interview, and may be used as the basis of occupational suitability judgments which parallel independent empirical findings (although not yet evaluated for criterion validity). How then do we account for this discrepancy? We believe there is a very straightforward answer. Quite simply, almost none of the enormous number of research studies has examined personality either with respect to its accessibility for evaluation in the interview, or its relevance for different jobs. Thus, it may well be that the factors investigated in the majority of interview research are too susceptible to judgmental error to be effectively evaluated by this method of personnel selection. But this should not imply that the interview *per se* has no role in employee selection. As personnel managers and professional interviewers have

been telling us for quite some time, and as our research has substantiated, personality may be reliably and accurately assessed in an
employment interview, and moreover appropriate suitability judgments may be made on the basis of this information.

Although there is little in the interview literature directly addressing
the issue of personality assessment, there is one study which is highly
relevant to the present discussion – Landy's (1976) study of the validation of an interview procedure in police officer selection. Landy
examined the interview used by one police department to determine if
interview-based ratings predicted on-the-street performance for
police officers. A three-member panel interviewed nearly 400 applicants for the position of patrol officer, of whom 150 were ultimately
hired. The interview was structured, and focused on the assessment of
nine factors (appearance, communication skills, education, experience, employment history, social sensitivity, emotional stability,
responsibility, sincerity) identified by a job analysis. These factors
were shown to be rated, very reliably, and were subsequently correlated with highly reliable supervisor performance ratings of job
knowledge, judgment, initiative, dependability, demeanor, attitude,
relations with others and communications. The interview assessment
dimensions and the performance dimensions were each factor
analyzed to obtain orthogonal dimensions of higher reliability, and
these factor scores were correlated in the validity analysis. Results
indicated that three of the four performance factors were predicted
from the averaged interview ratings. Landy concludes from this study
that interview procedures predicted on-the-street police performance.
But in addition, consider some of the dimensions rated in Landy's
study (e.g. social sensitivity, emotional stability, responsibility,
sincerity). While these dimensions are by no means theoretically
based, substantively defined and validated personality traits, they are
dimensions of human behavior which are intended to be differentially
relevant across individuals, and relatively consistent for any given
individual across time and place. Thus, Landy's study suggests that
such dimensions may be reliably and accurately assessed in an
employment interview and, more important, they are predictive of
later job performance.

Obviously, a great deal more research is necessary to determine the
role of implicit personality theory in the employment interview. Such
investigations must begin with thorough job analyses to ascertain the
personality characteristics which are relevant for different jobs.

Systematic studies of the role of personality in work behavior must be undertaken. The inferential accuracy of implicit notions of behavioral covariation must be examined in the context of work related behavior. And the validity of judging applicant personality in the employment interview, for purposes of predicting later job performance, must be more clearly demonstrated. However, research thus far has indicated that a greater understanding of both implicit personality theory and decision making in the employment interview is acquired by integrating the investigation of these issues. Further research will increase our knowledge of how we perceive others and how we use this information in an applied decision-making problem.

Acknowledgements

Figure 7.1 is reprinted with permission from an article by D. N. Jackson, A. C. Peacock and R. R. Holden, in *Organizational Behavior and Human Performance* (1982), vol. 29, © Academic Press, Inc., 1982. Figures 7.2, 7.4 and 7.5 are reprinted with permission from an article by M. Rothstein and D. N. Jackson, in the *Journal of Applied Psychology* (1980), vol. 65, © American Psychological Association, 1980. Figures 7.6 and 7.7 are reprinted with permission from an article by D. N. Jackson, A. C. Peacock and J. P. Smith, in *Journal of Personality and Social Psychology* (1980), vol. 39, © American Psychological Association, 1980.

This work was supported by an Imperial Oil Ltd University Research Grant to Douglas N. Jackson and Mitchell Rothstein.

Mitchell Rothstein is now employed at Ontario Hydro, Toronto, Ontario, Canada.

References

Arvey, R. D. (1979) Unfair discrimination in the employment interview: legal and psychological aspects. *Psychological Bulletin 86*: 736–65.

Arvey, R. D. and Campion, J. E. (1984) Person perception in the employment interview. In M. Cook (ed.) *Issues in Person Perception*. London: Methuen.

Azen, S. P., Snibbe, H. M. and Montgomery, H. R. (1973) A longitudinal predictive study of success and performance of law enforcement officers. *Journal of Applied Psychology 57*: 190–2.

Bellows, R. M. and Estep, M. F. (1954) *Employment Psychology: The Interview*. New York: Rinehart.

Bernstein, V., Hakel, M. D and Harlan, A. (1975) The college student as interviewer: a threat to generalizability? *Journal of Applied Psychology 60*: 266-8.

Black, J. M. (1970) *How To Get Results From Interviewing*. New York: McGraw-Hill.

Blum, M. and Naylor, J. (1968) *Industrial Psychology*. New York: Harper & Row.

Bruner, J. S. and Tagiuri, R. (1954) Person perception. In G. Lindzey (ed.) *Handbook of Social Psychology*, vol. 2. Reading, Mass.: Addison-Wesley.

Campbell, J. P., Dunnette, M. D., Lawler, E. E. and Weick, K. E. (1970) *Managerial Behavior, Performance, and Effectiveness*. New York: McGraw-Hill.

Cheloha, R., Colangelo, A., Landy, F., Massenberg, M. and Vance, R. (1977) *Plan for Validating Ability Testing Procedures*. Harrisburg, Pa: Pennsylvania State Civil Service Commission.

Dunnette, M. D. and Borman, W. C. (1979) Personnel selection and classification systems. *Annual Review of Psychology 30*: 477-525.

Edwards, R. C. (1977) Personal traits and success in schooling and work. *Educational and Psychological Measurement 37*: 125-38.

Fear, R. A. (1978) *The Evaluation Interview*. New York: McGraw-Hill.

Feldman, D. C. and Arnold, H. J. (1978) Position choice: comparing the importance of organizational and job factors. *Journal of Applied Psychology 63*: 706-10.

Ghiselli, E. E. (1969) Prediction of success of stockbrokers. *Personnel Psychology 22*: 125-30.

Gough, H. (1976) Personality and personality assessment. In M. D. Dunnette (ed.) *Handbook of Industrial and Organizational Psychology*. Chicago: Rand McNally.

Guion, R. M. (1976) Recruiting, selection, and job placement. In M. D. Dunnette (ed.) *Handbook of Industrial and Organizational Psychology*. Chicago: Rand McNally.

Guion, R. M. and Gottier, R. F. (1965) Validating of personality measures in personnel selection. *Personnel Psychology 18*: 135-64.

Hackman, J. R. and Oldman, G. R. (1976) Motivation through the design of work: test of a theory. *Organizational Behavior and Human Performance 16*: 250-79.

Hakel, M. D. and Schuh, A. J. (1971) Job applicant attributes judged important across several diverse occupations. *Personnel Psychology 24*: 45-52.

Jackson, D. N. (1972) A model for inferential accuracy. *Canadian Psychologist 13*: 185-95.

Jackson, D. N. (1974) *Personality Research Form Manual*. Port Huron, Mich.: Research Psychologists Press.

Jackson, D. N. and Paunonen, S. V. (1980) Personality structure and assessment. *Annual Review of Psychology 31*: 503-51.

Jackson, D..N., Chan, D. W. and Stricker, L. J. (1979) Implicit personality theory: is it illusory? *Journal of Personality 47*: 1–10.

Jackson, D. N., Peacock, A. C. and Holden, R. R. (1982) Professional interviewers' trait inferential structures for diverse occupational groups. *Organizational Behavior and Human Performance 29*: 1–20.

Jackson, D. N., Peacock, A. C. and Smith, J. P. (1980) Impressions of personality in the employment interview. *Journal of Personality and Social Psychology 39*: 294–307.

James, L. R. and Jones, A. P. (1974) Organizational climate: a review of theory and research. *Psychological Bulletin 81*: 1096–112.

Katz, D. and Braly, K. (1944) Racial stereotypes of one hundred college students. *Journal of Abnormal Social Psychology 28*: 280–90.

Keenan, A. (1976) Interviewers' evaluation of applicant characteristics: differences between personnel and non-personnel managers. *Journal of Occupational Psychology 49*: 223–30.

Korman, A. K. (1977) *Organization Behavior*. Englewood Cliffs, N. J.: Prentice-Hall.

Landy, F. J. (1976) The validity of the interview in police officer selection. *Journal of Applied Psychology 61*: 193–8.

Landy, F. J. and Trumbo, D. A. (1980) *Psychology of Work Behavior*. Homewood, Ill.: Dorsey.

Langdale, J. A. and Weitz, J. (1973) Estimating the influence of job information on interviewer agreement. *Journal of Applied Psychology 57*: 23–7.

Latham, G. P., Saari, L. M., Pursell, E. D. and Campion, M. A. (1980) The situational interview. *Journal of Applied Psychology 65*: 422–7.

Lay, C. H. and Jackson, D. N. (1969) Analysis of the generality of trait inferential relationships. *Journal of Personality and Social Psychology 12*: 12–21.

Lay, C. H., Burron, B. F. and Jackson, D. N. (1973) Base rates and information value in impression formation. *Journal of Personality and Social Psychology 28*: 390–5.

Lopez, F. M. (1975) *Personnel Interviewing*. New York: McGraw-Hill.

Mayfield, E. C. (1964) The selection interview: a re-evaluation of published research. *Personnel Psychology 17*: 239–60.

Peskin, D. B. (1971) *Human Behavior and Employment Interviewing*. New York: American Management Association.

Peters, C. H. and Terborg, J. R. (1975) The effects of temporal placement of unfavorable information and of attitude similarity on personnel selection decisions. *Organizational Behavior and Human Performance 13*: 279–93.

Reed, P. C. and Jackson, D. N. (1975) Clinical judgment of psychopathology: a model for inferential accuracy. *Journal of Abnormal Psychology 84*: 475–82.

Rothstein, M. and Jackson, D. N. (1980) Decision-making in the employment interview: an experimental approach. *Journal of Applied Psychology 65*: 271–83.

Schmitt, N. (1976) Social and situational determinants of interview decisions: implications for the employment interview. *Personnel Psychology 29*: 79–101.

Schneider, D. J. (1973) Implicit personality theory: a review. *Psychological Bulletin 79*: 294–309.

Schneider, D. J., Hastorf, A. H. and Ellsworth, P. C. (1979) *Person Perception*. Reading, Mass.: Addison-Wesley.

Shaw, E. A. (1972) Commonality of applicant stereotypes among recruiters. *Personnel Psychology 25*: 421–32.

Siess, T. F. and Jackson, D. N. (1970) Vocational interests and personality: an empirical integration. *Journal of Counseling Psychology 17*: 27–35.

Spriegel, W. R. and James, V. A (1958) Trends in recruitment and selection practices. *Personnel 35*: 42–8.

Tom, V. R. (1971) The role of personality and organizational images in the recruiting process. *Organizational Behavior and Human Performance 6*: 573–92.

Ulrich, L. and Trumbo, D. (1965) The selection interview since 1949. *Psychological Bulletin 63*: 100–16.

Vroom, V. H. (1966) Organizational choice: a study of pre- and post-decision processes. *Organizational Behavior and Human Performance 1*: 212–26.

Wagner, R. F. (1949) The employment interview: a critical summary. *Personnel Psychology 2*: 17–46.

Webster, E. C. (1964) *Decision-making in the Employment Interview*. Montreal, Canada: McGill University Industrial Relations Center.

Weiner, Y. and Schneiderman, M. C. (1974) Use of job information as a criterion in employment decisions of interviewers. *Journal of Applied Psychology 59*: 699–704.

Wiggins, J. S. (1973) *Personality and Prediction: Principles of Personality Assessment*. Reading, Mass.: Addison-Wesley.

Woodruff, C. K. (1980) Data processing people – are they really different? *Information and Management 3*: 133–9.

Wright, O. R. (1969) Summary of research on the selection interview since 1964. *Personnel Psychology 22*: 391–413.

Wright, O. R., Carter, J. L. and Fowler, E. P. (1967) A differential analysis of an oral interview program. *Public Personnel Review 28*: 242–6.

8 Person perception in the employment interview

Richard D. Arvey *and*
James E. Campion

Selecting employees almost always means interviewing them, and the interview is an exercise in person perception. The process of reviewing a candidate's credentials (often based on an application form), conducting an interview, evaluating the qualifications of a candidate, and making a decision to hire or not hire is essentially a perceptual and decision-making task within an applied context.

Industrial and organizational psychologists have been studying this process for more sixty years in an effort to determine the reliability and validity of these perceptual judgments and also to discover the various psychological variables which influence these judgments.

The present chapter will review and summarize this history with special emphasis on recent research findings. We shall focus more specifically on the issue of fair treatment and bias in the employment interview as it concerns minority group members. Fortunately, our task is made more manageable by the efforts of earlier reviewers who have periodically provided comprehensive reviews of the employment interview.

Our plan is to present first a model or schema of the variables and processes inherent in the employment interview. Second, we summarize the research findings as reported by earlier reviewers and, third, we bring these reviews up-to-date by reviewing research published in the past few years. Finally, we offer some suggestions about possible research avenues and potential methodologies which could be profitably utilized in future exploration of this phenomenon.

The employment interview: a model

One way of viewing the variables and processes involved in the employment interview is shown in Figure 8.1 (for elaboration of a similar model, the reader is referred to Schmitt, 1976). Figure 8.1 shows there are a number of applicant characteristics which may influence the perception of the interviewer and influence the resulting decision. In addition, there are a number of interviewer and situational factors which may also influence the perceptual and judgmental processes. Most of these classes of variables have been the object of research bearing on decision-making in the interview. Some of these variables will probably interact to influence subsequent decisions. For example, knowing the race and sex of an applicant may differentially shape the expectations, stereotypes and behaviors of an interviewer which in turn may affect the interview outcome. We have intentionally omitted any hypotheses about direction of cause among these variables. We simply do not yet have sufficient knowledge, even after sixty years or so of research, to pinpoint accurately causal relationships between these variables.

Prior research reviews

Wagner (1949)

The first comprehensive review of the research on the employment interview was published by Wagner in 1949. Wagner began his review by noting that one of the earliest investigations of the interview was pubished in 1911. In that article, Binet reported low reliability for interview-based assessments of intelligence collected from three teachers who had evaluated the same five children. However, the earliest industrial application was in 1915 when Scott reported low reliability for evaluations given by six personnel·managers who had interviewed the same thirty-six sales applicants. These disappointing results have become persistent themes for research on the selection interview.

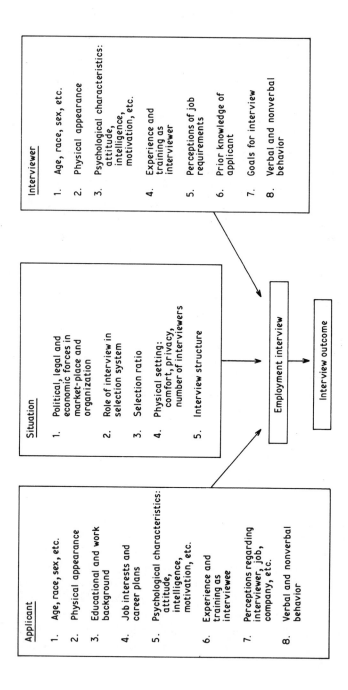

Applicant

1. Age, race, sex, etc.
2. Physical appearance
3. Educational and work background
4. Job interests and career plans
5. Psychological characteristics: attitude, intelligence, motivation, etc.
6. Experience and training as interviewee
7. Perceptions regarding interviewer, job, company, etc.
8. Verbal and nonverbal behavior

Situation

1. Political, legal and economic forces in market-place and organization
2. Role of interview in selection system
3. Selection ratio
4. Physical setting: comfort, privacy, number of interviewers
5. Interview structure

Interviewer

1. Age, race, sex, etc.
2. Physical appearance
3. Psychological characteristics: attitude, intelligence, motivation, etc.
4. Experience and training as interviewer
5. Perceptions of job requirements
6. Prior knowledge of applicant
7. Goals for interview
8. Verbal and nonverbal behavior

Employment interview

Interview outcome

Wagner located 106 articles dealing with the employment interview. However, only twenty-five reported any empirical work, and the remaining articles were non-empirical and represented a 'hodgepodge of conflicting opinions'. This early review was organized around several issues. One issue concerned the reliability and validity of interview judgments. Reliability was typically assessed by correlating evaluations of different interviewers who had assessed the same job candidates. Validity was typically assessed by correlating interview judgments with some measure of on-the-job performance. When the measure of performance was collected simultaneously with the interview judgments (e.g. interviews conducted with present employee groups), the design was called a concurrent study. In contrast, predictive designs involved following up at a later date those individuals who had been hired and put on the job. In his review, Wagner noted that reliabilities ranged from 0.23 to 0.97 with a median r of 0.57 for the 174 sets of ratings which were reported. Of the twenty-two validity coefficients summarized by Wagner, the range was from 0.09 to 0.94 with a median r of 0.27. Wagner noted that this was not a particularly high validity value.

Another issue addressed by Wagner was the ability of interviewers to integrate information. He suggested that while interviewers may be useful in eliciting from candidates information which may not be obtained through other data gathering mechanisms, this information may be best combined in a statistical rather than clinical fashion.

Wagner was favorably impressed by research results from standardized or patterned interviews and recommended their use. He also suggested interviewers consider using several 'new' techniques. For example, he suggested that the interviewer might sit on the sidelines and evaluate the candidates as they perform job tasks, such as giving a speech or participating in a group discussion – a procedure which today comprises an important component in the assessment center approach. He also recommended using the interviewer to rate the applicant while he (the applicant) carries out some practical job-related task, such as building a simple object. Again, this technique has found wide acceptance today in the work sample approach to assessing applicant qualifications.

In conclusion, Wagner recommended that the interview may be useful in three situations: (i) where rough screening is needed, (ii) where the number of applicants is too small to warrant more expensive procedures, and (iii) where certain traits may be most accurately assessed by the interviewer. He also recommends the use of a stand-ardized approach with an emphasis on assessing traits which have been demonstrated to be job related.

Mayfield (1964)

Fifteen years later, Mayfield (1964) summarized the interview research literature since the Wagner (1949) review. He noted that the literature still indicated relatively low reliabilities and validities for the employment interview. However, he went on to recommend a greater emphasis on studying the decision-making processes inherent in the interview and on factors that influenced the interview judgments. Moreover, he suggested that research should focus on dividing the interview into smaller chunks and studying one or two variables at a time in a more controlled fashion. Thus, he suggested a reorientation toward more microanalytical research. After reviewing the literature, Mayfield felt that the research findings tended to support several general statements.

(1) General suitability ratings based on unstructured interviews have low reliability.

(2) Material is not covered consistently in unstructured inter-views.

(3) Different interviewers are likely to weight the same informa-tion differently.

(4) Structured interviews result in higher inter-rater reliability.

(5) Interview validity is low.

(6) If the interviewer has valid test information available, his prediction based on the interview plus test information is usually no better and frequently worse than a prediction based on the test alone.

(7) Interviewers can reliably and validly assess intelligence, but have not been shown to be effective in evaluating other traits.

(8) The form of the question affects the answers given.

(9) The attitude of the interviewer affects the way he interprets the interviewees' responses.

(10) In unstructured interviews, interviewers tend to talk more than in structured interviews.

(11) Interviewers are influenced more by unfavorable than favorable information.

(12) Interviewers make their decisions quite early in unstructured interviews.

Ulrich and Trumbo (1965)

Published only six months after Mayfield's (1964) review, Ulrich and Trumbo (1965) reached many of the same conclusions. After agreeing that the interview lacked reliability and validity, Ulrich and Trumbo argued that it can be useful nevertheless. They suggested that researchers should examine the information gained from the interview separately from information gained from other sources such as employment tests.

These authors also supported Wagner's recommendation for a structured approach to the interview. They argued that interviews were especially useful for certain types of decisions. Specifically, their review indicated that the interview could be useful in assessing interpersonal relations and career motivations. Finally, they reviewed more recent microanalytic and decision process research and concluded these approaches were very promising.

Wright (1969) and Schmitt (1976)

Wright (1969) and later Schmitt (1976) summarized many research studies of decision-making processes of the employment interview. Both Wright (1969) and Schmitt (1976) relied heavily on the significant research conducted by Webster (1964) and his colleagues at McGill University. The studies summarized by Schmitt and Wright were, indeed, microanalytical. In fact, Wright (1969) suggested that researchers might profit by returning to the earlier orientation of dealing with the interview more as a totality because the small microanalytic approach would lead to fragmentation and meaningless results. In a similar vein, Schmitt (1976) indicated that, with few exceptions, the studies reviewed suffered from a lack of integration and from limited generalizability.

It is worthwhile here to summarize in more depth some of the specific variables and findings reviewed by Schmitt. Schmitt organized his review around specific variables and their impact on decision-making in the interview.

(1) Information favorability   A recurring research theme revolved

around the relationship between an interviewer's final decision and the kind of information presented in the interview. Schmitt's review of the available data suggested that interviewers reach a final decision quite early in the interview – typically within the first four minutes (Springbett, 1958). Also, data revealed that interviewers weigh negative information more heavily than positive information (Springbett, 1958; Hollman, 1972). Webster (1964) suggests that this phenomenon may result from a tendency for interviewers to receive feedback only about 'bad' employees and consequently to be more sensitive to negative or 'knock-out' factors.

(2) Temporal placement of information   Schmitt reviewed several studies dealing with presentation of specific positive or negative information during the interview. Some of these studies (Farr, 1973) indicated that order has a significant impact and that early impressions are more important than factual information in determining interviewers' judgments. He suggested that interviewers make up their minds early in the interview and then lose attention. Anderson (1960) found that after interviewers form a favorable decision, they spend more time talking than the interviewee, perhaps to 'sell' the candidates on the company. Schmitt suggests that the reason structured interviews are more reliable is that such a format may force the interviewer to pay more attention, which subsequently enhances his agreement with other raters.

(3) Interview stereotypes   A considerable number of studies reviewed by Schmitt had to do with the stereotypes interviewers have of ideal job candidates. Research by Sydiaha (1961), Bolster and Springbett (1961) and Hakel *et al.* (1970) tended to confirm the notion that interviewers possess stereotypes of ideal successful applicants against which real applicants are judged. However, London and Hakel (1974) presented data suggesting that these stereotypes diminish or are altered as the evaluation of an applicant progresses.

(4) Job Information   Several studies reviewed by Schmitt indicated that as interviewers receive more information about the job to be filled, inter-rater reliability increase (Langdale and Weitz, 1973), and there is a reduction in the impact of irrelevant attributes on decisions (Wiener and Schneiderman, 1974).

(5) Individual differences in the decision process   Schmitt reviewed several

studies investigating whether interviewers use and weigh information differently from one another in the interview. Hakel *et al.* (1970) found evidence indicating that actual interviewers gave different weights to academic standing and job experience factors in evaluating applicants than undergraduate students serving as raters. Valenzi and Andrews (1973) found wide individual differences in cue utilization resulting in considerable inter-rater differences in evaluating applicants.

(6) Visual cues   Schmitt's review suggested that nonverbal sources of information were more important than verbal cues and that a combination of both kinds of cues were maximally responsible for obtained differences in ratings of job candidates (Washburn and Hakel, 1973).

(7) Attitudinal, sexual and racial similarity   In 1976, Schmitt reviewed a handful of studies which investigated the importance of attitudinal and racial similarities between the interviewer and interviewee in influencing the resultant decision. Generally, the findings suggested that attitudinal and racial similarity affected evaluations of candidates (Wexley and Nemeroff, 1974; Rand and Wexley, 1975). In addition, several studies (Cohen and Bunker, 1975; Dipboye *et al.*, 1975) demonstrated that interviewers tended to give lower evaluations to female applicants. However, both males and females were more likely to be recommended for traditionally role congruent jobs.

(8) Contrast effects   Schmitt reviewed a number of studies on the effect of the quality of the preceding interviewee on interview ratings. There appear to be mixed findings in this area. Some studies found a significant, strong, and practical effect (Wexley *et al.*, 1972), while other studies suggest that the effect is either non-significant or trivial (Hakel *et al.*, 1970; Landy and Bates, 1973), especially when professional interviewers are used.

(9) Structured interview guides   Again, Schmitt found evidence that the use of a structured interview guide increases inter-interviewer agreement.

(10) Miscellaneous   Carlson *et al.* (1971) conducted a study showing that experienced interviewers were no more reliable than inexperienced interviewers, but that a requirement to accept a given number of applicants influenced the decisions of experienced interviewers

more than the decisions of less experienced interviewers. Also, Carlson (1967) investigated the relative importance of appearance and personal history information.

The review by Schmitt was comprehensive and is illustrative of the kinds of variables and processes investigated in exploring the employment interview during the past ten years or so.

Arvey (1979 a, b)

In 1979, Arvey summarized the research literature concerning evidence of bias in the employment interview with regard to blacks, females, handicapped and the elderly. Because of the increased probability that the interview will be subjected to legal scrutiny, Arvey reviewed the legal aspects of the interview. Eight legal cases concerning the employment interview were summarized. It appears that litigation has revolved around two basic themes:

(a) Do particular kinds of questions convey an impression of an underlying discriminatory attitude or intent? That is, references to 'girls', inquiries into non-job-related areas, such as marital status, parenthood, child care, etc. when these same questions are not asked of male candidates, may be sufficient to convince a court that discriminatory 'animus' or intent was operating.

(b) Does the inquiry operate in such a way to demonstrate a differential impact or adverse impact on protected groups? If so, is the particular information valid or job related? Organizations should avoid interview questions that affect differentially minority groups, unless such questions are job related.

In his review, Arvey identified processes causing differential evaluations according to sex, race, etc.: (i) stereotyping, and (ii) differences in behavior during the interview. Arvey suggested that stereotyping might lead to less favorable evaluations of minority members through three different mechanisms:

(1) The stereotypes of minority group members may be essentially negative in nature (e.g. blacks are dirty, uneducated, etc.).

(2) The stereotypes of a candidate may not 'match' the stereotypes of the job. For example, the perception of females as passive, emotional, etc. may not fit the stereotype of a given job and its requirements.

(3) The stereotypes may shape the kinds of expectations and standards interviewers have of job candidates during the interview.
For example, an interviewer may evaluate a female candidate
on a different set of criteria, e.g. beauty, poise, typing skills.

An additional explanation for differential evaluations of minority
group and candidates in the interviews could be that minority applicants behave in ways that are different and unfamiliar to interviewers.

Arvey reviewed seventeen studies investigating the effects of *applicant sex* in interview evaluations. The studies showed fairly consistently
that females are generally given lower evaluations than males when
both have similar or identical qualifications. A typical study is that of
Dipboye *et al.* (1975). Thirty male professional interviewers and thirty
male undergraduates evaluated twelve resumés for the position of
'head of a furniture department' and gave a rating about hiring each
applicant. Applicants' sex, physical attractiveness and scholastic performance were manipulated through the information provided within
the various resumes (i.e. brief summaries of the applicant's qualifications and past history). While a main effect was observed where male
applicants were evaluated higher than female applicants, the effect
accounted for only 1 per cent of the rating variance. Studies by Dipboye
et al. (1977), Haefner (1977), Rosen and Jerdee (1974) and others have
demonstrated a similar effect. However, a few studies have observed no
effect or findings in the opposite direction. For example, studies by
Muchinsky and Harris (1977) and Kryger and Shikiar (1978) indicated
that females were given higher evaluations than males.

In addition to reviewing studies dealing with sex as a main effect,
Arvey reported that research had also focused on several variables
predicted to interact with sex to influence the evaluations given. The
variable given the greatest attention was the type of job for which the
candidates were being considered. Evidence supported the notion that
females are given lower ratings for jobs typically 'masculine' in nature,
whereas males are given lower ratings when being considered for typically 'feminine' jobs (Shaw, 1972; Cohen and Bunker, 1975; Cash *et al.*
1977).

A second variable commonly investigated in combination with sex
was applicant competence or qualifications. Arvey reported that when
qualifications were included, sex tended to account for a relatively small
percentage of rating variance. A hypothesized interaction between sex
and qualifications, where competent females would receive lower
evaluations than competent males, was given only mixed support.

Finally, attractiveness was investigated in combination with sex. Arvey's review indicates that attractive candidates are typically preferred regardless of sex.

Somewhat surprisingly, Arvey could only locate three studies dealing with *race* of the applicant in interview evaluations. Even more surprising there was little evidence that unfavorable evaluations were given to black candidates compared to whites (Wexley and Nemeroff, 1974; Rand and Wexley, 1975; Haefner, 1977).

In addition, Arvey reviewed two studies investigating the effects of candidates' *age* on interviewer evaluations and found a relatively strong and pervasive effect of applicant age (Rosen and Jerdee, 1976; Haefner, 1977).

Finally, Arvey reviewed four studies investigating the effects of applicants *physical* and/or *mental handicap* on interview evaluations. Evidence supported the notion that handicapped applicants received lower evaluations in terms of hiring, but higher evaluations on motivational variables. Arvey suggests that interviewers might attribute higher motivation, effort levels, etc. to handicapped individuals who file applications for jobs through an attribute of greater effort to overcome disabilities.

In his conclusion, Arvey identifies a number of areas which need research attention.

(1) Methodological problems   Arvey called attention to the over-reliance on resumé and paper-and-pencil methodologies in this area. He suggested that greater efforts should be made to study 'real' interviews and to utilize more full stimulus fields. More use of videotaped and face-to-face interviews are needed. Arvey also suggested that researchers begin to explore Bayesian methodologies and concepts. Between- and within-subject designs need to be contrasted with regard to the information they yield regarding differential evaluations in the interview.

Arvey suggested that researchers need to tap subject pools other than undergraduate and graduate students and that subjects be given the opportunity to view more than *one* particular female, or handicapped individual in studies of this sort. Otherwise, any significant effect observed could be unique to the specific stimulus with which individuals were presented, and be due to other uncontrolled characteristics (hair color, height, etc.).

(2) More research on race, age and the handicapped   Arvey specifies that more research is needed with each of these minority groups.

(3) Process research   Arvey indicates that little is known about *why* differential evaluations are made and what goes on in the interview to influence the evaluations. In essence, he called for more research concerning the perceptual processes which might account for the phenomenon observed.

Review of recent research

This section consists of our summary of the recent literature concerning the employment interview. Basically, process research which has been published since the Schmitt (1976) article will be reviewed. Similarly, research dealing with bias and discrimination in the interview since Arvey's (1979) article will be reviewed.

This review will focus first on the general issues of interviewer reliability, validity and methodological concerns. Subsequently, we review the research on a topic-by-topic basis dealing with many of the topics and variables discussed earlier by Schmitt.

Reliability and validity

Recent research has not been as pessimistic about the validity and reliability as in prior years. Interviews conducted by a board or panel appear to be promising as a vehicle for enhancing reliability and validity. For example, reasonably favorable results were reported by Landy (1976) for the validity of board interviews for police officer selection. Data were gathered in a one-year period during which 399 white male applicants were interviewed and 150 applicants hired. The ratings made by the interviewing board at the end of each interview comprised the predictor variables. A principal-components analysis of the averaged interview trait ratings indicated that there were three major components. A principal-components analysis of supervisory ratings of performance identified four oblique performance factors. A validity analysis demonstrated that rated performance could be predicted from averaged interview-factor scores but not from the averaged overall recommendations of the interviewers. When the validity coefficients were corrected for restriction of range on the predictors, four of the twelve coefficients were significant. However, given the number of validity coefficients computed, and the statistical manipulations involved, these results are not that impressive.

A more positive outcome was reported by Anstey (1977) in a thirty-year follow-up on the British Civil Service Selection Board procedure. Using Civil Service positions obtained thirty years later as a criterion measure, he found the validity coefficient for the interview was 0.35 for a sample of 301 employees. When the coefficient was corrected for restriction of range on the predictor it rose to 0.66. As in the previous study the procedure employed here utilized a board interview.

Potential advantages of using group techniques for the interview were also reported by Rothstein and Jackson (1980). They had judges listen to a recording of a simulated interview and make judgments about (i) the possibility that an applicant would manifest certain related behaviors, and (ii) the suitability of the applicant for two occupations – accountant and engineer. They found that the group consensus judgments attributed a pattern of linked behaviors to the applicants that correlated with the known characteristics of those applicants.

However, less encouraging data were reported by Waldron (1974) who used nine psychologists to interview and predict the overall success of 118 candidates for the Royal Australian Navy. The interview did not yield any incremental validity to the predictions made separately from four tests and a life history form.

In another board interview study, Reynolds (1979) investigated the reliabilities for the oral interview used by the Louisiana Department of State Civil Service. Using the evaluations of three rater panels who interviewed sixty-seven job applicants, he found that individual reliabilities varied from 0.54 to 0.66 across the seven rating dimensions; when averaged across the three raters the reliability varied from 0.78 to 0.85. The reliability coefficient for the composite final score across the sixty-seven applicants was 0.90.

Several studies also investigated the general validity of the interview. Heneman *et al.* (1975) found low validities for predicting the job success of social workers. These authors investigated the effects of interview structure, biographical information and interviewee order on interviewer validity. Fifty-four undergraduates in personnel management and thirty-six social work supervisors rated six currently employed social workers assuming the role of job applicants in videotaped interviews. Where the criterion measure based on a job analysis of the social worker position was used, validity coefficients failed to achieve statistical significance. Analysis of variance revealed that only interviewee order had an appreciable affect on interviewer validity. However, the results obtained may not be generalizeable beyond the six presently employed social workers who served as interviewees in the study.

Another study published during this time was reported by Latham *et al.* (1980). These investigators utilized the critical incident technique to develop what they refer to as a situational interview. Critical incidents are reports by experienced employees or supervisors of unusually effective or unusually ineffective job behavior. These critical incidents were converted into interview questions in which job applicants were asked to indicate how they would behave in a specific situation. Each answer was rated independently by two or more interviewers on a 5-point Likert-type scale with benchmarks developed by job experts to facilitate objective scoring. They found inter-observer reliability coefficients of 0.76 and 0.79 for hourly workers and foremen, respectively. Similarly, the internal consistencies of the interview for the hourly workers and foremen were 0.71 and 0.67, respectively. The respective concurrent validity coefficients were 0.46 and 0.30. In another study, predictive validity coefficients of 0.39 and 0.33 were obtained for women and blacks, respectively. This research suggests that careful linking of job analysis and interview content can have beneficial effects on interviewer reliability and validity.

The themes suggested by research investigating the overall reliability and validity of the interview seem to be twofold:

(a) The use of board or panel interviews appears promising as a means of improving the validity and reliability of the interview. Perhaps sharing different perceptions with each other forces interviewers to become more aware of irrelevant inferences made from or about non-job-related variables.

(b) Use of directly related job analysis and other job information as a basis for interview questions is a useful method of improving the accuracy of the interview. This theme has been suggested previously by Schmitt (1976) and others (e.g. Langdale and Weitz, 1973).

Methodological issues Two methodological issues have received research attention in recent years: The use of college students as interviewers and the use of pencil-and-paper stimulus 'interviews'.

Related to the first issue, recent research suggests that the threat to generalizability by using students as interviewers seems minimal. Bernstein *et al.* (1975) found no differences between professional interviewers and college students with respect to variances, inter-rater agreement and main effects. These authors reviewed six studies and found that the only difference between college students and 'real' interviewers was that college students were more lenient in their ratings.

Similar findings were reported by Dipboye *et al.* (1975) who found no differences between professional interviewers and college students in their investigation of sex bias in the interview. Finally, McGovern *et al.* (1979) found that college students were equally as sensitive as professional personnel representatives to eye contact, voice tone and body movements in making interview evaluations. Thus, this issue appears not to be as critical as previously believed.

Because many previous studies of the employment interview have not been based on actual interviews but instead on pencil-and-paper stimulus materials, such as transcripts of interviews, application and resumé data, photographs, etc. a serious paradigmatic question may be raised about the external validity or generalizability of studies using these methods to actual interview contexts. Several recent studies suggest that the two kinds of settings and methods yield different results.

Gorman *et al.* (1978) raised the question regarding external validity: 'Can we learn anything about interviewing real people from interviews of paper people?' They had graduate students and experienced interviewers make judgments based on interviews and on test data alone. Based on the results, the authors concluded that the paper-and-pencil paradigm gives different results from judgments based on actual interviews.

In a related study, Okanes and Tschirgi (1978) had sixty-seven employment recruiters make pre-interview judgments based on a review of grades, job experiences, campus activity and faculty references. Following 470 actual interviews of the same candidates, the data indicated significant shifts from an 'unable to determine' rating category. Further, half the responses from the 'probably recommend' category shifted, with the majority going to 'probably not recommend'. Very large increases occurred in the 'probably not recommend' category. Thus, interviewers tended to be more negative in their evaluations following face-to-face interviews. This finding suggests two possibilities: (i) that references, resumés, etc. tend to be homogeneously positive, and raters cannot make accurate discriminations; and (ii) interviewers may use face-to-face interviews as a major source for 'knock-out' or negative factors. A study which yielded somewhat contradictory results on this issue was conducted by Ferris and Gilmore (1977). In this study, 120 psychology students evaluated either a male

or female applicant's resumé, or heard the applicant being interviewed, or saw a videotape of the interview, and then assigned a
favorability rating to the applicant. Results indicated that mode of presentation had no effect.

Pre-interview information should not be regarded as irrelevant. In a
provocative article, Dipboye (1980) argues that post-interview decisions are determined to a large extent by the impressions of applicants
formed by the interviewers before the interview. He suggests that pre-
interview evaluations influence the way the interviewer conducts the
interview and, in turn, the way the interview is conducted tends to
evoke interviewee behaviors that confirm the interviewer's pre-
interview evaluations. Also, Dipboye (1980) argues that interviewers
tend to notice, recall and interpret interviewee behavior in a manner
which is consistent with their previous impressions.

An additional methodological note was provided by Schuh (1978).
He suggested that note taking and avoiding interruptions are important in increasing interviewer listening accuracy. A videotaped interview of an applicant for a management position was viewed by 102
employment interviewers and 128 managers who were either required
or forbidden to take notes, and were either interrupted or not. On a
25-item listening accuracy test, the highest rate of accuracy (79 per cent)
was in the note taking and no interruption condition.

Finally, a study conducted by Newman and Kryzstofiah (1979) compared results from resumé research (a) when the study was conducted
unobtrusively, and (b) when employees were aware that their
responses were for a research study. Resumés of a black and a white job
applicant were sent to 240 employment managers who under one condition believed that these were actual job candidates. One year later, these
same companies were contacted and employment managers (perhaps
different persons) asked to participate in a study where resumés for
black and white applicants were presented again. These managers were
asked to report their expected response. When managers knew they
were contributing to a piece of research, and provided self-reports of
expected responses, these responses were prone to treat the black and
white candidates equally, and somewhat more favorably. In contrast,
employment managers who were unaware of their role in the study
tended to make employment decisions based more on the race of the
applicant.

In sum, studies investigating the interview and interview processes
seem to reflect a growing methodological sophistication. There is

increasing recognition for the need to capture more realistic stimulus situations and interviewer responses. There is a growing concern about the potential contamination of research results by method variance.

Decision-making studies

There were several studies reporting evidence for various rating errors in the interview. Kopelman (1975) studied the influence of preceding interviewees' performance on the assessment of a third candidate and found evidence of contrast bias in evaluations of videotaped interviews of candidates applying for medical school. Contrast effect counted for 11 per cent of the decision variance and was most influential in the assessment of candidates of intermediate quality. Additional evidence for the contrast effect was provided by Schuh (1978) who had 120 employment interviewers and 180 managers view videotaped interviews of four applicants for a management trainee position.

Farr and York (1975) investigated the influence of amount of information on primacy–recency effects in recruitment decisions. Seventy-two college recruiters evaluated hypothetical candidates described in a written booklet. The analysis indicated that recency effects occurred when interviewers were asked to make repeated judgments during the interview, whereas primacy effects were obtained when only a single judgment was required of each interviewer. The amount of information presented about each applicant had no effect upon judgments.

First impression error was investigated by Tucker and Rowe (1979). They asked seventy-two students to read and evaluate interview transcripts after examining a letter of reference. Results suggested that interviewers who first read an unfavorable letter were more likely to give the applicant less credit for past successes and to hold the applicant more personally responsible for past failures. Results also indicated that the decision to hire is closely related to interviewers' interpretations of past outcomes.

Finally, Keenan (1977) reported evidence suggesting that interviewers' personal feelings about candidates influenced their general evaluations of them. In a study of 551 graduate recruitment interviews conducted by 103 interviewers, Keenan found fairly strong relationships between interviewers' liking of the candidate and overall evaluations. The relationship between ratings of candidates' intelligence and general evaluation was only slightly reduced when the effect of liking was held constant. This was interpreted as suggesting that there are both affective and cognitive components in interviewers' evaluations of candidates.

London and Poplawski (1976) found sex differences in rating when they presented 120 male and 120 female undergraduates with information about two groups of hypothetical company employees. Their hypothesis that distinctiveness in amount and favorability of information would result in differential stereotypes about the two groups was not confirmed. However, they did find that female subjects gave consistently higher ratings.

Finally, Leonard (1976) studied the relationship between cognitive complexity and similarity error in an interview context. Sixty-four undergraduates conducted interviews with confederates who played roles as job applicants. Similarity was manipulated by the confederate roles and by information given to the subjects. Subjects high on cognitive complexity were more likely to evaluate similar applicants more positively, suggesting that cognitive complexity may moderate the impact of similarity error.

In sum, these recent studies tend to confirm earlier research, demonstrating that interviewers do indeed tend to produce ratings or evaluations which are influenced by contrast, primacy–recency, first impressions, personal feelings and other factors. On the positive side, some research again indicates that when evaluations are in the form of specific prediction of job behavior, less distortion is found.

There have been three studies published which investigated interviewer decision time. Huegli and Tschirgi (1975) examined a sample of 183 recruiting interviews conducted by sixteen interviewers at Ohio University. Interviews and decision times were recorded. The interviewers also completed a questionnaire describing their decision-making during the interview. Findings indicated that 77 per cent of the interviewers reported making decisions during the interview itself but only 33 per cent during the first half of the interview. This finding is at variance with previously reported studies which indicated that decisions were made very early in the interview. Huegli and Tschirgi also found that 'hire' decisions were made sooner than 'don't hire' decisions; however, interview length was unrelated to the hiring decision. Finally, decisions were unrelated to time of day.

A second study in this area was by Tucker and Rowe (1977) who conducted an experiment to determine whether consulting the application blank prior to the interview would delay the initial decision. Twenty-eight experienced recruiters interviewed a role-playing job candidate.

Half the interviewers were provided with an application blank prior to the interview and half were not. Results indicated that withholding the application blank did not slow down the initial decision nor did it reduce the interviewer's confidence in the decision.

In a third study, Tullar *et al.* (1979) investigated the effects of interview length (15 or 30 minutes) and applicant quality (high or low) on interviewer decision time. Sixty experienced employment counselors observed a videotaped interview and made a decision as soon as they felt they had sufficient information. The interviewers took significantly more time to make the decision for the high quality candidates and for the longer interview.

Interviewer training

Several recent studies have been conducted investigating the effects of training on interviewer evaluations. For example, recent work by Vance *et al.* (1978) investigated the use of behavioral rating scales in reducing interviewer error. Behavioral rating scales reflect the relevant dimensions of expected job behavior, and have anchor points to illustrate in specific behavioral terms the behavior the candidate is expected to demonstrate to achieve ratings at the various points on the scales. Audio recordings of interviews were rated by 112 undergraduates assigned to one of four conditions in a factorical design. One independent variable was whether interviewers utilized the behavioral rating scales or a typical graphic rating scale to make their predictions. Use of the behavioral rating forms tended to reduce rater error and to increase rater accuracy. The second independent variable was whether the interviewers were trained or not trained to reduce rater error tendencies. However, no significant effects for training were found.

Heneman (1975) also investigated the effect of interviewer training on interview reliability and validity. Thirty-six students, half of whom were trained, viewed six videotapes of either structured or unstructured interviews. While the results showed no significant interviewer validity, there was one significant finding involving inter-rater reliability. When untrained subjects observed an unstructured interview, reliabilities were lower. The training program consisted of a 90-minute lecture on use of job descriptions, rating scales and how to avoid rating errors.

This apparent failure of interview behavior is not, however, consistent with earlier findings (Wexley *et al.*, 1973; Latham *et al.*, 1975). The earlier work suggested that intensive workshops, including practice with feedback and group discussions, help to eliminate rating errors of contrast, halo, similarity and first impression.

A recent field study shedding some indirect light on the impact of training interviewers was reported by Mayfield *et al.* (1980). After training life insurance managers to interview candidates using a particular kind of structured interview format and questions, their responses to a standard taped interviews were analyzed in one study, and the actual ratings on specific interview items for 163 real job candidates were analyzed in a second study. Results demonstrated that it was possible for managers to reach agreement on some of their evaluation ratings, that ratings had a stable factorial structure which made good intuitive sense, and that many of these ratings were related to the final selection decision.

It is apparent that much, if not all, of the research dealing with interviewer training has focused largely on the psychometric aspects of interviewer ratings and evaluations as indicators of the success or failure of the training program. Other dependent variables should also be considered. For example, interviewer *behavior* during the interview should be examined. Do interviewers ask fewer 'leading' questions during interviews as result of training? Are they less nervous? Do they elicit more information from interviewees? Do they follow a logical sequence during the interview? Are interviewees more comfortable with interviewers who have completed training? Note that these kinds of questions have relatively little to do with the psychometric aspects of their ratings (e.g. halo, etc.) but are more *behavioral* in nature. It may be profitable to focus on these kinds of questions when examining interviewer training.

Minority characteristics

Since the review by Arvey (1979a) several studies have investigated the effect of interviewee handicap on interviewer judgments. Stone and Sawatzki (1980) conducted a study where ninety students, enrolled in a Masters of Business Administration program, observed one of six taped interviews which portrayed three conditions of disability (psychiatric, physical and no disability) and two levels of work history (good or bad). Results indicated that applicants who were described as having two hospitalizations for nervous breakdowns had a lower probability of being hired. More obvious was the finding that applicants with good work histories were given significantly higher evaluations.

A study by Hastorf *et al.* (1979) reviewed acknowledgement of handicap as a tactic in social interaction. Subjects observed two videotapes of handicapped individuals being interviewed and then chose the one with whom they would prefer to work with on a co-operative task. The results suggested that subjects prefer to work with interviewees who acknowledge their handicap.

In another study, Snyder *et al.* (1979) found that subjects avoided a person wearing a metal leg-brace and chose to view movies with normal subjects, when avoiding the handicapped person could masquerade as a movie preference.

An excellent review of the literature involving employment decisions regarding the handicapped was provided by Rose (1980). In his review, Rose indicates that there are four classes of variables potentially related to discrimination against the handicapped. These are: (i) the nature of the handicap, (ii) other personal attributes of the applicant or worker, (iii) the nature of the job or occupation being considered, and (iv) characteristics of the potential employing organizations, particularly the characteristics of the hiring and assessment procedures used by the organization. In addition, Rose delineates the methodological limitations of the research published in this area.

Applicant sex was examined as a potential factor influencing interview decisions by Simas and McCarrey (1979). Eighty-four male and female personnel officers who were classified into either high, moderate or low authoritarian groups evaluated male and female applicants in simulated videotaped recruitment interviews. The high authoritarian personnel officers of both sexes rated the male applicants more favorably than female applicants and indicated that they would make more job offers to the male applicants. Thus, this study is in line with the research reported earlier.

Rosen and Merich (1979) investigated the effects of applicant sex in selection decisions under conditions of strong or weak fair employment policy statements. Seventy-eight municipal administrators evaluated a resumé of either male or female applicants in a simulation where instructions indicated a strong organizational emphasis on fair employment practices, or in a condition where only lip-service was paid to fair practices. Results indicated strength of policy statements did not affect preference for male or female applicants. However, interviewers recommended lower starting salaries for females under the strong fair employment condition. The authors interpreted this within a reactance theory framework. That is, the administrators may have assigned lower starting salaries as a reaction against the hiring constraints imposed by the strong affirmative action policy.

The study by Ferris and Gilmore (1977) reviewed earlier revealed a marginally significant effect for male applicants to be given slightly higher favorability ratings than female applicants.

The impact of male and female applicant attractiveness was investigated by Heilman and Saruwatari (1979). These authors hypothesized that because attractive women are regarded as more feminine than unattractive women and attractive men are regarded as more masculine than unattractive men, attractive women would be at a disadvantage when being considered for stereotypically 'male' jobs, or jobs believed to require predominantly masculine talents for successful job performance. In this study, forty-five male and female college students evaluated application forms and photographs of male and female candidates who had been judged to be attractive or unattractive. The candidates were evaluated for either a clerical or management position on a number of dependent variables, such as qualifications, hiring recommendation, starting salary, etc. Analyses revealed that attractive females were given higher evaluations when being considered for the clerical job compared to unattractive females, but attractive females were rated lower when considered for the management job. In contrast, for male candidates attractiveness always led to higher evaluations regardless of the job.

Recent studies dealing with effects of applicant sex on interviewers' decisions reflect a growing awareness that other variables may interact with sex of the applicant. The phenomenon may be more complex than was previously supposed. For example, Heilman (1980) reported the results of an investigation in which interviewers evaluated a female candidate's application form as well as interviewing seven additional candidates. The proportion of females in the applicant pool was 12.5, 25, 37.5, 50 or 100 per cent. Results indicated that when women represented 25 per cent or less of the total pool, the female applicant was evaluated more unfavorably than if the pool reflected a large percentage of female applicants. These results were interpreted as supporting the idea that situational factors can reduce the adverse influence of sex stereotypes in employment settings.

In a study involving a design where fictitious but realistic resumés were mailed to actual employers, McIntyre et al. (1980) examined the pattern of responses made by organizations. Resumés of minority (black or female) and non-minority job candidates were sent to 458 companies. Their data indicated that males were given preferential treatment compared to females. In addition, results indicated that the black applicants were given more favorable treatment than white applicants. This is one of the few studies examining the impact of race on interviewers' decisions. The results are in line with those noted by Arvey in his earlier review.

An earlier study conducted by Newman (1978) discussed the results of sending bogus resumés for black and white applicants to 240 companies. (This was the 'unobtrusive' condition discussed in the Newman and Krzystofiah (1979) study above.) These data indicated a definite trend for larger companies to discriminate in favor of blacks. As noted previously, Newman and Krzystofiah (1979) found that this tendency did not generalize to situations where employment managers were aware of their role in the study. It should be noted, however, that these last are studies of recruitment rather than of actual interviews.

An unpublished doctoral study by Mullins (1978) used videotaped interviews to examine interviewer ratings of high and low quality candidates role played by black and white males. The study used a between-subjects design where 176 white business administration students viewed videotaped interviews. Results indicated that the most important variable influencing interview ratings was applicant quality but that the black applicant was significantly favored over the white applicant. The study is difficult to interpret, however, because the differences obtained may be a function of the specific individuals used in the stimulus condition.

One additional study focused on linguistic patterns as related to interview judgments. Kalin and Rayko (1978) had 203 students evaluate audiotapes of job applicants for four jobs varying in social status. Five applicants spoke with an English–Canadian accent and five applicants spoke with a definite foreign accent (Italian, Greek, Portuguese, West African or Slovak). Applicants with foreign accents were given lower ratings for the higher status jobs, but higher ratings for the lower status jobs.

No studies were found which investigated the effects of applicants' age in the interview. This variable needs investigation. In addition, no studies have fully examined the stereotyping process as it affects the interview. For example, McCauley et al. (1980) review the different definitions and conceptualizing of stereotyping and propose a Bayesian model. This model might be a useful framework to examine bias in interview situations. As yet, little has been done to examine stereotyping or any other processes which might contribute to differential evaluations.

Nonverbal behavior

An area of considerable recent research interest has been the study of interviewees' nonverbal behavior. For example, Amalfitano and Kalt (1977) examined eye contact effects on job interviewers' evaluations. Photographs were taken of a male and a female adopting two contrasting gaze directions: looking straight into the camera, and looking downward. Forty-four job interviewers in an employment agency were randomly assigned to one of the four photographs. Each subject was told to assume that he or she was interviewing the person for a job as a management trainee. Not surprisingly, the results showed interviewees were more likely to be hired if they looked straight ahead rather than down. In addition, those who looked straight ahead were rated as being more alert, assertive, dependable, confident, responsible, and as having more initiative.

In another study, Imada and Hakel (1977) examined the influence of nonverbal communication and modes of observation. Seventy-two female subjects serving as an interviewer, direct observer or television observer viewed an applicant whose nonverbal behavior was either 'immediate' or 'nonimmediate'. 'Immediacy' was manipulated through eye contact, smiling, posture, interpersonal distance and body orientation. Results again indicated that nonverbal communication had a significant effect on interviewer impressions and that 'immediate' nonverbal behavior consistently produced more favorable ratings.

In another study, Young and Beier (1977) examined the effects of nonverbal behavior of job applicants on subsequent hiring evaluations. Thirty-two interviewees were instructed to use one of four styles of nonverbal behavior during the videorecording of a short job interview with a standard content. Videotaped interviews were watched by twenty-two raters who assessed nonverbal cue usage, and by fifty judges who evaluated the applicants as prospective employees. Applicants who demonstrated greater amounts of eye contact, head movement, smiling and other nonverbal behaviors were rated higher on job acceptability. In fact, these nonverbal behaviors accounted for more than 80 per cent of the rating variance.

Tessler and Sushelsky (1978) investigated the effects of eye contact and social status on the evaluation of applicants in the employment interview. The dependent variable was interviewers' perception of how well the applicant was suited for a job requiring self-confidence. Using sixty undergraduates acting as interviewers, the results indicated statistically significant effects for eye contact and social status.

In another study, McGovern and Tinsley (1978) had fifty-two personnel representatives review videotaped job interviews, in which verbal content was identical but the interviewee's nonverbal behavior was varied. An interviewee in the 'low nonverbal' condition showed minimal eye contact, low energy level, lack of affect, low voice modulation and a lack of speech fluency. The interviewee in the 'high nonverbal' condition demonstrated opposite behavior. Nonverbal behavior was found to have a significant effect on almost every rating made by the subjects. Twenty-three of the twenty-six subjects who saw the 'high nonverbal' candidate, would have invited him or her for a second interview. All twenty-six who saw the 'low nonverbal' candidate would not have recommended a second interview. This study was later replicated by McGovern et al. (1979) using college students as subjects; the obtained results closely paralleled these results obtained with the professional interviewers.

In another study, Sigelman et al. (1980) examined the effects of verbal and nonverbal interview behavior of eighty-eight mentally retarded adults on employability rating given them by a panel of six students in a personnel management course. Verbal and nonverbal behaviors were relatively independent with the former accounting for most of the predicted variance in the criterion variables. Persons whose speech was intelligible, who spoke at length, and who responded appropriately to questions were most likely to make a favorable impression.

A similar research finding was reported by Sterrett (1978) who showed videotapes of a male job applicant displaying various intensities of body language to 160 managers in the insurance industry. The hypothesis that different body language intensities would result in differential perceptions of eight traits typically considered in the employment interview (ambition, motivational drive, self-confidence, self-organization, responsibility, verbal ability, intelligence and sincerity) was *not* supported. Thus, these results are somewhat contradictory to other findings.

Hollandsworth *et al.* (1979) performed a discriminant analysis to determine the relative importance of verbal and nonverbal dimensions of communication during 338 on-campus interviews conducted by seventy-three different college recruiters. The criterion variable was a 4-point rating on the question 'Would you hire?' The results showed the following order of importance among the independent variables: appropriateness of verbal content, fluency of speech, composure, body posture, eye contact, voice level and personal appearance.

In sum, it appears that interviewees' nonverbal behavior influences interviewers' evaluations. However, nonverbal behavior has less influence generally than what the candidate actually says. One problem common to many of these studies is that interviewers may infer from the interviewee's nonverbal behavior to his verbal skills. Thus, while researchers may manipulate the verbal–nonverbal variable in an orthogonal manner, interviewers may not view the two as independent.

It is also possible that these factors do not operate in a linear fashion to influence interviewers. For example, it may be that interviewers first screen on verbal dimensions, and subsequently shift the perceptual-judgmental process into more nonverbal domains.

Interviewee variables

There are two studies which examine the impact of interviewees' self-perceptions on interview outcome. King and Manaster (1977) had ninety-eight female undergraduates complete a body image satisfaction scale, self-cathexis scale, Janis–Field–Eagly self-esteem scale, and a job interview performance expectation scale, prior to participating in a 15-minute simulated job interview. After the job interview, subjects rated their own performance. Independently, two judges rated each subject's videotape performance. Interviewees' expectations for job interview success were significantly related to both body satisfaction and self-esteem. High self-esteem interviewees tended to overestimate how well they had performed in the interview. However, actual interview performance was not related to either self-esteem or body attitudes.

In another study, Keenan (1978) asked job candidates in 551

employment interviews to give estimates of the level of their motivation to succeed immediately before and after each interview. Their level of state anxiety was also measured by a state-trait anxiety inventory before each interview. At the end of the interview, interviewees indicated how much they liked the interviewer personally. They estimated both the likelihood of their being successful in the interview and the likelihood that they would accept the job with that company. Interviewers were asked to evaluate each candidate and to estimate his or her chances of being offered a job. Not surprisingly, when candidates liked interviewers personally, they were more optimistic about their chances of success and were more willing to accept potential job offers. Candidates were also more confident of success at the end of the interview when their pre-interview motivation had been high. However, interviewer evaluations of candidates were most favorable when the level of the interviewee pre-interview motivation had been intermediate. The job candidates' state of anxiety was unrelated to favorability of interviewers' evaluations.

These last two studies suggest that interviewees' pre-existing motives and expectations influence their own perceptions of performance during the interview. Interviewees with high motivation to do well, high self-esteem etc. may tend to aggrandize their actual performance and, in some cases, they may detract from their interview performance.

Relatively few studies have investigated psychological variables and perceptions of the interviewee as they influence the interview process. Yet it makes intuitive sense that these factors will influence interview judgments.

Perceptions of interviewer

It is becoming increasingly apparent that interviewers must become more aware of their own impact on job applicants. In a recent article, Rynes *et al.* (1980) reviewed research that examined the influence of organization recruitment practices on applicant attitudes and job choice behaviors. It was found that recruiting representatives, administrative practices and evaluation procedures are all potentially important influences on job-seeker attitudes and behaviors.

The influence of the interviewer on interviewee attitudes and behavior was recently demonstrated by several investigators. Keenan and Wedderburn (1975) demonstrated the effects of the interviewer's nonverbal behavior on interviewees' impressions. They found that the interviewer's use of nonverbal approval in role played interviews with twenty-four undergraduates resulted in a more favorable interviewee impression when compared to nonverbal disapproval. Contrary to expectations, interviewees' talking rate was not affected.

In a follow-up study, Keenan (1976a) found that nonverbal approval by interviewers in mock interviews also resulted in the interview being evaluated as more relaxed and the interviewee as having made a better impression when judged by undergraduate observers.

In a related study, Schmitt and Coyle (1976) asked 237 college students who had been interviewed for jobs at a college placement center to describe their reactions to the interviewer and their subsequent decisions. Results indicated that perceived interviewer personality, manner of delivery and adequacy of information influenced the interviewees' evaluations of the interviewer, the company and the likelihood of job acceptance. Finally, Fisher *et al.* (1979) surveyed ninety undergraduate seniors and explored effects of information favorability and source on applicant perceptions of source credibility and job offer acceptance. Results indicate that interviewers were the least credible source and that giving negative job information enhanced source credibility but decreased job offer acceptance.

It is obvious that research investigating the characteristics of the interviewer and the subsequent impact on interviewee behavior and perceptions is sorely lacking. Equally lacking is research which investigates the role of tight or open labor markets on subsequent interviewer behavior and impact on interviewees. For example, in recent years the Houston labor market for professional engineers in the oil industry has been incredibly competitive. Since individuals with the required skills are relatively rare, the role of interviewers and recruiters is considerably changed and reflect a 'sell the company' perspective. The nature of job interviews is thus quite different.

Interviewee training

There have been numerous studies exploring how interviewees might be taught to present themselves more effectively in the employment interview. An early example of this was reported by Stevens and Tornatzky (1976) who assigned twenty-six clients from a drug abuse treatment program to a workshop stressing behavioral interview skills, such as preparing for an interview, application completion, grooming, nonverbal communication and phrasing of answers to interview questions, or to a control group that received no treatment. A six-month follow-up showed no significant attitudinal differences between the two groups but those who participated in the interview work day obtained higher paying jobs.

Hollandsworth *et al.* (1977) developed a job interviewee skills workshop based on behavioral procedures such as modeling, role playing and directive feedback, and compared it with a traditional lecture discussion group approach, as well as a no treatment control group. Forty-five college seniors were randomly assigned to one of three groups. Subjects participated in a videotaped, simulated job interview prior to and following each workshop. Analyses of self-report and behavioral measures indicated that the group learning the behavioral procedures made significant gains in percentage of time of eye contact maintained during the interview. The discussion group was found to be superior to the behavioral and control groups in ratings of ability to explain individual skills, and expressions of feeling and personal opinion relevant to the interview. Also, interviewees in the discussion group demonstrated a significant increase in speaking time. Thus, both procedures seem to have an impact on increasing interviewee effectiveness in the interview.

In a follow-up study, Hollandsworth and Sandifer (1979) developed a workshop combining the most effective components of behavioral and discussion group methods; they trained forty-six Masters level counselors who subsequently conducted over 320 workshops for approximately 4100 secondary and post-secondary students. Data generated by these counselors indicate that the workshop was easily employed as a training procedure. Also, student participants reported high levels of satisfaction with the procedure.

Keith *et al.* (1977) also investigated training with sixty-six rehabilitation clients and found experimental support for training effects in improving knowledge of job openings and the number of job leads obtained. Further, eight of the nineteen trainees obtained jobs, whereas only six of forty-seven control group members were able to find employment. Finally, Speas (1979) assigned fifty-six prison inmates to one of four treatment conditions or to a waiting list control-group condition. The four instructional techniques were model exposure, role-playing, model exposure plus role-playing, and model exposure and role-playing with videotaped feedback. Judges' ratings of videotaped simulated pre- and post-treatment interviews and personnel interviewers' ratings of follow-up interviews served as criterion measures. Post-test results indicated that both the model plus role-playing and the model exposure plus role-playing plus videotaped feedback treatments were significantly more effective than the control procedure on all dependent variables.

Lastly, two research efforts focused on what the interviewee can do to impress the interviewer. Harlan *et al.* (1977) administered questionnaires to 274 managers, supervisory personnel, clerical workers and high school students, and asked them to indicate whether or not they would discuss various types of work-related factors if they were interviewed as applicants for employment. A systematic tendency was found for respondents to prefer to discuss 'motivator' rather than 'hygiene' factors (Herzberg *et al.*, 1959). Responding to a modified version of the questionnaire, twenty professional employment interviewers indicated that it is, in fact, wise to emphasize motivator and de-emphasize hygiene factors if the applicant wants to maximize the likelihood of being offered a job.

In a second study, Campion (1978) investigated college recruiter evaluations of 170 job applicants. His findings suggested that undergraduate grade point average (i.e. rating of student's academic performance), membership in a fraternity or sorority, and membership in a professional society were significantly related to interviewers' overall general impression, personal liking and chances for further consideration in the interview.

This domain of investigation might profit by researchers becoming more acquainted with literature available on impression management. The recent text by Schlenker (1980) provides a review of the theory and research in impression management which may facilitate future research efforts in this area.

Summary and conclusions

It is clear that research dealing with the employment interview is progressing. A number of themes emerge when reviewing what has been happening in this area over the past five years or so.

(1) Research investigating possible bias in the interview has been increasing   One theme which has been fairly consistent is the increased interest in the employment interview as a potential vehicle for discrimination against women and minority group job candidates. While

attention has focused predominantly on group membership, and how it affects interview decisions, more recent research has investigated the way other variables interact with protected group status to determine interview decisions. However, as we noted earlier, much more research needs to be conducted in this area. With the potential for increased legal challenges to the interview device, there is a pressing need for more research in this area before court decisions are made on the basis of preliminary and perhaps methodologically flawed studies.

(2) More variables associated with the interview have been under investigation   Our review has revealed a number of studies dealing with variables which previously received little research attention. For example, researchers have begun to probe such topics as nonverbal behavior, interviewees' perceptions of interviewers, interviewees' self-perceptions and interviewee training. For the most part, these are interviewee factors rather than interviewer factors. It is somewhat surprising that so little research has been conducted in the past dealing with applicant perceptions. Perhaps researchers felt that it would be somewhat intrusive to ascertain the perceptions, reactions, and so forth of actual candidates.

(3) Researchers are becoming more sophisticated in their research methodologies and strategies   As mentioned earlier, interview research in the past utilized resumé designs for the most part. However, recent research efforts are incorporating more realistic stimulus sets into the designs. The use of videotape to capture the employment interview as it progresses is more frequent, due possibly to the lower costs and greater flexibility of these technologies.

Moreover, researchers are realizing the limitations of resumé and other pencil-and-paper methodologies and conducting research to demonstrate the differences in results using these methodologies compared to more realistic stimulus and response settings. Some of the ethical issues associated with conducting research unobtrusively and without informed consent are being discussed (e.g. Newman and Kryzstofiah, 1979). Yet it is possible that results may have little relevance to actual employment interviews and associated evaluation processes unless interviewers and interviewees remain unaware of the purposes of the interview.

(4) Research continues to be microanalytic in nature   The research reviewed

here has most certainly been microanalytic. Researchers have examined a narrow range of variables when conducting their research on the employment interview. In our view, this approach still continues to have some usefulness despite Schmitt's (1976) admonition about conducting research which is too narrow. In our opinion, research efforts should focus on capturing more real or actual behavioral and evaluation processes, but should also continue to focus on relatively small components of the interview and interview process.

(5) Researchers investigating the employment interview have neglected related research in the person perception literature   In reviewing recent research, one is struck by the almost complete lack of attention which has been paid to the person perception literature by researchers in this area. It is almost as if industrial and organizational psychologists have studied the employment interview in isolation from the rest of the field of psychology, perhaps even ignoring the fact that the phenomenon under investigation is essentially a perceptual process. Thus, one of the recommendations we can offer to researchers in this area is to pay far greater attention to what is going on in other areas of person perception. Specifically, researchers could profit by examining the interview in the light of various theoretical models and frameworks which stem from other areas. These include the following:

(a) Attribution models   The employment interview and the evaluation judgments made by interviewers are surely a function of the attribution they make about interviewees. Hastorf *et al.* (1979) summarized the literature in this area some time ago; attribution theory suggests interviewers judge the success or failure of interviewees, and attribute such success or failure in turn to internal factors associated with interviewees or to external factors beyond the control of the interviewee. Moreover, attribution models differentiate between factors which are assumed to be stable (e.g. ability, difficulty of task) or relatively unstable (e.g. effort, luck). The implications which stem from attribution models are clear: interviewers will form judgments about interviewees according to the attributions they make about the causes of the candidate's past achievements. However, attribution theory has been virtually ignored in the investigation of the employment interview process.

(b) Impression formation and management   A large body of literature has accumulated about the way individuals form impressions and how impressions may be managed. For example,

Schlenker (1980) summarizes a large number of studies dealing with the impact of nonverbal behavior on perceiver impression and judgments. These studies have been conducted largely by social psychologists. Similarly, Hastorf *et al.* (1979) indicate that an area under investigation is how perceivers combine evaluation data. The same kind of question appears in the employment interview – How do interviewers combine informational cues? Yet, some of the scaling and weighting models developed by psychologists in person perception research have received little or no attention from industrial psychologists.

(c) Implicit personality theory   The notion that individuals have their own idiosyncratic models of personality which differ from those of other judges is seldom recognized as a more general phenomenon by researchers dealing with the employment interview. With the exception of Hakel (1969), few researches in industrial psychology pay much attention to this perceptual model.

In short, the mainstream of research dealing with the employment interview has typically been without the benefit of more broadly applicable person-perception models. The price has been somewhat short-sighted and situationally bound research, without the guidance of broader based theories.

A final word

The employment interview continues to be widely used. While many industrial and organizational psychologists are well aware of its limited reliability and validity, few would advocate not interviewing candidates for jobs in their own organizations (e.g. research assistants, secretaries, etc.). Thus, research on the interview continues and will continue as long as it is a widely used technique. One direction industrial psychologists should move toward is that of converting the findings and results stemming from research into applied guidelines for interviewers and interviewees. There is a dearth of guidelines and suggestions concerning the improvement of interview effectiveness based on research findings. Instead, many guidelines, suggestions, 'how to interview' workshops, and techniques are founded on intuition, beliefs and what seems more comfortable, rather than on research results. Greater efforts should be made to merge research with application.

References

Amalfitano, J. G. and Kalt, N. C. (1977) Effects of eye contact on the evaluation of job applicants. *Journal of Employment Counseling 14*: 46–8.

Anderson, C. W. (1960) The relation between speaking times and decision in the employment interview. *Journal of Applied Psychology 44*: 267–8.

Anstey, E. (1977) A 30-year follow-up of the CSSB procedure, with lessons for the future. *Journal of Occupational Psychology 50*:149–59.

Arvey, R. D. (1979a) *Fairness in Selecting Employees*. Reading, Mass.: Addison-Wesley.

Arvey, R. D. (1979b) Unfair discrimination in the employment interview: legal and psychological aspects. *Psychological Bulletin 86*: 736–65.

Bernstein, V., Hakel, M. D. and Harlan, A. (1975) The college student as interviewer: a threat to generalizability. *Journal of Applied Psychology 60*: 266–8.

Binet, A. (1911) Nouvelles recherches sur la mesure du niveau intellectual, etc. *L'Annu Psychol XVII*: 182.

Bolster, B. I. and Springbett, B. M. (1961) The reactions of interviewers to favorable and unfavorable information. *Journal of Applied Psychology 45*: 97–103.

Campion, M. A. (1978) Identification of variables most influential in determining interviewers' evaluations of applicants in a college placement center. *Psychological Reports 42*: 947–52.

Carlson, R. E. (1967) The relative influence of appearance and factual written information on an interviewer's final rating. *Journal of Applied Psychology 51*: 461–8.

Carlson, R. E., Thayer, P. W., Mayfield, E. C. and Peterson, D. A. (1971) Research on the selection interview. *Personnel Journal 50*: 268–75.

Cash, T. F., Gillen, B. and Burns, D. S. (1977) Sexism and 'beautyism' in personnel consultant decision-making. *Journal of Applied Psychology 62*: 301–7.

Cohen, S. L. and Bunker, K. A. (1975) Subtle effects of sex role stereotypes on recruiters' hiring decisions. *Journal of Applied Psychology 60*: 566–72.

Dipboye, R. L. (1980) Self-fulfilling prophecies in the selection recruitment interview. Unpublished manuscript.

Dipboye, R. L., Arvey, R. D. and Terpstra, D. E. (1977) Sex and physical attractiveness of raters and applicants as determinants of resumé evaluations. *Journal of Applied Psychology 62*: 288–94.

Dipboye, R. L., Fromkin, H. L. and Wiback, K. (1975) Relative importance of applicant sex, attractiveness, and scholastic standing in evaluation of job applicant resumés. *Journal of Applied Psychology 60*: 39–43.

Farr, J. L. (1973) Response requirements and primacy–recency effects in a simulated selection interview. *Journal of Applied Psychology 57*: 228–33.

Farr, J. L. and York, C. M. (1975) Amount of information and primacy–

recency effects in recruitment decisions. *Personnel Psychology 28*: 233–8.

Ferris, G. R. and Gilmore, D. O. (1977) Effects of mode of presentation, sex of applicant, and sex of interviewer on simulated interview decisions. *Psychological Reports 40*: 566.

Fisher, C. D., Ilgen, D. R. and Hoyer, W. D. (1979) Source credibility, information favorability, and job offer acceptance. *Academy of Management Journal 22*: 94–103.

Gorman, C. D., Clover, W. H. and Doherty, M. E. (1978) Can we learn anything about interviewing real people from 'interviews' of paper people? Two studies of the external validity of a paradigm. *Organizational Behaviour and Human Performance 22*: 165–92.

Haefner, J. E. (1977) Race, age, sex, and competence as factors in employer selection of the disadvantaged. *Journal of Applied Psychology 62*: 199–202.

Hakel, M. D., Dobmeyer, T. W. and Dunnette, M. D. (1970) Relative importance of three content dimensions in overall suitability ratings of job applicants' resumés. *Journal of Applied Psychology 54*: 65–71.

Harlan, A., Kerr, J. and Kerr, S. (1977) Preference for motivator and hygiene factors in a hypothetical interview situation: further findings and some implications for the employment interview. *Personnel Psychology 30*: 557–66.

Hastorf, A. H., Wildfogel, J. and Cassman, T. (1979) Acknowledgement of handicap as a tactic in social interaction. *Journal of Personality and Social Psychology 37*: 1790–7.

Heilman, M. E. and Saruwatari, L. E. (1979) When beauty is beastly: the effects of appearance and sex on evaluations of job applicants for managerial and non managerial jobs. *Organizational Behaviour and Human Performance 23*: 360–72.

Heneman, J. G. III (1975) The impact of interviewer training and interview structure on the reliability and validity of the selection interview. *Proceedings of Academy of Management 231–3*.

Heneman, H. G., Schwab, D. P., Huett, D. L. and Ford, J. L. (1979) Interviewer validity as a function of interview structure, biographical data, and interview order. *Journal of Applied Psychology 60*: 748–53.

Herzberg, F., Mausner, B. and Snyderman, B. B. (1959) *The Motivation to Work*. New York: Wiley.

Hollandsworth, J. G. and Sandifer, B. A. (1979) Behavioral training for increasing effective job-interview skills: follow-up and evaluation. *Journal of Counseling Psychology 26*: 448–50.

Hollandsworth, J. G., Dressel, M. E. and Stevens, J. (1977) Use of behavioral versus traditional procedures for increasing job interview skills. *Journal of Counseling Psychology 24*: 503–9.

Hollandsworth, J. G., Jr, Kazelskis, A., Stevens, J. and Dressel, M. E. (1979) Relative contributions of verbal, articulative, and nonverbal communication to employment decisions in the job interview setting. *Personnel Psychology 32*: 359–67.

Hollman, T. D. (1972) Employment interviewers' errors in processing positive and negative information. *Journal of Applied Psychology 56*: 130–4.

Huegli, J. M. and Tschirgi, H. (1975) An investigation of the relationship of time to recruitment interview decision making. *Proceedings of Academy of Management*: 234–6.

Imada, A. S. and Hakel, M. D. (1977) Influence of nonverbal communication and rater proximity on impressions and decisions in simulated employment interviews. *Journal of Applied Psychology 62*: 295–300.

Kalin, R. and Rayko, D. S. (1978) Discrimination in evaluative judgments against foreign-accented job candidates. *Psychological Reports 43*: 1203–9.

Keenan, A. (1976a) Effects of the nonverbal behavior of interviewers on candidates' performance. *Journal of Occupational Psychology 49*: 171–6.

Keenan, A. (1976b) Interviewers' evaluation of applicant characteristics: differences between personnel and non-personnel managers. *Journal of Occupational Psychology 49*: 223–30.

Keenan, A. (1977) Some relationships between interviewers' personal feelings about candidates and their general evaluation of them. *Journal of Occupational Psychology 50*: 275–83.

Keenan, A. (1978) The selection interview: candidates' reactions and interviewers' judgments. *British Journal of Social and Clinical Psychology 17*: 201–9.

Keenan, A. and Wedderburn, A. A. (1975) Effects of the nonverbal behavior of interviewers on candidates' impressions. *Journal of Occupational Psychology 48*: 129–32.

Keith, R. D., Engelkes, J. R. and Winborn, B. B. (1977) Employment-seeking preparation and activity: an experimental job-placement training model for rehabilitation clients. *Rehabilitation Counseling Bulletin 21*: 259–65.

King, M. R. and Manaster, G. J. (1977) Bossy image, self-esteem, expectations, self-assessments, and actual success in a simulated job interview. *Journal of Applied Psychology 62*: 589–94.

Kopelman, M. D. (1975) The contrast effect in the selection interview. *British Journal of Educational Psychology 45*: 333–6.

Kryger, B. R. and Shikiar, R. (1978) Sexual discrimination in the use of letters of recommendation: a case of reverse discrimination. *Journal of Applied Psychology 63*: 309–14.

Landy, F. J. (1976) The validity of the interview in police officer selection. *Journal of Applied Psychology 61*: 193–8.

Landy, F. J. and Bates, F. (1973) Another look at contrast effects in the employment interview. *Journal of Applied Psychology 58*: 141–4.

Langdale, J. A. and Weitz, J. (1973) Estimating the influence of job information on interviewer agreement. *Journal of Applied Psychology 57*: 23–7.

Latham, G. P., Saari, L. M., Purcell, E. D. and Campion, M. A. (1980) The situational interview. *Journal of Applied Psychology 65*: 422–7.

Latham, G. P., Wexley, K. M. and Purcell, E. D. (1975) Training managers to minimize rating errors in the observation of behavior. *Journal of Applied Psychology 60*: 550–5.

Leonard, R. L. (1976) Cognitive complexity and the similarity–attraction paradigm. *Journal of Research in Personality 10*: 83–8.

London, M. and Hakel, M. D. (1974) Effects of applicant stereotypes, order, and information on interview impressions. *Journal of Applied Psychology 59*: 157–62.

London, M. and Poplawski, J. R. (1976) Effects of information on stereotype development in performance appraisal and interview contexts. *Journal of Applied Psychology 61*: 199–205.

Mayfield, E. C. (1964) The selection interview: a re-evaluation of published research. *Personnel Psychology 17*: 239–60.

Mayfield, E. C., Brown, S. H. and Hamstra, B. W. (1980) Selective interviewing in the Life Insurance Industry: an update of research and practice. *Personnel Psychology 33*: 725–39.

McCauley, C., Stitt, C. I. and Segal, M. (1980) Stereotyping: from prejudice to prediction. *Psychological Bulletin 87*: 195–208.

McGovern, T. V. and Tinsley, H. E. (1978) Interviewer evaluations of interviewee nonverbal behavior. *Journal of Vocational Behavior 13*: 163–71.

McGovern, T. V., Jones, B. W. and Morris, S. E. (1979) Comparison of professional versus student ratings of job interviewee behavior. *Journal of Counseling Psychology 26*: 176–9.

McIntyre, S., Moberg, D. J. and Posner, B. Z. (1980) Preferential treatment in preselection decisions according to sex and race. *Academy of Management Journal 23*: 738–49.

Muchinsky, P. M. and Harris, S. L. (1977) The effect of applicant sex and scholastic standing on the evaluation of job applicant resumés in sex-typed occupations. *Journal of Vocational Behavior 11*: 95–108.

Mullins, T. W. (1978) Racial attitudes and the selection interview: a factorial experiment. Unpublished doctoral dissertation, University of Houston, Texas.

Newman, J. M. (1978) Discrimination in recruitment: an empirical analysis. *Industrial and Labor Relations Review 32*: 15–23.

Newman, J. M. and Kryzstofiah, F. (1979) Self-reports versus unobtrusive measures: balancing method variable and ethical concerns in employment discrimination research. *Journal of Applied Psychology 64*: 82–5.

Okanes, M. M. and Tschirgi, H. (1978) Impact of the face-to-face interview on prior judgments of a candidate. *Perceptual and Motor Skills 46*: 322.

Rand, T. M. and Wexley, K. N. (1975) Demonstration of the effect, 'similar to me', in simulated employment interviews. *Psychological Reports 36*: 535–44.

Reynolds, A. H. (1979) The reliability of a scored oral interview for police officers. *Public Personnel Management 8*: 324–8.

Rose, G. L. (1980) Employment decisions regarding the handicapped: experimental evidence. Presentation at American Psychological Association, Montreal, Canada.

Rosen, B. and Jerdee, T. H. (1974) Influence of sex role stereotypes on personnel decisions. *Journal of Applied Psychology 59*: 9–14.

Rosen, B. and Jerdee, T. H. (1976) The influence of age stereotypes on managerial decisions. *Journal of Applied Psychology 61*: 428–32.

Rosen, B. and Merich, M. F. (1979) Influence of strong versus weak fair employment policies and applicants' sex on selection decisions and salary recommendations in management simulation. *Journal of Applied Psychology 64*: 435–9.

Rothstein, M. and Jackson, D. N. (1980) Decision-making in the employment interview: an experimental approach. *Journal of Applied Psychology 65*: 271–83.

Rynes, S. L., Heneman, H. G. III. and Schwab, D. P. (1980) Individual reactions to organizational recruiting: a review. *Personnel Psychology 33*: 529–42.

Schlenker, B. R. (1980) *Impression Management*. Monterey, Calif.: Brooks/Cole.

Schmitt, N. (1976) Social and situational determinants of interview decisions: implications for the employment interview. *Personnel Psychology 29*: 79–101.

Schmitt, N. and Coyle, B. W. (1976) Applicant decisions in the employment interview. *Journal of Applied Psychology 61*: 184–92.

Schuh, A. J. (1978a) Contrast effect in the interview. *Bulletin of the Psychonomic Society 11*: 195–6.

Schuh, A. J. (1978b) Effects of an early interruption and note taking on listening accuracy and decision making in the interview. *Bulletin of the Psychonomic Society 12*: 242–4.

Shaw, E. A. (1972) Differential impact of negative stereotyping in employee selection. *Personnel Selection 25*: 333–8.

Sigelman, C. K., Elias, S. F. and Danker-Brown, P. (1980) Interview behaviors of mentally retarded adults as predictors of employability. *Journal of Applied Psychology 65*: 67–73.

Simas, K. and McCarrey, M. (1979) Impact of recruiter authoritarianism and applicant sex on evaluation and selection decisions in a recruitment interview analogue study. *Journal of Applied Psychology 64*: 483–91.

Snyder, M., Kleck, R., Strenta, A. and Mentzer, S. (1979) Avoidance of the handicapped: an attributional ambiguity analysis. *Journal of Personality and Social Psychology 37*: 2297–306.

Speas, C. M. (1979) Job-seeking interview skills training: a comparison of four instructional techniques. *Journal of Counseling Psychology 26*: 405–12.

Springbett, B. M. (1958) Factors affecting the final decision in the employment interview. *Canadian Journal of Psychology 12*: 13–22.

Sterrett, J. H. (1978) The job interview: body language and perceptions of potential effectiveness. *Journal of Applied Psychology 63*: 388–90.

Stevens, W. and Tornatzky, L. (1976) The effects of a job-interview skills workshop on drug-abuse clients. *Journal of Employment Counseling 13*: 156–63.

Stone, C. I. and Sawatzki, B. (1980) Hiring bias and the disabled interview: effects of manipulating work history and disability information of the disabled job applicant. *Journal of Vocational Behavior 16*: 96–104.

Sydiaha, D. (1961) Bales' interaction process analysis of personnel selection interviews. *Journal of Applied Psychology 45*: 393–401.

Tessler, R. and Sushelsky, L. (1978) Effects of eye contact and social status on the perception of a job applicant in an employment interviewing situation. *Journal of Vocational Behavior 13*: 338–47.

Tucker, D. H. and Rowe, P. M. (1977) Consulting the application form prior to the interview: an essential step in the selection process. *Journal of Applied Psychology 62*: 283–7.

Tucker, D. H. and Rowe, P. M. (1979) Relationship between expectancy, causal attributions, and final hiring decisions in the employment interview. *Journal of Applied Psychology 64*: 27–34.

Tullar, W. L., Mullins, T. W. and Caldwell, S. A. (1979) Effects of interview length and applicant quality on interview decision time. *Journal of Applied Psychology 64*: 669–74.

Ulrich, L. and Trumbo, D. (1965) The selection interview since 1949. *Psychological Bulletin 63*: 100–16.

Valenzi, E. and Andrews, I. R. (1973) Individual differences in the decision process of employment interviewers. *Journal of Applied Psychology 58*: 49–53.

Vance, R. J., Kuhnert, K. W. and Farr, J. L. (1978) Interview judgments: using external criteria to compare behavioral and graphic scale ratings. *Organizational Behavior and Human Performance 22*: 279–94.

Wagner, R. (1949) The employment interview: a critical summary. *Personnel Psychology 2*: 17–46.

Waldron, L. A. (1974) The validity of an employment interview independent of psychometric variables. *Australian Psychologist 9*: 68–77.

Washburn, P. V. and Hakel, M. D. (1973) Visual cues and verbal content as influences on impressions after simulated employment interviews. *Journal of Applied Psychology 58*: 137–40.

Webster, E. D., (ed.) (1964) *Decision-making in the Employment Interview*. Montreal: Industrial Relations Center, McGill University.

Wexley, K. N. and Nemeroff, W. F. (1974) The effects of racial prejudice, race of applicant, and biographical similarity on interviewer evaluations of job applicants. *Journal of Social and Behavioral Sciences 20*: 66–78.

Wexley, K. N., Sanders, R. E. and Yukl, G. A. (1973) Training interviewers to eliminate contrast effects in employment interviews. *Journal of Applied Psychology 57*: 233–6.

Wexley, K. N., Yukl, G. A., Kovacs, S. Z. and Sanders, R. E. (1972) Importance of contrast effects in employment interviews. *Journal of Applied Psychology 56*: 45-8.

Wiener, J. and Schneiderman, M. L. (1974) Use of job information as a criterion in employment decisions of interviewers. *Journal of Applied Psychology 59*: 699-704.

Wright, O. R., Jr (1969) Summary of research on the selection interviews since 1964. *Personnel Psychology 22*: 341-413.

Young, D. M. and Beier, E. G. (1977) The role of applicant nonverbal communication in the employment interview. *Journal of Employment Counseling 14*: 154-65.

Name index

Adams, H.F., 158
Addington, D.W., 127
Adinolfi, A.A., 146
Adorno, T., 20
Ajzen, I., 53, 105, 106
Akert, R.M., ix, 129, 132, 137, 146, 154
Allen, A., 40
Allen, R.B., 41
Allport, G.W., 1, 11, 18, 37, 129, 146, 155
Amalfitano, J.G., 225
Anderson, C.W., 208
Anderson, N.H., 49, 50, 51, 52, 53, 54, 57, 58, 59, 60, 61, 64, 71, 76, 88, 90, 91, 92, 93, 94, 95, 96, 97, 98, 104, 106, 107, 108
Andrews, I.R., 209
Anstey, E., 214
Archer, D., ix, 129, 132, 137, 146, 154
Aronson, E., 62, 64
Arvey, R.D., ix, 168, 210, 211, 212, 213, 221
Asch, S.E., 1, 11, 54, 55, 57, 77, 90, 91, 96, 97
Ash, M.G., 4
Ausubel, D.P., 148
Azen, S.P., 174, 176

Bates, F., 209
Beach, B.H., 97
Beach, L.R., 97
Beakel, N.G., 129
Beck, G.D., 151

Beier, E.G., 127, 225
Beldoch, M., 127
Bell, D., 108
Bellows, R.M., 169
Bem, D.J., 40
Berlew, D.F., 158
Berman, J.S., 42
Bernardin, H.J., 152
Bernstein, V., 170, 181, 215
Berscheid, E., 66
Bettman, J.R., 78
Binet, A., 145
Birnbaum, M.H., 64, 78, 81, 87, 91, 103
Black, J.M., 170, 171, 196
Block, J., 29, 33, 43
Blum, M., 176
Bolster, B.I., 71, 208
Borman, W.C., 152, 170, 181, 196
Boucher, J.D., 127
Boyd, J.B., 153
Braly, K., 180
Breedlove, J., 158
Brehmer, B., 102, 104
Bridgman, P.W., 16
Brien, M., 76
Brigham, C.C., 147
Briscoe, M.E., 56
Bronfenbrenner, U., 159
Bruner, J.S., 87, 118, 120, 126, 177
Brunswik, E., 101, 104
Buck, R.W., 129
Buckley, S., 161
Bugenthal, D.E., 127, 129, 130

242

Subject index